FORESTS ON FIRE

Ecology and Politics in the Himalayan Tarai

FORESTS ON FIRE

Ecology and Politics in the Himalayan Tarai

By

Ajay S. Rawat

Director Research

Centre for Development Studies

Nainital, U.P.

COSMO PUBLICATIONS

1998 **INDIA**

First Published 1998

ISBN 81-7020-840-8

Published by:
MRS. RANI KAPOOR
for COSMO PUBLICATIONS Div. of
GENESIS PUBLISHING PVT. LTD.
24-B, Ansari Road,
Darya Ganj,
New Delhi-110002, INDIA

Typeset at
Cosmo Publications

Printed at
Mehra Offset Press

Dedicated
to
Shri Rajendra Singh Bhandari

Contents

FOREWORD

The Book 'Ecology and Politics in the Himalayan Tarai' is interesting in many ways. To begin with it is a study about an area in Uttar Pradesh (India) which prior to the advent of Independence was known for its dense forests, swamps and malarial climate, thus making it inhospitable for human habitation.

This situation resulted in thriving wildlife and therefore an ideal ground for big game during the days of the Raj. Proliferation of maneating tigers and leopards in the area shaped up gamesman like Jim Corbett, who excelled himself in sparing the local population of the awe and terror of wild beasts.

Tarai besides being the play field of the renowned Jim Corbett also provided sanctuary for the plunderers and dacoits of Kumaon and Rohailkhand. Tarai also harboured the India Robinhood Sultana Bhantu. That in such a milieu the tribals-Tharus and Buxas - thrived is again an awe- inspiring story.

Tarai, the land of adventure of yore, has undergone a sea change during the post-Independence era. The dense forests are only a memory of the past. Today there are sprawling fields which have turned the area into a granary of Uttar Pradesh. The Tharus and Buxas, the lords of the land of those idyllic days, are no doubt still there, but are enveloped only in the habitats of the settlers.

The new settlers during the past few decades they have been in the Tarai have not only found a home and hearth for themselves, but have also tasted affluence, a factor which has made them to launch many a new ventures. This burgeoning entrepreneurship besides having helped the industrialization of the area, has also brought in some problems in its train. While on the one hand there are reports of the ever increasing air and water pollution, on the other, there are also undercurrents of social discontent. The study also highlights the causes and results of militancy which had over-whelmed the region at one time though its memory still haunts the residents of the area.

The study in addition to focussing on all these facets of the problems in their historical perspective also suggests remedial measures to them. That makes it lively, positive and constructive.

I hope, this area study would be of immense interest not only to the lay reader world over, but also to the academicians and policy planners as also the functionaries executing those policies.

As such the study is an original and novel effort to bring to lime light an area hitherto shrouded in darkness and mystery.

Department of Agriculture & Cooperation
Ministry of Agriculture
Krishi Bhawan, New Delhi.

(J.C. Pant)
SECRETARY

PREFACE

Human activities have already caused significant deterioration to earth's atmosphere resulting into the so called green house effect and the ozone layer depletion. Extensive felling of trees for accelerating economic growth and consumption of energy has increased soil erosion and contaminated fresh water bodies leading to the break up of the ecological cycle upon which life support system depends.

The situation in the Himalaya is more alarming where the ever increasing population at the subsistence economic level is faced with a continuous decline of forest and concomitant loss of natural resources. The onslaughts of Man have been particularly severe in the forests of the highest but a comparatively young and fragile mountain system of the world, the Himalaya including the Central Himalayan region. Here the situation poses a greater risk than usually perceived, for these lofty peaks are the source of the great Ganga river system where one third of the Indian population resides.

The Tarai region in Kumaon is an integral part of the Central Himalaya. The eco-systems here are highly dynamic as also productive, the biomass productivity may be one of the highest in the entire country. But then this area until recently was highly inhospitable to Man, if not very nearly hostile to human existence. Many a times during the British rule, efforts were made to colonize it for agricultural purposes. But all these efforts failed. The scourge of malaria and vagaries of climate thwarted these attempts at human habitation. It was notorious for its most unhealthy, malarial climate and also for the number of tigers it harboured. Continuous heavy rains created ditches, ponds and swamps, which became the breeding grounds for mosquitoes. Nature was thus successful in shielding this area from human abuse.

As the Second World War drew to an end, the scarcity of food caused by it compelled the Central and Provincial Governments to take up urgent and immediate measures to increase the production of staple food grains. Consequently herculean efforts were initiated in the Tarai and Bhabhar region to reclaim it. The Government was trying to cope up with this situation? that India achieved Independence. Thus after 1947, a wave of settlers from West Punjab (now Pakistan) and East Pakistan (now Bangladesh) came to settle down in Tarai and Bhabhar and with these new settlers dawned a new era of permanent settlement in this region.

Consequent upon the demographic change, the demand for agricultural land rose abruptly. Grow More Food Movement and the Green Revolution simultaneously gripped the nation and thousands of hectares of forest area in Tarai and Bhabhar was brought under agriculture. As a result the immense capacity of Tarai to hold ground water disappeared. Its natural ecosystems, which earlier controlled and modulated the floods in a big way by first holding a large quantity of water and then breaking the force of the flood waters, can no longer perform these essential flood control functions. With heavy monsoon rains in upper catchment areas water rushes down the hill slopes and then flows through the Tarai without any obstacle. It causes havoc not only locally, but all along the agricultural plains. Flash floods have become a regular occurrence after reclaiming the Tarai region. The actual damage caused to crop, property and life itself is enormous, but more ominous is the resultant loss of natural production and shrinkage of agricultural land caused by the deposition of sand and other materials after the floods.

There is still another dangerous effect of the destruction of the Tarai ecosystem. The Tarai area with its natural forest cover in the past acted like a huge reservoir or like a huge sponge which stored the abundant rain water of the monsoon and later released it during the lean period. This natural irrigation system which irrigated the plains after the monsoons has dried up after the reclamation of Tarai.

Tarai has assumed a new importance today. Subsequent to

the militant activities and the political upheaval the timber mafia has become active and wreaked colossal damage upon the forests. In the prevailing circumstances, forest dwellers, the Gujjars and the settlers in Khattas known as 'Ghamtappus' or baskers in the sun as well as the tribals have been reduced to a miserable situation of deprivation, so much so that their very survival is at stake.

Industrialization which followed abundance in food grain production has not been an unmitigated blessing. Whereas it has affected agricultural production and caused social dissensions, on the other hand it has worsened the environment. Social harmony has been a victim of this turbulence. Previously discontent was contained only in the Khattas, Gujjar settlements the tribals, peasants and the taungya cultivators. The recent short spell of militancy gave a big jolt to social equanimity. These factors have resulted in turmoil in Tarai, which if not handled properly with speed may fester further. The sooner we realise it, the better for the whole nation. Carving out Udham Singh Nagar, a new district out of the Tarai area of the existing Naini Tal district recently was only a politically motivated move which may do little to solve the problem. Instead this political gimmick has polarized the people into regional groups thus adding to the turbulence of the area. Moreover it has made the kulaks very sceptical about the future of Tarai and has added to the woes of the marginalized population.

This study designed to analyse these trends is a pioneer endeavour on the growth and development of Tarai Bhabhar, and the associated problems consequent upon the reclamation of this region. It is primarily based upon extensive field study, which at times was at personal risk. Archival material, revenue department records and records of the forest department have been used to supplement it . This study was undertaken in connection with the work of the project that I had taken up as a Fellow of the Nehru Memorial Museum and Library, Teen Murti House New Delhi.

I must avail this opportunity to express my gratitude to Shri J.C. Pant, Prof. Rabindra Kumar, Shri S. Deb Roy, Dr. R.S.

Tolia, Shri H.S. Balwaria, Shri J.S. Nayal and Shri Giriraj Shah for their invaluable suggestions and persistent encouragement. Acknowledgements are also due to Miss Archana Arora, Shri Daljeet Singh Goraya, Smt. Shanti Nabiyal, Shri Ramesh Lal Sah, member of the department of Agro-Economics, U.P. Agricultural University, Pant Nagar and Shri Govind Singh Rautela the typist whose efforts have facilitated the culmination of this work.

1

History and Growth of Tarai-Bhabhar

The term Tarai and Bhabhar in Kumaon region is applied to the broad belt of foothill country at the northern margin of the plains. This terrain is of recent origin and is composed largely of the detritus washed away by swift flowing streams from the southern face of the adjoining Siwalik hills. There is an abrupt change of gradient at Bhabhar on the upper rim of Tarai, which leads to a vast deposition of coarse material, i.e., boulders and shingles by the swift flowing streams in Bhabhar, while the finer material- sand and clay- is carried further and has been responsible for creating the Tarai region. This submontane zone thus comprises a characteristic post tertiary depositional phenomenon along the foothills distinguishable into the sub-regions of Tarai and Bhabhar.

E.A. Smythies has described Bhabhar as, "It consists of the stony tract of the country that runs along the foot of the

Kumaon Himalaya between the Sharda river on the Nepal frontier on the east, and the Baur river and Kaladhungi town on the west. The width of the belt varies form 4.83 to 24.42 km,the ground is usually undulating with a gentle but constant slope to the south, the average altitude being about 241.76m at the foot of the hill, and about 227.84m at the junction of Bhabhar and Tarai". About Tarai E.T. Atkinson has commented that, "It comprises a long and narrow strip of country running for about 145 km. It is bounded on the north by Bhabhar, on the south by Pilibhit, Bareilly, Moradabad and Rampur districts, on the east by the Sharda river and on the west by the Bijnor district."

The Tarai, which was at one time swampy and notorious for its malarial climate, was the traditional habitat of the Tharu and Buxa tribes. The earliest cultivators in the Tarai area were these two indigenous tribes, whereas in Bhabhar land was cultivated by the hill men. They were known as gentlemen farmers by the British administrators. The majority of them had land in the hills and therefore they migrated to the hills during summers. Consequent upon the end of the Second World War as also partition of the country following Independence, this area has now developed into a zone of mechanised farms and affluent farmers. The tribals, now living amidst a fast changing socio-economic scene, are facing various types of socio-cultural problems.

In Bhabhar the most important characteristic feature is the absence of surface water due to porous substratum. The availability of this prime resource arranged either through irrigation or perennial rivers is, therefore, a conditioning factor of population concentration and economic activities. This sub-region is mostly inhabited by people belonging to the interior of Kumaon.

Natural Vegetation

The vegetation can be classified under the following heads:

1. Savannah type vegetation in the marshy Tarai Zone usually below 257.87m.

2. Sub-tropical deciduous forests extending all along the southern foothill zone of Bhabhar and Tarai, along the Dun* areas and over the outer slopes of the Siwalik ranges upto 899 m elevation. The principal species are sal (Shorea robusta), khair (Acacia catechu), shisham (Dalbergia sisoo), sain(Terminalia tomentosa), haldu (Adina cordifolia), teak and eucalyptus. Narrow belts of this type of vegetation penetrate into valleys of the Kali, Sarju, Ramganga(E), Gola, Kosi and the Ramganga (W) rivers upto 102.30 m elevation.
3. Sub-tropical pine forests occur in extensive patches above 1017.73 m elevation where edaphic and climatic conditions are suitable.

Drainage of Bhabhar and Tarai

Most of the rivers(except for Kosi** which enters the plains at Ramnagar, Gola*** which enters the plains near Raṇibagh and Kali**** which enters the plains near Tanakpur) that pass through Bhabhar and Tarai, originate in the Siwalik ranges.These small and big streams, that originate in the Siwalik ranges along the outer face of the Himalaya, play a significant role in irrigating agricultural land in the waterless

---

** At some places the Siwaliks are separated from the Lesser Himalaya by longitudinal tectonic valleys generally called 'Dun'. The surface of these valleys is on the whole level, but sometimes broken into steps at different heights. In Naini Tal district the occurence of such a feature is observed. (Joshi etal., Kumaun Himalaya, p. 24).*

*** Kosi also known as Kosila takes its rise in the high ranges of Bhatkot, north-west of Kausani in Almora district and generally flows south-east and southwards for the major part.*

**** Gola originates in the north-east mountainous region of district Naini Tal. Initially it flows southwards, frequently changing its direction to west and north-west and taking a sudden change in direction to south and south-east while entering the plains.*

***** Kali separates Kumaon from Nepal. It originates near Lipu Lekh pass and enters the plains near Tanakpur. It is then known as Sharda.*

tract of Bhabhar. The principal ones among these flowing from west to east are the Phika. Dhela, Dabka, Baur, Bhakara, Nandhaur and the Kamin. Among these the Dabka, Baur and Nandhaur are relatively larger streams. These rivers frequently branch off into various channels or coalesce with other streams and thus create a great complexity in the drainage pattern. Most of the rivers usually shrink to insignificant proportions during the dry weather, but carry great volume of water during the rains.

The rivers and streams passing through Bhabhar ultimately meander into Tarai. Apart from the rivers and rivulets coming from Bhabhar, there are several streams in the Tarai zone, which originate at its swampy northern fringes, i.e. the 'spring line', due to a high water table. These rivulets are also characterized by heavy volume of water flow during the rainy season and frequently break into numerous channels, so much so that it is often difficult to distinguish the main stream. The most important among such Tarai streams are Saniha, Lohiya, Kamin, Deoha, Kailas, Bahgul and Bhakra.

Early History

Prior to the reign of the Mughal King Akbar, i.e. during the latter half of the 16th century, the history of Kumaon in connection with its lowland possessions, Bhabhar and Tarai, is not recorded and hence shrouded in oblivion. However, tradition has it that during the epic period, Bhabhar and Tarai areas were the abodes of the famous sages. Sitabani, near Kotabagh, is supposed to have been the 'ashram' of the sage Valmiki where Sita lived in exile. During the Mahabharata period, this tract was under the Vidharbha Kings, who were renowned for their cattle wealth. It is said that the Pandavas sojourned here during their period of secret exile. Keechak, the general of the Vidharbha King, was slain by Bhimsen, somewhere in the south-west of the present township of Kichha. Again, Arjun defeated the army of the Kauravas, which was forcibly taking away the cattle of the Vidharbha King, in this terrain. Extensive ruins near Kashipur indicate that this area was populated in the remote past. Huien-Tsang, the Chinese traveller, who came to India during the seventh century, has referred to Kashipur as 'Govisana'. During the Gupta period, the Tarai and Bhabhar areas formed an integral part of the Kumaon kingdom, which was then being ruled by the Katyuris. This dynasty at the zenith of its power is supposed to have ruled from Kabul to Nepal and is the earliest ruling dynasty known to authentic history of Kumaon.

However, with the end of the golden period of Gupta dynasty, especially after Harsha of Kannauj, a sordid political confusion gripped the land. Perhaps an adverse climatic change attended by some natural calamity worsened the situation and the Tarai was led to desolation. Progressive decay set in, farms and fields were deserted and the region relapsed into dark jungle by A.D 1100. According to the medieval historians, "It was hither and thither interspersed with patches of grazing and cultivation".

With the advent of Muslim rulers in North India, they started encroaching upon this territory. Soon it became a scene of perpetual struggle between the Kumaon Rajas and the neighbouring Muslim rulers. As the tradition has it the Tharus and Buxas, who are now regarded as indigenous races of Tarai, migrated to this region during this period. It is said that in the 13th Century the Delhi Sultans, Nasirudin Shah and Balban, invaded this terrain. Later Feroze Shah also launched an attack on this area. During the Mughal rule, Tarai formed a part of their kingdom while Bhabhar was independent. 'Ain-i-Akbari' records 21 Mahals in the Tarai. During Akbar's rule, entire Kumaon was supposed to furnish a quota of 3,000 cavalry and 50,000 infantry.

Kumaon was being ruled by the Chand dynasty during Akbar's reign and Raja Rudra Chand (1567-96 A.D.), a scion of this family, was Akbar's contemporary. The Kumaonis under Raja Rudra Chand distinguished themselves in some expedition against Nagor and in recognition of this victory and bravery, Akbar conferred a grant on Raja Rudra Chand. The portion of the Tarai, that came into the possession of Rudra Chand through this grant, was called the 'Chaurasi Mal' or 'Naulakhiya Mal'. The former appellation was derived from the fact that it was 84'kos' in length and the latter owing to the revenue of nine lakh rupees which was assessed upon it. It was bound on the east by the river Sharda, on the west by the Pili Nadi, on the north by Bhabhar and on the south by the plains and constituted the following fiscal sub-divisions:-

1. Sahajgir, now known as Jaspur.
2. Kota, now known as Kashipur.
3. Mundiya, now known as Bajpur.
4. Gadarpur, now known as Gadarpur.
5. Bhuksar, now known as Rudrapur and Kilpuri.
6. Bakshi, now known as Nanak Matta.
7. Chinkee, now known as Surbna, Baheri.

Raja Rudra Chand himself established the township of Rudrapur and appointed governors throughout the parganas. It was one of these governors, Kashi Nath Adhikari, who later founded the township of Kashipur.

During the rule of his immediate successor, Luxmi Chand (still during the reign of Akbar), the royal armies of the Mughals appear to have re-visited the Tarai. Their places of encampment are identified at Tanda and more especially at Peepulhutta, where there is a mango grove called the Badhsahee Bagh. Fourth in the descent from Rudra Chand was Tremul Chand, Raja of Kumaon, who ruled during the years 1625-1638 A.D. During a part of this period, the Tarai is said to have attained a high degree of prosperity and to have actually yielded nine lakhs of rupees from various sources of revenue to the Kumaon treasury. But this prosperity was short-lived. As the tract incurred the envy of its neighbours and even before the death of Tremul Chand encroachments began to be made by the Kuttair Hindus. His successor, Baz Bahadur Chand finding himself in danger of total dispossession from these fertile lowlands, repaired to Delhi and entered into the military service of Emperor Shah Jahan.

He accompanied the Imperial expedition against Kabul and Kandhar and exhibited exemplary courage in these campaigns. On the return of the royal armies to Delhi, Baz Bahadur Chand was rewarded with special favours. Not content with obtaining merely favours and a title, he adhered to the original object of his visit, and procured the full recognition of his right to 'Chaurasi Mal',together with an order, addressed to the Viceroy of the 'Sooba', for effectual assistance against the Kuttair Chiefs. With the aid of Nawab Rustum Khan, the founder of Moradabad, he succeeded in expelling his enemies from the Tarai. Afterwards he established the township of Bajpur.

The second recognition of the right by royal Firman to Baz Bahadur Chand may be said to date from the year 1678 A.D. during the reign of Aurangzeb. The history of the succeeding 50 years of this tract remains shrouded in obscurity. Nothing eventful is known of Baz Bahadur's successors until the reign of Raja Kalyan Chand in 1731 A.D.

In the earlier part of his rule, Kalyan Chand had to face the aggressions of Nawab Mansoor Ali Khan, Subedar of Oudh, who attempted to cede Surbna and Baheri to his domain, but by a successful appeal to the emperor Muhammad Shah, the nominal integrity of his Tarai possession was preserved to the Raja of Kumaon. During his latter years, he had to encounter a stronger enemy. In the years 1744-48 A.D.the Rohillas of Rohilkhand invaded Kumaon twice. The first eruption was contained in the very heart of the hills near the source of the river Ramganga where Pratap Shah, the Raja of the neighbouring Garhwal Kingdom rebuffed the further progress of the Rohillas. The second invasion was checked at the entrance of the hills where the Rohillas force was routed by the Kumaoni army under the command of Shibdeo Joshi. However, the complete expulsion of these invading forces from the plains of Tarai was a formidable task, hence recourse was taken to the Imperial help. Kalyan Chand himself approached the Mughal Emperor, who was camping at Sumbhal those days and implored him for aid against his enemies. The appeal of the Kumaoni Raja was heard, though the powerful Rohillas were not a force to reckon with at that time (1747 A.D.). Moreover the power of the Imperial Government had been weakened due to the onslaughts of the Marathas and the invasion of Nadir Shah.

The result of Kalyan Chand's visit to Sumbhal was renewal of the 'Sunud' for the Chaurasi Mal and the vacation of the territory by the Rohillas with the exception of the eastern tract at Surbna and Baheri. Soon after his return to the hills, Raja Kalyan Chand died in the year 1748 A.D. He was succeeded by his son Deep Chand, then an infant who was placed under the guardianship of Shibdeo Joshi at the request of the dying Raja. Deep Chand after ruling Kumaon for a period of nearly 27 years, was murdered by his cousin Mohan Chand in the year 1775 A.D. The Tarai remained in a state of prosperity during the early period of Raja Deep Chand's reign. In the first sixteen years of his reign, Deep Chand on the advice of Shibdeo Joshi built forts at Rudrapur and Kashipur to keep a vigil over the Rohillas. During this period, the plains of northern India including Rohilkhand were the scene of constant disturbance and change. Together with this the weakening influence of the later Mughals slackened the central control. The Tarai thus became the sanctuary of emigrants from the lower country, who had fled from extra-taxation, and the multiplied masters, which the wars of that period had created. At that time the principal cultivators in Tarai were the Tharus, Buxas and Barwaiks, with a considerable admixture of settlers from the plains, both Hindus and Muslims.

Shib Deo Joshi died in 1764 A.D. at Kashipur. With his demise though Bhabhar remained with the hill Rajas, the control over Tarai slipped gradually into the hands of the Rohillas and Raja Deep Chand was reduced to the state of a nominal Zamindar or Jagirdar in Tarai.

The years between 1764 and 1775 A.D. were a period of dissensions in Kumaon, which resulted in the Gurkha invasion. It took place after sixteen years in 1791 A.D. After the death of Shib Deo Joshi, the affairs of Kumaon were thrown into confusion by the intrigues of the Rani, wife of Deep Chand, on the one hand, and Mohan Singh Rautela, his cousin on the other. Mohan Singh after putting the Rani to death, succeeded in murdering Deep Chand and then his two sons in 1778 A.D. He then proclaimed himself as Raja Mohan Chand, but the ministers, especially the Joshis, who were hostile to Mohan Singh, joined hands with Lalit Shah, the ruler of Garhwal and helped him in invading Kumaon with a big force in 1779 A.D. Mohan Singh was defeated. Lalit Shah thereupon installed his second son Pradyumna Shah on the throne of Kumaon and Harsh Deo, the leader of the Joshis, was made the Prime Minister of Pradyumna Shah.

After this settlement, Lalit Shah proceeded on return journey to Garhwal, but died enroute in 1780 A.D. Thereafter his eldest son, Jai Krit Shah, ascended the throne of Garhwal. He ruled from 1780-85 A.D. On his demise in 1785 A.D., Pradyumna Shah was installed as ruler of Garhwal. Harsh Deo Joshi ruled Kumaon on behalf of Pradyumna Shah. During his absence, Mohan Singh again came to the foray. War ensued between him and the Joshis, who remained loyal to the ruler of Garhwal. Mohan Singh was killed, the Joshi faction was completely routed when they were defeated near Bhim Tal. Thereafter, Lal Singh became supreme, and the Joshis were persecuted.

The Gurkha Invasion

Meanwhile a neighbouring power, the Gurkhas, was watching with interest the state of affairs in Kumaon. It capitalized on the discontent of the Joshis. With the aid of the defeated Harsh Deo Joshi, the Gurkhas invaded Kumaon and, owing to the confusion into which the country had been lately thrown by the struggle of the rival factions, succeeded in subduing it.

Between 1781 A.D. and 1802 A.D., the Gurkhas were preoccupied in restoring order in the hilly tract and could not pay attention to the lowland territories of Kumaon. Resultantly the control of the Tarai remained in the hands of the Rohillas. The Gurkha invasion of Kumaon and the civil strife which preceded that event, drove down a number of hill people to the Tarai and the townships of Kashipur and Rudrapur together with the adjoining villages of Tarai, became the emigrant settlements.

With the commencement of the British rule in Rohilkhand since 1802, there was a sea change in the course of events in Tarai and Bhabhar. The British Government started taking active interest in its affairs. This tract had by then become a small mart for the Bhotia traders from the hills. To give a new impetus to trade, the British Government decided to hold annual trade fairs in Bhabhar. The first trade fair of this kind was held from 9th November 1802 to 8th December 1802. It seems that these trade fairs could not generate a favourable response, because in later records there is no mention about them and soon these fairs must have discontinued.

British Occupation

The British occupied Kumaon in 1815 and thereafter in 1818, Mr. Traill, the then Commissioner of Kumaon, was concerned about the development of Tarai and Bhabhar as an agricultural tract. But little headway was made due to the lack of water supply. However according to a report prepared in 1837 by the district administration it appears that the revenue of Kotabagh and Chhakhata was Rs. 6,380. In these two pattis, 29 villages lying along the foot of the hills had been cultivated from olden times by people from the hills as their inalienable right. The headman or Padhan received two ploughs (hal) of land as their remuneration which they held during their tenure of office. The hal was the area a pair of bullocks could plough in a day and for this amount,the tenant-at-will paid five rupees. Beside these villages, a few others had been brought into cultivation since 1815 by granting proprietary right to any individual who cleared the waste. The new proprietors leased the land to the tenants-at-will at a rate ranging from rupees two to four per hal. Nevertheless considering the present state of affairs, there was but little cultivation in 1837 in Kotah Bhabhar, though it was then the richest portion of the area. Lalji Chakrayat was the principal land holder and he aided development in Bhabar by settling colonies of cultivators and arranging for their support.

In the Chhakhata Bhabhar from the foot of the hills to Tanda in the plains there were some patches of cultivation close to the 'guls' or water courses. Harak Singh Mahar, the patwari was the most influential person in the area during that period.

But it was not until 1850, when Sir Henry Ramsay conceived a plan for providing the Bhabhar with a net-work of irrigation canals by channelizing water from the river Kosi, that regular cultivation was made possible on a wide scale. Debi Das Kayasth in 1898 wrote, "...the canals, bridges, roads and bungalows which are seen to this day in Bhabhar are his work."

Henry Ramsay administered Kumaon for 44 years. In August 1840, he was appointed as Junior Assistant Commissioner of Kumaon division and on 10th February 1856, he became Commissioner of Kumaon. He retired from this position in 1884. During the whole tenure of his service, so great was his zeal for the welfare of the people that he seldom took leave and most of his furloughs were medical.

Ramsay started and settled the township of Haldwani in Bhabhar during his service tenure in Kumaon and planned for the habitation of the Tarai area. During those days this tract was plagued with malarial fever and bowel troubles. Ramsay, therefore, pioneered to undertake precautionary measures in this direction. As soon as he assumed office, he took measures to check malaria and other diseases. Concomitantly Tarai was connected by well maintained roads. Wells were dug in most of the villages. The worst swamps were dewatered and channels for irrigation were taken out from the principal streams. Consequently at the time of his retirement, there were 219.36 km of masonry canals in the Tarai and Bhabhar area and by 1897, the total length of running masonry canals had increased to 243.28 km. Maximum construction was done in this period and a Tarai Improvement Fund was started in 1880 from which funds were provided for the repair of roads, bridges and other works.

Tarai and Bhabhar assumed a new importance in 1857. Although Naini Tal itself remained undisturbed, Haldwani was attacked by the neighbouring Rohilla chief of Bareilly. Following which a number of recalcitrant people took refuge in the dense forests of Tarai. The 66th Gurkha and the 8th Irregular Cavalry, reinforced by the Nepal contingent, succeeded in quelling the disturbances. After 1857 thousands of inhabitants from the neighbouring districts settled in Bhabhar and Tarai.

During Henry Ramsay's period, Tarai and Bhabhar were personally administered by the Commissioner Kumaon as Tarai and Bhabhar Estate. After his retirement, Bhabhar came under Almora district and Tarai formed a separate district administered by a Superintendent. In February 1891, the Commissioner of Kumaon, Colonel Erskine proposed certain alterations in the district boundaries, the principal object of which was to bring the administration of Bhabhar and Tarai under one officer, keeping in view the administrative feasibility. In 1891, Naini Tal became a separate district and Bhabhar and Tarai were brought under the Deputy Commissioner of Naini Tal. Their amalgamation was proposed in September 1894, and in 1895 an Assistant Commissioner was appointed as incharge of the two Government Estates, while in 1900 a special permanent officer known as Kham Superintendent was appointed in Tarai and Bhabhar. The real prosperity of the area was however most marked in the period 1870-1890. During that period the cultivated area in Tarai and Bhabhar was 79,421.51 ha. The same period also witnessed an increase in the population by leaps and bounds. From 1890 the population steadily decreased.

Prior to this in 1895, G. Adams, the then Senior Member of the Board of Revenue made an inspection of the area from Haldwani upto the river Sharda and observed in his inspection note that, "the circle of Talla Des or Tanakpur on the bank of the Sharda was practically cut off from the rest of Bhabhar and that it was of easy access from Champawat and Lohaghat, even then through which there was a considerable trade with Tibet". As such he suggested that if the road to Champawat and

Lohaghat was improved, it would benefit the existing mart of Tanakpur greatly. Thus in 1896 The Tanakpur-Bhabhar was transferred to Almora. But it was a short-lived arrangement, as the Bhabhar and Tarai were amalgamated into one unit at the end of 1900. Further, on 1st October, 1910 Almora Bhabhar was transferred to the Tarai and Bhabhar of Naini Tal district.

The only great land owner in Kashipur during those days was the Rautela (The younger brother of the Chand King was known as Rautela), Raja of Kashipur. The family was founded by Lal Singh, the younger great-grandson of Raja Baz Bahadur Chand of Kumaon and the brother of Mohan Singh, who became Raja in 1777, but was killed the next year by the Joshi faction as mentioned earlier. In addition to the Zamindari villages in Kashipur, the Rautela Raja owned extensive property in Bijnor In the Bhabhar there were a few wealthy landholders, but none of them had very extensive possessions. The main among them were the Mahar Thokdars of the Chhakhata pargana.

From the British occupation of Kumaon upto the year 1844, Kashipur and Jaspur were separate revenue divisions and formed part of Moradabad district. In 1844, the revenue divisions of the Moradabad district were rearranged, following which Bajpur, Kahsipur and Jaspur, along with sundry villages from Thakurdwara, Sarkara, Moradabad and Afzalgarh were constituted in one pargana under the name of Kashipur. Shortly before 1857, Bajpur was brought under Tarai and in 1869 a number of other villages followed suit. In October 1870, the entire pargana of Kashipur was given over to the Tarai.

During the British period there were five types of villages. In the first place there were directly managed or the Kham villages. Most of the villages fell under this category.Next came the old settled villages along the foot hills, which were settled before the British conquest and had been held from time immemorial by bodies of 'hissedars' under a 'Padhan'. Thirdly, there were those villages which were held under a regular settlement in the ordinary 'bhaichara' tenure of the plains, known in Bhabhar as 'mustajiri'. These were transferred from Moradabad in 1860. Fourthly, there were the villages which were at one time held as settled villages and the settlers enjoyed proprietary rights. They were later on relinquished to or ceded to the Government. Lastly, there were the 'Muqaddami' villages which were managed directly by the Government through the agency of a' Muqaddam' or headman.In the case of new cultivations no rent was charged for the first two years.

The villages of Tarai and Bhabhar after Independence were broadly classified into the following categories.

1.	Kham villages	711
2.	Buxari villages	55
3.	Hissedari villages	85
4.	Thekedari villages	35
5.	Mustajiri villages	53
6.	Colonization villages	175
7.	Muafi villages	two whole and 19 partly

In Kham villages the State Government was the proprietor under the Government's Grant Act. The U.P. Tenancy Act was in force which made rights of the lesses inheritable. Under Rule 4 of the rules relating to the management of Government Estates, the Kham tenants had a right of extension - they could bring wastelands adjoining their fields under their plough. They were termed as settled or Bandobasti and were directly managed; the Government having made a settlement with the individuals to pay a fixed amount of land revenue for a period of years.

The U.P. tenancy Act did not extend to the Buxari villages. The Buxas were allowed shifting cultivation and were recorded in Class X(L) of the Khatauni. Since 13 Buxari villages were acquired for colonization, their number was reduced to 42.

As for Hissedari villages, they had intermediaries, the Zamindars. The U.P. Tenancy Act was not applicable to these villages, but the U.P. Land Revenue Act was in force. As regards the Zamindari villages the maximum were in Kashipur division. It contained 183 villages of which only fourteen were held in direct management under the Superintendent of Tarai and Bhabhar, the remainder being held in Zamindari tenure.

In Thekedari villages, land was leased out to Thekedars or contractors for 30 years with the right to sublet but not to transfer, the period of lease being renewable for further terms of 30 years.

In Zamindari villages there was a category called Mustajiri villages. The Mustajirs were hereditary contractors of Government villages and collected revenue direct from each cultivator. The Mustajirs had full proprietary rights; they paid a fixed rent to the Government and had the right to let out, mortgage or donate land.

In Colonization villages, the State Government exercised proprietary rights. The tenants had hereditary rights and the U.P. Tenancy Act was applicable. The lease terms and conditions encouraged cooperative farming.

Muafi villages had intermediaries like in Hissedari villages. The U.P. Land Revenue Act was applicable to these villages.

With the promulgation of Zamindari and Land Reforms Act in 1969 all these categories including the distinctive Buxari villages were terminated.The present categories are as follows:

1. Lessees with transferable rights and grove holders have become Bhumidars,or owners of the land.
2. Lessees with only heritable rights have been classed as Sirdars.
3. Sub-tenants of disabled persons or retired army personnel are termed as Asanus.
4. Sub-tenants of able bodied persons are categorized as Adivasis.

As for trespassers on Government land , while they do not get any right under the new law directly, they can obtain it after regularization proceedings under the existing Government orders.

The different forms of tenancy in the Bhabhar,generally speaking, resembled that of the hills. In the hills landed propriety was termed as 'Thhat' and the grants in 'Thhat' conveyed free-hold tenancy over land as well as its produce. The land seldom changed proprietors and most of the occupants derived their claim to the soil, solely from the prescription of long established and undisturbed possession.

Where the land grant was already held in property by others, those occupant proprietors, if they continued on the estate sank into tenants of the new grantee, who moreover by the custom of the area was permitted to take one third of the estate into his immediate cultivation. Of the remainder of the estate,the right of cultivation rested with the original occupants, who were then termed as 'Khaikars' or occupants and not 'Thhatwan' or proprietors.They were under proprietors whose rights as the original occupant cultivators had been usurped by or granted to some persons previously.

'Sirtan' formed the third category of the agriculturists. He was tenant at will holding tenancy under an agreement,sometimes written and sometimes verbal. However, he had no claims to any permanency or privileges. Sometimes artisans, ploughmen and the like were given land to cultivate free of rent or at nominal rent in return for their services. They were also classed as 'Sirtans'.

For the realization of land revenue, besides the Government functionaries, there was another official, known as 'Padhan' in Bhabhar, who was associated with the revenue collection. Padhan was responsible for the collection of revenue in his village which he made over to the Patwari. Additionally in his position as headman he was also entrusted with certain minor public duties. The Padhan was remunerated with assignment of land or 'Padhanchari' money. This remuneration was known as ' Hak Padhani'. The office of the Padhan was hereditary.

Rules For Management of Tarai and Bhabhar Villages :

In 1903 it was observed that some tenants were leaving Tarai, because they had to pay rent even on the barren land. Thus in 1906 rules were framed for the management of Kham villages. They were as follows:

1. "A village Padhan was responsible for cultivation of villages by bringing in tenants and making proper distribution of land among them,
2. fixing and getting entered in the papers of Patwaris at each harvest rents on land cultivated by tenants.
3. realizing and crediting rents in the Tahsil,
4. arranging for the cultivation of land of such tenants, who have relinquished their holdings or absconded,
5. enumerating and getting entered in Patwari's papers cattle of tenants and others,
6. realizing grazing dues fixed by Patwari and crediting them in Tahsils,
7. Arranging material for supply of wood, bamboos, grass and other articles to tenants,
8. arranging material for erection of huts for tenants,
9. arranging for supply of coolies to officers on tour,
10. distribution of water to tenants for irrigation pur poses and other matters."

Thus an effort was made to remove the grievances of the tenants; whereas on the one hand measures were taken to realise full dues from them, at the same time steps were taken to make sure that they are not made to pay unduly. The Padhans were desired to make sure that the tenants got good harvest, so that they may continue to stay back in Tarai.

The same year terms and conditions were also laid down

by applicants for land in the Government Estate of Tarai and Bhabhar which were as follows:

1. "That whole villages may be given to them so that the interference of others may not affect their cultivation and management,
2. that the canals or 'guls' which may be necessary for the purpose of irrigation may be constructed at the expense of the Government and no water rates recovered from them,
3. that the headmens' dues at the rate of 10% on collection may be paid to them for the first year and the reduction in rents on land may also be allowed,
4. that moderate rent rates may be fixed for the first three years,
5. that for the first three years they may be given the right to give land to cultivators free, or on rents or on 'batai' system as they may think fit, since in the first year different allowances have to be made to the tenants.
6. that they may be supplied forest products free of charge, timber for houses and agricultural implements, grass for thatching and grazing purposes and wood for fuel,
7. that they may be allowed guns for protection of crops,
8. that arrangements may be made for drinking water wells,
9. that tenants may be permitted to bring in cultivators freely from Zamindari villages and other districts,
10. that 'takawi' loan may be advanced to the tenants on their Padhan's security without interest."

Meeting these requirements, according to the applicants for land in Tarai was necessary to make their occupation attractive. Enumeration of these conditions on the part of the Government showed its desire to meet them and thus encourage settlers in Tarai.

To attract settlers these proposals were more or less accepted and to hold up the cultivators further a trust known as the Kumaon Bhabhar Cultivators Trust Fund, Naini Tal District was formed in 1906. The money of the trust was used for the purpose of defraying the cost of medicines for distribution among cultivators of this area.

Concomitantly sanitary conditions were also being improved by providing good drinking water wells. Statistics available for the years 1905-1908, of the cleaning operations of these wells indicate the Government's drive to give the people ample supply of potable water all the year round. The data is detailed below:

Improvement of Tarai Wells

Year	Cleaned & repaired	Treated successfully	Treated unsuccessfully	Total
1905-6	14	20	21	55
1906-7	-	44	14	58
107-8	130	33	27	190
TOTAL	**144**	97	62	303

To improve the economic condition of the inhabitants of Tarai and Bhabhar, two ginning mills were started in Kashipur, since the Kashipur cotton was regarded as the best indigenous cotton in United Provinces. Its chief merit was its lustre. This cotton fetched good price particularly in Bombay.

Horticulture schemes were also started in Tarai and Bhabhar. Mango and leechi orchards were introduced and by 1910 there were five well established orchards in this area. They were at Haldwani, Kaladhungi and Ramnagar in Bhabhar and Gadarpur and Sitargnaj in the Tarai. On 2.6.1913, the Commissioner Kumaon sanctioned another garden in Kichha apart from the above-mentioned five gardens.

Rules for Tenants Leaving Kham Villages:

Rules were framed as early as 1906 for the Tarai and Bhabhar tenants desirous of leaving the Kham villages. They were as follows:

1. "Tenants who have paid up all rents and 'takawi' dues to the Government and all money due to the Padhan or Hissedar are at liberty to leave the Government Estate subject to the following conditions:

    (a) Their huts again become the property of Government and under no circumstance must the roof be tampered with or taken away.

    (b) They shall not take away their agricultural implements and carts made from material supplied free by Government until after payment for the said material.

    (c) They must send a written relinquishment to the Superintendent before the 15th of April after which detailed relinquishments can be rejected and the tenant can be held responsible for the rent of his holding for the ensuing year.

    (d) No property of any kind can be removed from the village until the Peshkar has certified that all money dues to Government, the Padhan and Hissedars have been paid in full.

    (e) In the case of any dispute about money due to a Padhan or Hissedar be unable to prove the debt, the tenant must be allowed to remove his property as soon as the Government demand and takawi have been paid in full.

2. The relinquishment will be sent at once to the Peshkar for report:

    (a) As to whether any money is due to the Government,Padhan or Hissedar.

    (b) The reason of the tenants wishing to relinquish his holding, the Peshkar must submit his report within

20 days of receiving his order.

3. Should any tenant attempt to remove a cattle or his property from the village before his accounts have been settled in full or until some responsible person has given security for the amount due from him to the Government, Padhan or the Hissedar, he will be treated as an absconder and his cattle and property will be retained until the amount in full has been paid or until he has furnished such security.

4. Other property will be handed over to the Padhan, who will give a receipt (a) to the Peshkar, (b) to the owner. The Padhan will be held responsible for the safe custody of such property.

5. Under no circumstances whatsoever can a tenant wishing to leave the Estates be prevented from doing so, but subject to the above rules, his cattle and property can be retained.

6. Nothing under these rules shall prevent the Superintendent from

   (a) Accepting relinquishment after 15th April.

   (b) Allowing a tenant to take away his agricultural implements etc. free of charge provided that the tenant is going to another Government village with sanction of the Superintendent".

(Source: Kumaon Commissionery Naini Tal)

By laying down these rules the Government admitted the right of a Tarai and Bhabhar tenant to leave his farm at his will. At the same time with a view to discourage them from doing so it laid down certain stiff rules also, e.g. they could not take away any implement and equipment made out of the material supplied free of cost to them by the Government.

Before these rules were framed, correspondence ensued between the Joint Secretary, Board of Revenue, Northern-Western Provinces(which also included present Uttar Pradesh) and the Commissioner Kumaon in this connection. In his letter dated, 26 August, 1904, the Joint Secretary wrote to the Commissioner, Kumaon that , " It is however impossible to allow defaulting tenants to leave the Tarai without taking some steps to recover money due from them to the Government. Particularly to ensure this the above rules were framed in 1906."

Appointment, ect. of Patwaris and Kanungos:

Patwaris and Kanungos were important officials of the revenue administration in Tarai and Bhabhar. They wielded more powers than their counterparts in other areas. Apart from revenue powers, they also had police powers. Kanungo in police matters had the power of police inspector and the Patwari in criminal cases was entrusted with the power of a sub-inspector.

The special rules regarding appointment of Kanungo and Patwari for the Bhabhar and Tarai were framed for the first time in 1897, but they did not actually come in force until 1906-1907. The important ones were as follows:

For Patwaris:

1. The Patwaris shall be appointed by the Deputy Commi--oner.
2. The Deputy Commissioner shall maintain a list of qualified candidates, from which appointments will invariably be made, unless a vacancy occurs in excess of the number of qualified candidates, in which case the Deputy Commissioner shall make temporary arrangements.
3. The qualification for enrollment in the list of the candidates shall be as follows:
   (a) A certificate from the Assistant Surgeon will be produced that the candidate is of sound physique.
   (b) A certificate of having passed the vernacular middle examination or some higher examination.

(c) A certificate of having passed the examination of the Hill Patwari School. No candidate shall be enrolled who is under 20 or over 25 years of age.

4. On enrollment the candidate will be required to file a security of Rs.500 and also to undergo such a course of practical training for a period of about six months as the Deputy Commissioner may order.

5. On appointment the Patwari shall live in his circle (patti) unless specially exempted, and shall not absent himself therefrom, except on duty, without permission.

6. (a) A Patwari shall not engage in trade, or money lending, nor borrow money,in his circle without the permission of the Deputy Commissioner; not unless exempted by the Deputy Commissioner, own, cultivate, or purchase land in his patti.

(b) In the event of a Patwari being transferred to a circle in which he has contracted debts, or in which he or any member of his family owns or cultivates land, he shall be bound to bring this fact to the notice of the Deputy Commissioner.

7. A grant will be annually made to the district from which rewards may be given by the Deputy Commissioner to such Patwaris as may in his opinion deserve the same.

8. If, after due enquiry, in which an opportunity for explanation shall be allowed to him, misconduct or neglect of duty is proved against a Patwari or Assistant Patwari, he may be fined a sum not exceeding three months pay, or suspended for a period not exceeding six months.

9. Appeals against orders of removal or dismissal shall lie to the Commissioner, and shall be preferred to him within 60 days of the order complained of. The Commissioner's order shall be final. In case of all punishment, other than removal or dismissal, the order of the Deputy Commissioner shall be final.

10. A Patwari shall ordinarily be retired on attaining the age of 50 provided that the Deputy Commissioner may in any case from time to time sanction such extension not exceeding a year at any one time, as he may think desirable, i.e., till he attains the age of 60."

(Source: Kichha Tahsil)

As the Patwari was a grass-root level official of the Government and as such likely to indulge in mal-practices like bribery etc. he was prevented from any personal profiteering activity in his patti. At the same time he was not to be posted to a place where he or his family had economic interests. To encourage the Patwaris to do good work there was provision for reward also.

For Kanungos:

1. "A person satisfying the following conditions, shall ordinarily be considered eligible for Supervisor Kunungos or Assistant Kanungos:

   (a) That, unless specially exempted by the Government, he has passed the middle class or some higher examination in the Government educational course. Exemptions may be applied for in the case of deserving Patwaris, who have sufficient education to be likely to make efficient Kanungos.

   (b) That he is of good physique, the physical fitness of the candidate should be certified by the Civil Surgeon of the districts.

   (c) That he is of good character and of a respectable family.

   (d) That he has himself resided for at least three years in the United Provinces.

2. When a vacancy occurs in a Kanungoship in consequence of the retirement or decease or appointment to another post of a hereditary Kanungo, the Deputy Commissioner shall appoint against that duly qualified

member of the family whom he considers to be best entitled, failing any duly qualified member, and in case non-hereditary* vacancies, the Deputy Commissioner shall appoint a duly qualified Patwari of the tehsil or other suitable candidate.

3. In no case shall a minor be appointed to Kanungoship.

4. A person appointed as Kanungo in a vacancy, whether hereditary or non-hereditary, shall be appointed on probation and shall not be confirmed before one year's satisfactory service.

5. The Deputy Commissionery may fine any Kanungo an amount not exceeding three month's of his salary or may suspend him for a similar period or reduce his pay for such a period as he deems advisable.

The Deputy Commissioner may transfer Kanungos as he thinks advisable. The Commissioner may, on the report of the Deputy Commissioner, order the removal or dismissal of a Kanungo for misconduct, incompetence or pecuniary discrepancies.

6. An appeal from the order of the Commissioner removing or dismissing a Kanungo shall be made to the Board of Revenue and shall be filled within 90 days from the date of the said order. In the case of minor punishments the Deputy Commissioner's order shall be final."

(Source Tahsil Haldwani)

There is clearly an effort to place the high-caste in the society in this position. Firstly a Kanungo should belong to a respectable family and secondly there was a provision of hereditary Kanungoship.

Police:

Upto 1891 there was no regular police in Tarai and Bhabhar,

* *Hereditary Kanungos were appointed only from those families in which the right had already been admitted by the Board or Government.*

their powers being delegated to the revenue officials as in the hills. In 1893 rural police was introduced and grain-paid chaukidars or watchmen were appointed. There were 386 village chaukidars of which 234 were for Tarai, 128 for Kashipur and 24 road chaukidars for patrolling on the roads from Bareilly to Haldwani, from Ramnagar to Kashipur and from Kahsipur to Kaladhungi. The grain- paid chaukidars proved inefficient and were replaced by cash paid chaukidars. Simultaneously Civil Police was also raised for the area with 19 investigating officers, 15 clerks and 174 constables. There was armed police which was raised during the same period, but this body formed as well as a reserve for the whole of Kumaon division. A force of 12 mounted policemen was posted in the region and their chief function was to patrol the Rampur State border. The force was under the control of Superintendent of Police, Kumaon Division who was assisted by one reserve and one visiting inspector for this district.

Later with the process of colonization, Tarai and Bhabhar were divided into eight circles, each having a police station with staff of investigating officers and constables. These circles generally corresponded with the parganas in which the stations were situated, the latter being located at Haldwani and Ramnagar in the Bhabhar and at Kahsipur, Bajpur, Gadarpur, Kichha, Sitarganj and Khatima in Tarai. Attached to these stations were six outposts, maintained for the purpose of road patrolling and not as reporting stations. Of these there were two in Bajpur Circle, at Sultanpur and Kaila Khera. The outpost of Rudrapur belonged to the Kichha Circle and that at Majhauli to Sitarganj. The remaining outposts at Kathgodam and Kaladhungi were dependent on Haldwani Circle. The average area of each circle was 582.75 square km for a population of 40,000.

Besides all this, there were Municipal Police supported by local funds at Haldwani and Kashipur and Town Police in the townships of Jaspur, Kaladhungi, Ramnagar and Ranibagh-Kathgodam. Both the Municipal and Town Police were enlisted under the provisions of Act V, of 1961 at the rate of one constable for every 100 houses. Presently in Tarai and Bhabhar, the police arrangements are similar to those as in the plains of U.P.

Forest Management:

The first attempt in this direction was made in 1826, when on the recommendation of Traill, Commissioner Kumaon, a proclamation was issued, prohibiting cutting of sal (Shorea robusta) on all the 'thaplas' or flats immediately adjoining the lower ranges along the whole extent of the Bhabhar. No other steps towards conservancy were however undertaken. The denudation of trees of all species appears to have continued steadily and reached its climax between 1855 and 1861, when the demand of the railways for sleepers attracted numerous contractors to these parts. They were given free choice to cut where and how they pleased; with the result that large number of trees were felled, many of whom for want of transport were left lying in the forest to rot. This reckless felling during this period was carried on to such an extent that for several years after the control of the forests was taken in hand by the Commissioner, the whole effort of the officials was directed towards clearing the timber thus left by the contractors. Fortunately the gravity of the situation was realized by the then Commissioner, Major Ramsay in 1861, and he took prompt measures to stop further denudation of the forest and to place this valuable property on a sounder and more permanent footing. In the following year Major Ramsay was appointed Conservator in addition to his ordinary duties. The farming of leases and indiscriminate felling of trees were stopped, forest officers were appointed and a system of conservancy was begun under which all trees considered fit for felling were marked by the officials before they were felled. Along with it fire conservancy also was started.

In 1868 the forests were first placed under the control of the officers of the Forest Department, but it was not until the 5th of September 1877, that the forests were gazetted as Government forests, and the area of the forest divisions was formally demarcated. With the exception of the occupancy rights on Zamindari villages, the Government maintained its full rights to forest produce over the whole of Tarai and Bhabhar.

During this period the Kumaon Iron Works Company was started in 1862 in Kumaon. Forest rules were relaxed in favour of this company , so as to allow it entire control over the fuel supplies. With the passing of the Forest Act in 1878, the Civil and Reserved Forests were separated. Subsequent to the passing of the Act other small areas, mostly situated outside the base of the hills, were reserved and placed under the management of the Forest Department. It was followed by the significant developments detailed below:

1. In 1890, the block of forest leased to the Kumaon Iron Works Company was taken back by the Government.
2. In 1899 the principal khair (Acacia cetechu) growing areas in Bhabhar viz. Garappu, Bakra, Goula, Sukhi and Kailas blocks were reserved with a view to the resuscitation of the kath (catechu) manufacture.
3. In 1899 some sal (Shorea robusta) forests in the blocks of Sawlde, Kothkhara, Surai, Banbassa and Makonia blocks were declared protected.

Grazing Rights :

Tarai an Bhabhar had been an unrestricted grazing ground for many years. In 1903 it was observed that grazing was causing great damage to the forests. Thus it was decided to have compact blocks available for grazing or having grazing reserves. In 1909 rules were finally framed for grazing dues.The important ones were as follows:

1. "The Forest Division shall receive full grazing dues from all villages situated within Reserved Forests . The Divisional Forest Officer shall enumerate the cattle and realize the fees from these villages.

2. The grazing dues shall be shared equally from all villages, which are situated outside the Reserved Forest, but within three km. of the boundary of blocks open to grazing.

3. In addition to these villages, any other villages situated at a greater distance from the forests may graze their cattle in the reserved blocks open to grazing, by obtaining permission before hand from the Special Forest Officer, Tarai and Bhabhar.

4. A list of all villages of which the grazing dues are to be shared, shall be prepared annually by the Special Forest officer on or before 1st October.

5. In the event of cattle from villages, which are not included in the shared list, being found grazing in the Reserved Forest, they shall be liable to be compounded, and their owners to prosecution, on receipt of intimation from the Special Forest Officer that such cattle have been found grazing in the reserves.

6. All enumeration of cattle of villages on the shared list shall be done by the Special Forest Officer.

7. In the case of sal (Shorea robusta) forests included in the open grazing areas, the Forest Department reserves the right to close any area to all cattle except those which can graze free by right therein."

By framing these rules the Government wanted to make it clear that grazing would no more be free and unrestricted. Thereby it also wanted to make it a source of earning.

Silviculture

During this period, silvicultural schemes were introduced in the forests of Central Himalaya and the rich forest wealth of Bhabhar and Tarai also received attention for sustaining annual revenues by selling forest products. Since 1912, the interest in proper management of forests increased and rough working plans for commercial fellings were drawn up for the hills. With the introduction of silvicultural schemes, contractors and labourers started settling down in Tarai and Bhabhar. These new settlers were however migratory.

For the forest products of Tarai and Bhabhar, the local market was limited, the chief centres being Ramnagar, Haldwani, Kaladhungi and Tanakpur in the Bhabhar and Kashipur, Bajpur, Gadarpur,Lalkuan, Kichha, Sitarganj and Khatima in the Tarai, absorbing large part of the products which passed through them to the plains. Bareilly, Moradabad, Meerut and Delhi were the principal markets outside where the forest products of Tarai and Bhabhar found their way. The main market products were trees of various species, mainly:

1. Sal (Shorea robusta) for timber and railway sleepers.
2. Sain (Terminalia tomentosa) and haldu (Adina cordifolia) which were sent largely to Wood Working Institute, Bareilly and to the North Western Railway Workshop at Lahore.
3. Sisoo (Dalbergia sisoo) was sent as logs to Bareilly and Pilibhit for furniture industry. There was also a demand for large logs by the Gun Carriage Factory at Jabalpur.
4. Semal (Bombax ceiba) was largely in demand for matches and packing cases. It was supplied to West Indian Matches Company at Clutterbuckganj, Bareilly, (4050 c.m. per annum), Saw Mills at Lalkuan, Indian Turpentine and Rosin Company in Bareilly (3240 c.m. per annum). Semal planks also found a ready market at Bareilly, Aligarh, Kanpur and Meerut for packing cases.
5. Khair (Acacia katechu) trees were generally in demand for the manufacture of Kattha(catechu) and by the 'chainees' from Gonda and other eastern districts. An agreement had also been concluded for the yearly supply of 6,000 trees of over 0.99 m in girth to the Indian Wood Products Company at Izzat Nagar at

Bareilly for the extraction of Kattha (catechu).

Thus forest product based industries were being encouraged. This besides helping industrialization also added to the earnings made from forest produce. With this end in view silvicultural schemes were introduced. Additionally the forests in Bhabhar and, to some extent, the Tarai as mentioned earlier provided grazing grounds for numerous herds of cattle and buffaloes. Large quantity of ghee and butter was made and sent from here to districts like Bulandshar, Meerut and Bareilly which depended largely on the supplies of cattle bred in the Bhabhar and to some extent in the Tarai area.

Rules for Supply of Timber to Tenants:

In 1936 rules for supply of free timber to tenants of the Tarai and Bhabhar Government Estates from Tarai and Bhabhar Estates Forest Division were finally framed. These rules were formulated to attract settlers as well as to manage scientifically the forests of these areas. The important ones were as follows:

1. "Tenants will be allowed to cut unmarked trees without permit for their bonafide personal requirements from the area open for this purpose.
2. No indents will be allowed with the exception of indents for timber for (a)Pucca houses, (b)Timber required by new settlers.
3. The sanctioned scale of timber to be allowed per 100 bighas* of cultivation for Bhabhar and Tarai was:
   (a) **Bhabhar:** For agricultural implements, 'Kachha' houses and cattle sheds including new houses, new cattle sheds and repairs to old houses and old cattle sheds, timber of the following species and according to the quantities laid down below will be given annually in the form of poles,props and rafters for houses and cattle sheds and larger trees for agricultural implements:

6/1/4 bighas = 1 acre = 0.40469 ha.

Sal	.099 c.m.	
Khair	.020 c.m.	
Sissoo	.0.13 c.m.	per 100 bighas of
Tun	.0054 c.m.	cultivation. (6.56 ha)
Dhauri & Kokat .	60 c.m.	

(Over 0.3m diameter)

(b) **Tarai:** for houses, including new houses and repairs to old houses and cattle sheds per 100 bighas of cultivation. This timber also includes timber required for agricultural implements, so no separate timber for ploughs will be given.

Sal	.06 c.m.	
Sissoo	.01 c.m.	
Khair	.016 c.m.	per 100 bighas of
	cultivation.	(6.56 ha)
Tun	.054 c.m.	
Dhauri and Kokat	.46 c.m.	

(over 0.07 m girth)

(c) **Masonry Building:** For masonry buildings, either for new or for repairs to old buildings either in the Bhabhar or in the Tarai, tenants must submit application through the Superintendent Tarai and Bhabhar Estates.No timber will be given unless recommended by him. The following scale indicating the amount of timber to be given in relation to the area under cultivation is given as a normal guide, but any case may be considered on its merits:

Up to 500 bighas(32.8 ha.)

Sal 4.6c.m. (measured in the log under bark)

Haldu 2.3 c.m.(measured in the log under bark)

For each subsequent 500 bighas

Sal 2.3 c.m. (measured in the log under bark)

Haldu 1.15 c.m. (measured in the log under bark)

(d) **Timber for New Settlers:** All applications must be submitted through the Superintendent, Tarai and Bhabhar and recommended by him, but the maximum amount of timber which will be given will be, four times the amount allowed under (3a) (3b) for the area it is anticipated by the Superintendent will be brought under cultivation in the first year".

(Source - Forest Division, Haldwani)

This so-called scientific management of forests put further restrictions on the residents in procuring their need for small timber. This also meant preventing waste of the forest produce. This arrangement as became evident a decade later added to the discontent of the local, who previously were used to procure their requirement without any let and hinder. These rules also added to the importance of the forest officials, a factor which fuelled further the antagonism of the locals.

Post War Reconstruction Boards:

Inspite of these restrictions there was a steady growth of settlers in Tarai and Bhabhar upto the dawn of the 20th century along with its first decade. It was primarily for the rise in population and easy availability of land there. But in 1918 owing to the epidemic of influenza, which swept this area, the population started dwindling. In 1920 these tracts were further ravaged by the epidemic of cholera. Shyam Lal Verma, a member of the Tarai and Bhabhar Development Committee in 1947, is of the view that both these areas could not recover after the above mentioned epidemics.

According to the 'Report of the Tarai and Bhabhar Development Committee, 1947', a series of dacoities over a period of 30 years preceding 1947 was also responsible for a steady decline of population. The forests in Bhabhar and Tarai afforded a safe sanction to bands of robbers from the very beginning. The British tried to settle them in agricultural pursuits, but could not succeed and Tarai and Bhabhar were frequently ravaged by the Mewati, Gujjars and dacoits from the Doab. Tarai was also a haunt of the Indian Robin Hood, Sultana Bhantu.

However, the establishment of a Post-War Reconstruction Board in January 1943, gave impetus to a plan for settling people here. I.W. Russell, the then Superintendent of Tarai and Bhabhar prepared a preliminary report on the scheme of settling soldiers in this area; but the scheme was abandoned on the critical comments of William Stampe, Irrigation Adviser to the Government of India, who considered the problem of Tarai drainage from an engineering view point, most 'difficult and insuperable'. But as the end of the Second World War was in sight, the question of the retrenched soldiers began to loom large and at the instance of the Government, a detailed topographical contoured survey was ordered. Radha Kant prepared a detailed scheme for the colonization of ex-servicemen in the Tarai and Bhabhar; but it could not be implemented until 1947. Released army personnel were allotted land in the villages around Bazpur, Kashipur, Haldwani and Kaladhungi etc.

As the Second World War drew to an end, the scarcity of food caused by it compelled the Central and Provincial Governments to take up urgent and immediate measures to increase the production of staple food grains. Consequently herculean efforts were initiated in the Tarai and Bhabhar region of Naini Tal district. The Government was trying to cope up with this situation when India achieved Independence and with it came the partition. Thus in and after 1947 waves after waves of refugees from Punjab and East Pakistan came to settle down in Tarai-Bhabhar and with these new settlers started a new era of permanent settlement in Tarai and Bhabhar areas of district Naini Tal.

Among the diverse groups of people that have settled in the Tarai and Bhabhar Region, at least the following 15 categories of migrants can be broadly identified.

1. Tribal settlers, mostly Tharus and Buxas.
2. Hill people of U.P.
3. Punjabi settlers who came before 1947.
4. Punjabi refugee settlers.
5. Subsequent Punjabi settlers as a consequence of chain migration (they are not necessarily refugees, but relations of the first wave of Punjabi migrants).
6. Bengali refugee settlers who had come from East Pakistan after 1947.
7. Bengali refugees from East Pakistan who came during 1963-64 owing to political disturbances.
8. Repatriates from Burma.
9. Ex-servicemen.
10. Agricultural graduates.
11. Political sufferers and freedom fighters who were given land by the Government (mostly from Eastern U.P.)
12. Bengali refugee settlers who came from Bangladesh after 1971.
13. Absentee landlords, including politicians, film stars, high officials, business-men and industrialists who managed to purchase land in the newly developed region.
14. Jat settlers.
15. Rai Sikhs.

These settlements have brought in a sea change in Tarai and Bhabhar. With the new settlements farms have replaced dense forests. Owing to the disappearance of forests, wild-life is almost on the verge of extinction. Coming in of new settlers have made the life of the original settlers of this place, e.g. Tharus and Buxas pitiable. The new-comers have by hook or crook deprived the tribals of their extensive land and have compelled them to make their living by working as labourers. The moisture and humus rich Tarai land has turned into a granary now, thereby making the new settlers neo-rich. Of late farm based industries also have started coming up. This has brought in social discontent in its trail. The tribals are already dissatisfied with their lot. Coming up of industries is dislodging the locals from their land. Gradually the neo-rich is increasing its clout. Punjab terrorists have worsened the situation.

In Tarai and Bhabhar there are today 10 Development Blocks, viz. Haldwani, Kotabagh, Ramnagar, Jaspur, Kashipur, Bajpur, Gadarpur,Rudrapur, Sitarganj and Khatima. There are eleven municipalities and eight Town Area Committees. The area and population of different urban localities is detailed below:

S.No	Urban localities	Geographical area in km2	Population 1981 Census	Population 1991 Census
(A)	**Municipalities**			
1.	Haldwani-Kathgodam	10.62	71300	102744
2.	Kashipur	5.46	51773	69889
3.	Ramnagar	2.46	26013	37288
4.	Jaspur	4.00	21242	39719
5.	Tanakpur	1.01	8818	1310
6.	Rudrapur	12.43	34658	61067
7.	Khatima	8.40	8493	11243
8.	Kichha	4.00	13606	21176
9.	Gadarpur	3.40	3615	9445
10	Bajpur	2.62	11366	16858
11.	Sitarganj	2.00	3212	16722

(B) Town Area Committees

1.	Kaladhungi	1.16	3112	4670
2.	Lalkuan	4.25	3155	5235
3.	Sultanpur	2.00	4769	5848
4.	Dineshpur	4.95	3308	6056
5.	Kaila Khera	4.98	3335	5020
6.	Mahua Dabra	5.20	3263	5338
7.	Mahua Dabra Ganj	2.80	4722	6605
8.	Shaktigarh	7.64	3151	3843

2
The Tribes of Tarai

Tharus :

The Sub-Himalayan Tarai of Kumaon is inhabited by two tribes Tharus and Buxas. They are the earliest settlers in the region and their antiquity has given them the claim of being the autocthons of Tarai. The Tharus live in the Khatima and Sitarganj blocks. Their population according to the 1991 Census is 66, 175. They are spread in 142 villages, but in fact the number of villages with exclusive or dominant Tharu population is about 88 out of the 142 villages inhabited by this tribe. In some of the villages their number is negligible.

Their Origin:

According to the tradition prevalent amongst the Tharus, their original home is Chittor and their progenitors are Jaimal

Fateh Singh and Tarran Singh of the Sisodiya clan of the Rajputs (1303 A.D.)

H.R. Nevill, is of the view that the Tharus are an aboriginal clan who claim royal descent from the female side of the rulers of this area. He states that in the remote past, when the ruler of this region was defeated by the forces of an invader, the women of the royal palace rather than fall into the hands of the enemy fled into the dense forests with the Saises and Chamars belonging to the place. From their union sprang the two indigenous races, the Tharus and Buxas, the former to have descended from the 'Chamars' or cobblers and the latter from the 'Saises' or black-smiths.

Crooke traces their origin to the word 'Tharu,' denoting a 'wine bibber'. This name is believed to have been given to the Tharus by one of the Kshatriya Rajas of the plains, who was astonished to witness the Tharus thirst or capacity to consume liquor. Nesfield holds the view that, "the word 'Thar', which in the colloquial dialect of the lowest classes means a man of the forest," is quite applicable to the Tharus, since it denotes their forest dwelling .

Tharu Villages :

The Tharu villages are generally scattered. In the past when land was in abundance they were always in search of a good site for their villages. A good site according to them was a tract of land on a raised level with close proximity to a river or some water source, but safe from water logging or inundation during the rainy season. The fertility was to be high and the tract had to be safe from the ravages of wild animals, epidemics and the haunt of evil spirits. If any of these conditions was lacking they were apt to abandon the site as had happened in the past. It is stated that the Tharu village, Tisaur in Sitarganj Tahsil had been shifted as many as four times from its original site due to inundation of land. This is not possible nowadays owing to the alienation of Tharu land by some of the big farmers who settled here after 1947. A number of villages in Sitarganj and Khatima tahsils were deserted in the past due to the menace of wild elephants, or epidemics or owing to the presence of evil spirits. At the time of abandoning the villages, the Tharus removed only their household goods to their new settlement and left behind their houses intact to become haunts of evil spirits.

Once a village is established, its boundary is usually marked by pillars or posts made of stones. In Tharus villages, fields separate one house from another. A narrow and unmetalled lane runs through a village. On either side of the lanes, the houses are arranged neatly on a higher elevation in a row. Mostly there is no clustering of houses in Tharu villages like in other Indian villages and their dwellings are conspicious owing to their cleanliness.

Another characteristic feature of the Tharu village is the community life. Here one person is related to others by more than one kinship ties resulting from blood and nuptial relationship. The Tharus represent a closely knit society. The Tharus of Tarai claim themselves as 'Rana Tharus' and according to Dr. S.K. Srivastava they have developed a bond of fellowship and corporate life through mutual obligation and co-partnership. They have a strong traditional panchayat organization to settle their disputes and to ensure adherence to their common code of conduct.

Tharu Religion and Rites:

With the passage of time the Tharus have become Hinduised and practice the Brahmanical form of religion; but traces of tribal religion can still be observed.

They have faith on benevolent and malevolent spirits. The former have to be appeased with prayers and supplications while the latter have to be contained, averted or exorcised by spells and threats or even through magic. Thus 'Pachhauwan', the benevolent spirit and 'Kharga Bhut', the evil spirit have become family deities of the Tharus.

Together with this there are hill spirits and jungle spirits which are propitiated as symbols of the forces of nature or at times are personified and propitiated as powers of the immediate environment of the Tharus. The two well known hill spirits are Parwatiya and Punyagiri which are supposed to reside in the northern hills. Parwatiya when offended inflicts people with sickness. Punyagiri is believed to be fond of children but if she is offended she inflicts them with chronic diseases and they can hardly survive her attack.

The jungle spirits on which the Tharus have faith are Banaspati and Arimal or Bharamal. Banaspati is supposed to reside over a pile of branches inside the village forest and whenever an individual happens to pass through that tract, he adds another branch to the pile as a token of gratitude and respect.

Arimal or Bharamal is symbolized by a pile of stones and is supposed to reside in close proximity to Banaspati. The villagers add a stone to the pile whenever they pass that way. This spirit is invoked when the cattle go astray and once the cattle are found, the individual who invokes the spirit offers sweets worth one and a quarter rupees. It is further believed that so efficacious is the spirit that if one fails to give the offering of sweets in the prescribed time, the offender will arouse the ire of the spirit and incur a heavier loss.

Ancestral Spirits:

The Tharus have tremendous faith on the spirits of their departed ancestors and address them as Budhe Babu or Niradhar. They are installed in every Tharu household and are propitiated on every religious rite. It is a common belief amongst them that when Budhe Babu possesses the children it makes them weep for days and the Tharu mothers then offers it rice and concomitantly the children are relieved from its hold.

Spirits of the Cattle:

The cattle spirits known as Karodew and Rakat Kaluwa are supposed to protect the animals of the Tharus from diseases and night predators. In the month of July offerings are made to the cattle spirits and it is regarded as the privilege of the head of the family to make this offering.

The Tiger Spirit:

It is believed by the Tharus that those persons who are killed by tigers become spirits and are known as 'Bagha Bhuts' or tiger spirits. This denotes the Tharus residing within or on the periphery of Tarai forests, which abounded in tigers during those days. Besides the cult of the dead, the Tharus have added to their pantheon of religious worship, the gods,goddesses and saints of other communities, like Hindus,Muslims and Sikhs. Some of the famous Gods of the Hindu pantheon, such as, Pandava, Mahadev and Nar Singh have been incorporated in their religion. Mahadev is regarded by the Tharus, like the Hindus as the God of destruction and Nar Singh as the reincarnation of Lord Vishnu. The belief in a Supreme Being, Thakur, is also borrowed from the Hindu philosophy. They consider Thakur, the Supreme God who is very benevolent and does no harm to mankind.

The Muslim 'Pirs' or holy men are also revered by the Tharus. Bala Pir is very popular amongst them and is supposed to guide and help them when troubled by evil spirits and during sickness of the children. They also rever Bale Miyan and Mithan Shah. Guru Nanak Deo is also worshipped by the Tharus like the Hindus.

The concept of village goddess is also prevalent among the Tharus. On the outskirts of every Tharus village, towards the east under a 'pipal' tree or a ' neem' tree is the abode of the village goddess Bhumsen. She represents collectively all gods, goddesses and spirits. The village goddess is installed on a mound of earth. In close proximity, and at lesser elevations on the mounds of earth other deities are installed by the Bharara (priest). The main deities which are installed with the village goddess are the seven mother goddesses, viz. Durga, Kalka, Sitala, Jwala, Parwati, Hulaka and Purwa. It appears that the superior position retained by the Tharu women is projected by the dominant mother goddesses.

Religious Rites in Agriculture:

The maximum time of the Tharus is spent in agriculture and associated pursuits because of which their important religious rites centre around agricultural operations. Different rituals and rites (a few of which are given below) are observed by the Tharus to protect their crop from animals, insects and pests:

(a) It is a common belief amongst the Tharus that if the seed sown does not germinate, only the Bharara can relieve them from this problem through his magical prowess. The Bharara on listening to the woe of the peasant takes a couple of rounds of the field sprinkling water and chanting 'mantras'. This ritual to augment germination is known as 'Bahurava'.

(b) Once the plants have blossomed to protect them from insect pests the Bharara energizes some milk with his magical power and keeps it at the Padhan's or village headman's residence. Later this milk is distributed amongst all the villagers and concomitantly the women of every house hold sprinkle this charmed milk over three corners of their fields leaving the fourth through which it is believed that the insects will escape.

(c) The Tharus believe that by spreading smoke over fields created by burning jaggery and ghee is also helpful in getting rid of pests and insects.

(d) To prevent crops from wild animals 'machans' are raised on poles which serve as watch posts. But in the villages which border forests, this technique is not very helpful. In such villages the help of Bharara is sought who first recites some mantras and after the chanting of the mantras sprinkles water over different corners of the fields. It is believed that after weaving this magical spell, the animals dare not enter the fields.

The Ceremony of Naya:

This ceremony is observed on a Monday or Thursday. It is celebrated when the corn begins to ripen in the fields. On this day the Tharus offer some ears of grain to their household deities to invoke their blessings before harvesting. It is also associated with the ceremony of the first tasting of the new grain. To celebrate the occasion men and women bring some stalks of grain from the fields and offer them to the household gods. The grains are then removed from the stalks and after grinding, 'puries' and sweets are prepared with them. Concomitantly these delicacies are offered to the gods to receive their final blessings before harvesting. Afterwards the food offered to the gods is shared amongst the family members and guests.

Religious Festivals :

Of all the festivals, Holi is celebrated with greatest fervour by the Tharus. The celebration of Holi or the spring festival starts from 'Puranmasi' or the full-moon in February. On the day of the commencement of Holi a small semal (Bombax ceiba) tree is burnt in an open space near the temple of the village goddess, Bhumsen. The next day the villagers led by the village headman or Padhan assemble near the temple of Bhumsen. The Padhan carries jaggery, ghee and clove in a brass plate together with a mug of water and fire. The villagers and the children, who accompany the Padhan, carry with them five cow dung cakes and musical instruments like cymbals and drums. They proceed singing and dancing. When the procession reaches the temple of Bhumsen, the Padhan takes off his shoes and places on the fire the offering he has brought for all the deities and Bhumsen. The cow dung cakes are then burnt in the holy fire. In the end jaggery is distributed among the people present there who sing Holi songs and dance.

After the function is over at the Bhumsen's temple, the villagers go to the Padhan's house for sweet and jaggery and then they return to their houses. The Holi festival is celebrated for about a month and a half and throughout the period there is much revelry, dancing and music. For dancing married men don their wedding costumes, but their womenfolk do not. The men tie anklets round their ankles for dancing. Men and women dance separately in circles of their own. Sometimes they dance together also, though it is very rare. However in both the forms one group sings and the other dances repeating the lines of the lead singer. The singers are accompanied by musical instruments like drums and cymbals.

On the eighth day after the commencement of Holi, the Tharus celebrate the function known as Khakarera. On this day an individual from every family in the village accompanied by the Pahdan carries seven balls of mud with seven thin wickers stuck in the ball. The Padhan also carries with him cloves, ghee, jaggery, five different kinds of grain (pachranga), flowers of tesu, leaves of barley as well as fire in a broken pitcher and goes in southern direction. After crossing the outskirts of the village, the Padhan places the offering on the fire in the name of goddess Bhawani and breaks the broken pitcher into pieces with a hammer. The onlookers raise slogans in the name of the goddess and clapping their hands they run towards the river to take a holy dip in it. In the end they all assemble at the Padhan's house and indulge in throwing coloured water at each other. The act is called 'Chhalari'. After they have finished with the amusement of throwing water at each other they sing Holi songs and eat jaggery and sweets offered to them by the Padhan.

The amusement and revelry of Holi comes to an end with the ceremony of Bari Charai which is observed in the month of April. The Bharara fixes an auspicious date either on a Monday or Thursday in the first or second week of April to celebrate Bari Charai.

The day before Bari Charai, there is community fishing; men, women and children go to a nearby river for fishing. The next morning, on the actual day of the Bari Charai, the Bharara makes an offering of jaggery, cloves and ghee to the goddess Bhumsen. Subsequently the women folk of the village do community cooking and prepare special dishes of fish, puri, sweet rice and other dishes according to the availability of food items. After cooking all the ladies of the village, go to some orchard for picnicking with the Padhaniya or the Padhan's wife as their leader. The Padhan as well as the Bharara and some men reach there, after which the Bharara invokes the Goddess Bhawani and offers her prayers. When the prayers are over, the ladies treat the Bharara with eatables as a special guest and he reciprocates by chanting some mantras for their health and happiness. After this ritual is over all those present assemble under a mango tree to have their food. Subsequently the Padhaniya initiates vulgar Holi jokes and the rest of the women follow suit. The Padhan, Bharara and the other men who are present there become the target of these obscene jokes. Soon the menfolk become so embarrassed that they flee the scene and play Chhalari and throw water on other men who happen to pass that way. The women on the other hand crack dirty jokes, sing crude, vulgar songs and indulge in other obscenities till sunset. The vulgarities are mostly manifested in a musical form and the accompanying instrument for maintaining the rhythm is the dhol or drum.

A fortnight after the Bari Charai festival, Chhoti Charai is celebrated. In this the local deities are propitiated by the villagers in the morning. Later the womenfolk from every household prepare different dishes in their houses, including fish and then they gather in an orchard with the food and picnic together. After partaking the food the women sing group songs for hours. The theme of the songs revolves around love stories and the pangs of separation which the lovers and the husband and wife have to undergo. Mostly there is a lead singer and the rest follow her.

Asadhi :

The festival is celebrated in the month of July, which synchronizes with the Hindu calendar month Asadh. The Bharara is called to invoke Bhumsen and other associated deities. This worship is both individual and collective. The main motive of propitiation is to protect the village from diseases and natural calamities. For pleasing the gods, the

Bharara makes an offering of ghee and jaggery on the holy fire and then sacrifices goats or fowls. For collective worship contributions are made by every family.

For individual or private worship, the patriarch of the family observes a fast until the required offerings have been made to the family deities by the Bharara. The rituals involved to please the gods in individual worship are very interesting. Amongst the pantheon of Tharu gods, goddess Durga who is a symbol of Shakti is held in high esteem. On this occasion goddess Durga is offered jaggery and ghee in the sacrificial fire and then a red flag is tied in the courtyard of the house in her reverence. The spirits of the ancestors and the spirits of the cattle-shed are also worshipped on this day.

Aunth :

This festival is celebrated in the month of Kunwar (September - October) after the harvesting of paddy. No special religious rites are performed on this festival except that the women prepare sweets and dishes of rice on this day to offer them to the spirits of the ancestors and the family deities for invoking their blessings.

Worship on the Occupation of a new House:

Before selecting the site for a new house, the Bharara is called for worshiping the goddess Bhawani. Subsequently the site is selected and again before the foundation stone is laid, the family deities are worshipped by the Bharara to seek their blessings. Sweets and jaggery are then distributed to rejoice the occasion. Once the house is completed, the Bharara fixes an auspicious date to occupy the house. Mostly the day falls on Thursday. Before the family enters the new house, the head of the family installs the ancestral spirits and the family deities. Then he makes an offering to them to invoke their blessings. The matriarch also offers the first cooked meal in the new house to the ancestral spirits and the family deities. After the offerings, food is partaken by the family and family friends.

It seems that the basic idea of the religious rites, ceremonies and worship of the Tharu gods, goddesses and spirits is to invoke their blessings against the fear of the unknown and the unforeseen and to ensure the welfare of the individual family as well as the community at the village level.

Birth Ceremony :

After conceiving a woman has to observe certain taboos till the time she delivers. She is not supposed to go out during the solar eclipse. But if it is important for her to leave the house she must smear some ash on her belly and must not expose it to the sun.

She is not supposed to visit places which are haunted. Not only that, she must not touch a corpse, pass through a cremation ground and even avoid social callings during nights.

It is important for every pregnant woman to don an amulet made and blessed by the village Bharara. This amulet with its magical powers can protect the child from evil spirits and can also ward off the evil eye in the mother's womb.

Village Panchayat:

The Tharus of Tarai are mostly Rana Thakurs. They have a strong traditional Panchayat organization for enforcing social discipline, settling their disputes and ensuring adherence to their common code of conduct. A Village Panchayat is a compact social unit constituted of different families in a village, which can execute certain functions which an individual family on its own cannot adequately and satisfactorily perform. The Village Community is responsible for maintaining law and order as well as in retaining their cultural heritage and identity. Whenever there is a cultural activity in the village like presentation of folk dances, folk songs and even folk tales, it is obligatory for the whole village to witness the performance.

It also helps in promoting the reciprocity of obligations in the socio-economic life of the Tharus. The members of the community are willing to help each other during social activities or in crisis. The main reason which can be attributed to it is the strong bondage of kinship among the Tharus.

The Buxas

The core area of the Buxas, known as Bhuksar, encompasses the Gadarpur, Bajpur, Kashipur and Ramnagar blocks in Western Tarai. But their main concentration is in the Bajpur and Gadarpur blocks of Tarai. The total Buxa population in the district, as per 1991 Census is 20,548 and they are spread in 86 villages.

Origin :

The Buxas claim royal descent from their female side. According to Amir Hasan, who had been closely associated with the welfare programme of the Buxas, "the Buxas of Bajpur claim descent from Raja Jagatdeo, a great warrior of Rajasthan, who was a worshipper of Durga and offered his head to her". The Buxas claim that they brought goddess Durga, now known as Kashipur Devi to Tarai and the coconut offered by them to propitiate her is symbolic of the head offered by Raja Jagatdeo.

Some Buxas are of the view that Raja Jagatdeo had two sons, Chittaur and Nandhur or Anandhar. It is believed that the Tharus are the scions of Chittaur and Anandhar is supposed to be the progenitor of the Buxas. There are yet others who maintain that Andandhar was brother and not the son of Raja Jagatdeo. His descendants are also Buxas with the only difference that these Buxas do not till the land, they only disperse seed on the soil and they abstain from meat and fish.

Some Buxas assert that they are Panwar Rajputs and their progenitor, Udayjit of Dhara Nagri wing owing to some misunderstanding with his elder brother Raja Jagatdeo was banished from home. He and his followers then took refuge near Banbasa on the Sarda river in Naini Tal district in Kumaon. Later the Raja of Kumaon solicited his help for defending the territories of Kumaon against the neighbouring powers. He was thus made the feudal lord of the Sub-Himalayan Tarai in

Kumaon. W. Crooke, the author of the book' The Tribes and Castes of North-Western Provinces and Oudh', also states that many Buxas claim that they came from Dakkhin, others from Delhi and that they were expelled from the Dakkhin by the Marathas . However on the basis of an anthropological survey conducted with the help of Dr. B.S. Pangtey it can be stated that the Buxas like the Tharus are of a Mongoloid stock.

Religious Beliefs :

The Buxas are amongst the most Hinduized tribes of India. They themselves claim to be Hindus and to support their viewpoint they state that like the Hindus they had a caste hierarchy in the past which later on merged into one class.

According to Buxa tradition they had migrated to Tarai in the medieval period to escape the wrath of the Mughals. When they arrived here they had to face several problems just like an uprooted community has to experience in an entirely new environment. The Buxas thus realized that for survival in this rugged and inhospitable tract it was essential to dispense with their caste and class barriers. Subsequently in one of the nocturnal marathon sessions which was held on the banks of the river Sarda, it was decided to merge all the castes and subcastes into one and to draw a veil of secrecy over their past. The decision was made obligatory and irrevocable. Since then the Buxa society is stated to have become classless. However on the basis of their Rajput ancestry from the female side, the Buxas are divided into four classes, viz. Rajbansi (or royal lineage), Suryabansi (of solar lineage), Chandrabansi (of lunar lineage) and Dujbansi(of Brahmin lineage). But this classification is merely notional and has no effect on the seemingly casteless structure of the Buxa society.

The Buxas worship most of the deities of the Hindu pantheon, but it is Lord Rama and his spouse Sita which command maximum reverence among them. Next to Rama is Lord Krishna who is extremely popular amongst the women and youth.

Sunderi Devi or Basundra Devi is also worshipped with great respect by the Buxas. She is a married goddess and according to the Buxas her original abode is in Dharanagar in Rajasthan from where the Buxas also claim to have migrated. When they moved into Tarai, they brought the goddess along with them. The Buxas believe that Sundari Devi is originally a tribal goddess who was later taken into the folds of Hinduism. Her devotees are known as 'Deviware' and constitutes one of the two sects into which the Buxas are subdivided. The others are called 'Guruware' who are worshippers of Guru Nanak Dev. For the Buxas, Guru Dev is Guru Nanak Shah and is worshipped on several occasions. The Buxas are aware of Guru Nanak Dev, but not of the tenets of Sikhism. At present the worshippers of Guru Nanak also worship the Devi and like to identify themselves with the Deviwares.

Muslim saints and thinkers have also made an impact on the Buxas. Crooke mentions two Muslim saints, Sarwar Lakhi and Kalu Sayyid who are worshipped by the Buxas. Zahir Auliyapir is also revered by the Buxas of Bajpur only and they maintain that he was originally a Kshatriya who later embraced Islam. During his worship, he is offered flowers and 'matkas' or earthen pots.

In Dehradun there are Mussani or Muswani Buxas who unlike other Buxas shun pork. Legend has it that Muswanis were originally Muswans or Mussalmans, i.e. Muslims working for the Rajput 'ranis' or queens who migrated to Tarai and subsequently mingled with the composite Buxa community which sprung after the merger of different castes and creeds. Interestingly some of the Buxas living in Dogadda Block of Garhwal invoke the Prophet, Hazart Mohammad and his daughter Bibi Fatima to cure diseases and ward away evil spirits.

Apart from the Hindu pantheon of gods and goddesses there are some indigenous Buxa deities also, which are worshipped by them. In every village in front of the Padhan's (village headman)house there is an elevated mud platform, measuring 1.5x 0.9 metres. This raised platform is the abode of Bhumsen, the master of land as well as protector of the village.

Bhumsen is the village god, whereas Bhumica is the family deity. Its abode is in every household and once every year, he is offered a ceremonial worship. The auspicious occasion chosen for the purpose is after the harvesting season when there is enough food-grain for feasting and rejoicing. Other families from the village are also invited for the celebration. Since different families fix different dates for the ceremony, the festivity lasts for a month.

The Buxa Village:

Unlike other tribes of India, The Tharus and Buxas live in an area which is highly developed and known as the agricultural bowl of India. Most of the agriculturists in Tarai are affluent, but the Buxas and Tharus have become an anachronism in Tarai today. Their whole mode of living with their primitive agriculture and mud-walled hutments are not in consonance with the true perspective of Tarai. Although the face of Tarai has changed dramatically after its colonization since 1947, there is hardly any improvement in the economic life of the Buxas and no material benefits have accrued to Buxa villages in the last 46 years.

The Buxa villages are built on one straight street plan generally of a considerable width between 12 to 18 metres and are very clean with the huts placed end to end. In majority of the villages there are two rows of houses, the doors of each row facing east with a wide courtyard in between. The cattle-sheds are normally at the back of the houses, though in some dwellings, the row of cattlesheds lie in front of the house with the courtyard being located between the house and the cattle shed. In some villages there is only one row of houses, but even in these dwellings, a spacious courtyard is conspicuous.

In the past the site of a Buxa village was selected near a water point in consultation with the priest. He used to give his approval after propitiating the god Bhumsen. Once the village site was identified, a suitable place was found to install the god

Bhumsen. Subsequently a site was selected for the 'Padhan's or village headman's house. Normally it was constructed near Bhumsen's abode. After this the huts for the villagers were constructed in such a manner that the row of the houses lay north-east with the doors facing towards the east. When the colony was completed, the priest was again invited to worship the god Bhumsen after which the families moved into their new homes. However with the vicissitudes of time the practice has discontinued.

Moreover in the present day situation with encroachment in Buxa villages, it is not possible for them to change their settlements at will.

In Buxa house wood is used liberally. Both the roof and walls are made of wooden frames. The roof is supported by horizontally fixed wooden logs made from sal (Shorea robusta) or haldu (Adina cordifolia) wood. These logs are in their turn supported by pillars made of khair (Acacia catechu) or bakain (Melia azadirachta). The walls made of wooden frames are later plastered with mud in such a manner that the wood frame is not visible. These plastered walls are subsequently decorated with pictorial representations, mostly religious and floral designs. The Buxa dwellings are very beautiful and blend with the background. In recent years some affluent Buxas have constructed cement houses which are very incongruous with their surroundings. In the old houses there are no separate bathrooms and lavatories. Mostly people take bath in the nearby river or well and for answering the call of nature they go to the forest.

Social Structure :

There are two important characteristics of the Buxa society, their already stated social equality and the privileged position of the Buxa women.However the Buxas do have among themselves a system of superior and inferior 'Gotra',though it hardly affects the social status of any family. As the Buxas are an agricultural community, there are economic disparities also due to the size of agricultural holdings and their cattle wealth.

But such economic disparities do not result in social inequality to a great extent. The Buxas are related to each other by consanguinous and affinity ties. The blood relations, parents and the succeeding progeny constitute a 'khandan'. The relatives by marriage or other associations are termed as 'Asnams'.

The Buxas of Kumaon Tarai as pointed out earlier are divided mainly into two socio-religious groups, the Deviware and the Guruware. Both the groups claim superiority over each other, though Deviwares, being the more dominant group, have been able to establish their superiority over the other group.

Intermarriage is prevalent among the two groups. However if a boy from the Devi worshiping family marries a Guruware girl, then the groom's parents perform certain ceremonies after the nuptial rituals to relieve their bride from the influence of the deities of her parents' home and to initiate her in their religious system. This is called 'devta utarna' and 'devta chharahna', descension and ascension of the deities. During the descension ceremony the deities of the bride's ancestral home are offered sweets to induce them to descend and relieve the girl. In the ascension ceremony which follows soon after, the newly wed is offered sweets and one of the elders of the family holds her hand and requests his family deities to accept her. After performing these rituals the bride is permitted to enter her in-laws kitchen. According to tradition when a girl from the Guruware sect is married into the Deviware, her presence in the kitchen without performing the purification rituals is said to displease the gods and they may forsake the family of the Guruwares. When a Deviware girl who is married into the Guruware sect visits her parents, she is also not permitted into the kitchen of her parents, because she is supposed to have become impure in the company of the Guruwares.

Apart from these two sects there are two more groups among the Buxas who are termed as Domares and the Pachhmia. The Domares are supposed to be scions of a Buxa who had eaten food from the hands of a nautch girl.It is said that once a Buxa musician played 'sarangi' with a nautch girl, because the instrumentalist who accompanied her was indisposed. This nautch girl had come to perform in a Buxa village during a religious ceremony. Since the accompanist was ill it was essential for the local musician to accompany the dancer lest the gods became angry.During the dance performance, both fell in love with each other and they spent the night together.

The next morning the incident became public and the erring couple were produced before the Panchayat, (a meeting of the elders). The dancer confessed before the elders that the Buxa had slept with her, but had not partaken her food. On the other hand the musician, who was so infatuated by the woman's charm, contradicted her by stating that he had eaten from the hands of the dancer. He thought by saying so he would get the woman. The dancing party however did not oblige him and they left after showing their displeasure. The Buxa Panchayat took a serious view of the fact that he had eaten food from the hands of a nautch girl and ostracised him and his family members. Although this incident took place in the hoary past, the stigma is still attached with this social group and even today they cannot marry or dine with the other Buxas. But secretly many Buxas eat or drink with them at their place though they would not accept this in public

The Buxas living in the north-western portion of Kashipur sub-division are known as Pachhima (westerners) or Pachhmia Buxas. This group is more akin to the Buxas of Dehradun district. The Buxas of Kumaon Tarai consider them as inferior. They do not give their daughters in marriage to the Pachhmias though their daughters are accepted in their families.

Gotras and Kheras :

The Buxas have a system of 'Gotras' on the pattern of the Hindu society. Besides 'Gotras' they also have 'Khera', literally meaning the place of residence, which connotes the place where the family originally lived.

Social Organization :

The Buxas have a well knit and strong village organization. They live exclusively in hamlets of their own. Previously non-tribals did not live in proximity of Buxa villages, but now with the encroachment upon tribal land, non-tribals have started to live in their vicinity. However, non-tribals have not been allowed to construct houses in the midst of Buxa villages owing to which the Buxa habitations have been able to retain their identity. The village unit is most important amongst the Buxa social organization and is more important than the family unit.

The affairs of the Buxa village are presided over by a strong functionary called the 'Padhan' or the village headman. He maintains discipline and solidarity in the village by virtue of his traditional position, authority and prestige of his office.

The institution of Padhan was created by the British for Kham administration.He acted as an intermediary between the people and the State. The Kham Superintendent used to settle an area for Buxa habitation and with the help of the Padhan he distributed land to the Buxas. The Padhan in turn used to collect rent from the cultivators on behalf of the Kham Superintendent.

In the past when the Buxas practised shifting cultivation, it was not possible for the administration to keep a count of them and consequently to register their names in revenue records. It was therefore considered expedient to deal with the head of the group and with the passage of time the Padhan became an intermediary between the people and the Kham Superintendent as well as the spokesman of his people.

The office of the Padhan was hereditary and the eldest son was accepted as his successor. With the coming of Independence the Kham administration was abolished and Gaon Sabhas (Village Council) have been set up with Pradhans or Padhans as their heads. In the present system the Padhan no longer enjoys the official status, but he still remains the head of his village and wields great influence. He is expected to be patron of all social occasions in the village like marriages, festival celebrations and social get togethers. All religious functions and programmes are organized under his supervision and he is the first to host a feast during festivals and later the revellers are entertained by other families of the village. The abode of Bhimsen, the village deity is in front of his house and most of the collective worship of the village folk is performed at his place. He acts as the guardian of the people and when the village is plagued with epidemics, he is expected to relieve the villagers from its wrath with the help of the deity Bharara.

The family and inter-family disputes are referred to him and he is expected to solve most of the problems at the village level. He settles them alone or with the help of the village elders.

When the Padhan is unable to settle a dispute at the village level, he refers the matter to the 'Takhat' or inter-village elders' council. The Takhat is an important social organization of the Buxas which provides guidelines in socio-religious and economic matters. It also lays some norms for social conduct and behaviour, ensures observance of traditions and settles village disputes like those of property, water, petty thefts, cattle lifting, sexual assaults and marital disputes.

The Takhat is presided over by a functionary who is also addressed as Takhat. He is assisted by different officials which are mentioned below:

(a) Munsif, who tenders advice to the Takhat and ssists him in dispensing cases.

(b) Daroga, is the Chief Executive officer of the Takhat. He summons the concerned parties to the sitting and ensures compliance of the decisions taken by the Takhat.

(c) Sipatus, are helpers of the Daroga who also act as messengers for issuing summons to the concerned parties.

The Takhat on his discretion also invites the Padhans of the village and other important Buxas during the hearing and their advice is taken into consideration while settling the disputes. The office of the Takhat is mostly hereditary and the eldest son usually succeeds his father. He may at times be called to assist his father during the meetings, or he even succeeds him during his life time.

The full bench of the Takhat does not usually meet for settlements of disputes. It is convened in full only when a dispute is of a serious nature and may have wide ranging repercussions or where matters of social conduct and general policy are involved. To avoid delay in disposing off cases, most of the Takhats appoint regional functionaries, who exercise jurisdiction over certain villages assigned to them and decide disputes at their level on behalf of the Takhat.

The power of the Takhat is gradually fading with the coming of the new settlers. They have begun interfering in the internal matters of the Buxas, so as to use them as a vote bank for their personal interests. In the past they have influenced decisions of the Takhat with the result that the youth is losing respect for it. The Buxas have a weakness for liquor and the new settlers take full advantage of this by inviting them for drinks and getting things done in their favour. During elections, the Buxas are terrorized by new settlers to vote in their favour with the result that there is hardly any voting right of the Buxas. This too has resulted in lowering the prestige of the Takhat.

Economic Activity :

More than 90 percent of the Buxas are involved in agriculture. In the past land was aplenty and they were masters of all they surveyed. But with the colonization of Tarai their habitats have shrunk in size. Some of the new settlers have illegally occupied their land, stolen their cattle and jeopardized their very existence. Today about 15 percent of the Buxas have become landless. The landless work mostly as agricultural labourers in big farms or they usually take land from other

Buxas on 'theka' or 'batai', i.e. letting out of land on rent or distribution of the agricultural yield on percentage basis.The Buxas normally do not like to approach non-tribals for leasing out land to them. They do not prefer to work for them. The landless Buxas are perpetually under debt. When the going gets tough, they migrate to other villages where till recently they used to get some land from the Padhan or other big Buxa land owners. However in the prevailing situation with the encroachment upon tribal land by the new settlers, this is not possible now.

The Buxa are extremely fond of fish. Fishing is almost a part of their routine. Each household has fishing nets and rods. A large number of men, women and children go for fishing in ponds,rivers and rivulets. They are so fond of fishing that they would not mind giving up urgent household chores and even suspending agricultural activity for fishing, especially group fishing.

Agriculture is the main vocation of the Buxas, though a negligible part of the population is involved in tailoring, as untrained Ayurvedic doctors, agricultural labourers and a very few in menial jobs.Even today the Buxas consider it below their dignity to go in for service, whether it is in Government, in the industrial sector or even private employment. Although the Buxas possess rudimentary knowiedge of carpentry and blacksmithy, they have not adopted these crafts to earn their livelihood or to supplement their income. However if efforts could be made by welfare agencies or social organizations to motivate them, these crafts could provide them a perennial source of income, especially to those who have been rendered landless.

The Buxa women help their men in their economic pursuits, especially agriculture. While ploughing is mainly done by men, women assist them in sowing and weeding. Harvesting as well as thrashing is done mainly by the women folk. They tend the cattle and keep poultry wherever possible.

The Buxa women are adroit in several handicrafts. They

prepare beautiful hand fans and baskets which are exquisite pieces of handiwork.They prepare mats from wild grass and are well versed in embroidery. The Buxa women are very dexterous in preparing utensils with mud and in decorating walls with designs made of mud. On festivals and religious occasions they prepare fine specimens of 'rangoli' ritualistic designs on the ground with cowdung, lime and pigments.

Rituals associated with Agriculture :

As Buxas are primarily agriculturists, several rituals are connected with agriculture. When rains are delayed, the Buxas invoke the rain god to quench the thirst of Mother Earth. Prayers are offered by the Bharara, the village priest, and children beat sticks and subsequently roll on the ground which is made wet with water.Together with this they chant, "snail, snail give us water and let it drain the fields". Concomitantly the children collect subscriptions in cash or kind and a community feast is held outside the village in a grove where offerings of foods are made to the rain god for rain.

Before planting or sowing paddy in 'kharif' and wheat and barley in 'rabi', Mother Earth is worshipped. Prayers are offered to Mother Earth in the field where the seedlings are to be planted and ghee and jaggery with incense is then burnt in the sacred fire. No rituals are however performed at the time of sowing other crops except for sugar-cane. Similarly no rituals are performed when seeds are sown to grow seedlings for transplantation.

Prayers are offered to the gods before harvesting the above mentioned crops. Two kilograms of grain are pounded into flour and big chappatis known as 'Tikkars' are prepared and offered to the gods with butter milk. Thereafter the crop is harvested and the first crop of the year is offered to 'Bhumia', the village deity. Later a community feast is held to celebrate the onset of harvesting.

When sugarcane is harvested, a 'havan' is performed at the grower's house and a few pieces of sugarcane are kept infront of the fire. Sowing and harvesting are mostly done on Wednesday, Thursday and Friday, as these days are supposed to be auspicious for the agricultural pursuits.

Deforestation and Tribes :

Destruction of forests has dwindled the forest base and concomitant loss of natural resources, thus adversely affecting the tribal economy. Further with the increase in agricultural land in Tarai, the tribals could not compete with the new settlers. While the new settlers commanded both money and muscle power, the Buxas were meek and steeped in poverty. By the sheer force of the domineering nature of the new settlers the Buxas were subjugated. In this they were also helped by the officials. In the initial stages, when Tarai and Bhabhar areas were colonized and rules were not being strictly enforced, a sizeable number of settlers encroached upon the territory of the tribals.According to the district administration in 1951, the Tharu and Buxa tribals owned about 250,000 ha of land, today only about 30,000 ha is in their possession. In most of the cases land grabbing was done through force or cajolery. The tribals were forced to gift, mortgage or lease land through affidavits. They were also subjected to harassment, so that ultimately they were forced to leave their villages or make a compromise with their tormentors by agreeing to be landless labourers and grow food crops in the land previously owned by them. It is a pity that even though in the revenue records they continue to be owners of the land, but so many years having passed in the meantime, they cannot obtain it.

The following methods were used by the new settlers to terrorise them:

(a) The tribal cattle were lifted at night or even during day time.

(b) Their animals were not allowed to graze on traditional forest land.

(c) Their fields were encroached upon and false cases were registered against them.

However the more belligerent amongst the new settlers just roared in with their tractors on fallow land to occupy it.

When the land alienation of tribals assumed serious proportion, the Social Welfare Department of the State Government appointed a study team to probe into the living conditions of the tribals. A detailed study report was prepared by it in 1978 which revealed that some 1300 settlers' families had grabbed land from the tribals, who had owned it for a century or so. The complicity of the authorities that be at this game of grabbing the Buxa land become evident when inspite of this report no action was taken against the land grabbers.

The land grabbing was done more often than not with the connivance of the revenue and police officials. Moreover the land revenue authorities have not been able to keep pace with the rapid development of agriculture in Tarai and Bhabhar in maintaining the records. They are in an absolute mess and it has been observed that in several cases the recorded tenant is not the actual occupant of the land. The worst affected by this motivated inefficiency of the revenue authorities are the tribals. This inefficiency is at the root of most of the difficulties of the tribals. Innocent as they are, they do not know the wily ways of the unscrupulous officials.

It is significant that besides tribal land, the trespassers did not spare even Government land, which they have recklessly occupied owing to the nonchalant attitude of the authorities, or in connivance with them. In a belated bid to correct the entries and to accept the reality of the situation, the Government adopted a policy of regularization of trespassed land, vide G.O. No. 1-35(12)66, dated July 6, 1967 of the U.P. Government. But this compromising attitude of the Government has encouraged the criminal elements to encroach further upon forest and tribal land.

Land grabbing was also done through unscrupulous money lending by 'banias' (local traders),'banjaras' (roving traders) who trade mostly in cereals) and some of the new settlers, who could not use muscle power. They snared the tribals into usury and took possession of their land and crop through deceit. The most prevalent mode was to acquire land through unregistered mortgage deeds in the face of the provision in the Zamindari Abolition and Land Reforms Act of 1969, which states that tribals can sell land to nontribals only after obtaining permission from the District Collector.This mortgage deed in reality is a camouflage for deceit and for giving a legal colour to the forgery. In the deed, the loan recorded is twice or thrice of the amount actually given and with the accrued interest it is impossible for the tribals to repay it. The land ultimately passes into the possession of the money lender and never reverts to the original owner, though in revenue records, it would still be in the name of the tribals.

Thanks to this provision of the land of the tribals being legally in their name in the revenue records, inspite of the same being in possession of others through deceitful means; the tribals can still reclaim the same if helped by the Government. Even being aware of fact, the risk is worth taking, for guardians of the law so far have failed to make their impact felt.Some of the land grabbers have now achieved social status with their money power and have also gained important positions in political parties. Consequently the Government officials are unable to take any serious and effective action against these illegal occupants.

This process of money lending has reduced the tribals to a hopeless condition.Even though they have become landless, they cannot be benefited by the U.P. Landless Agricultural Labourers Debt Relief Act of 1975, as on paper they continue to be land owners. This act covers all such persons whose main source of livelihood is agricultural labour. The legislation provides relief to landless agricultural labourers including members of Scheduled Tribes, from illegal and unregistered debts. It exempts them from decrees and attachments in connection with realization of debts which were not executed upto March 1975. But the Tharus and Buxas do not come within the ambit of this act, because on paper they own land in their name.

The incidence of indebtedness has assumed serious dimensions. While in the old days the money lenders were content with the high rate of interest or payment in kind, the present day money lenders have an eye on this land.Before 1950, when the money lender caused harassment to the tribals, the Kham Superintendent used to interfere and exempt the tribals from either payment of interests or fix easy installments of repayments.

Everything however has changed with the influx of outsiders. The money lenders from cities in and outside Tarai discovered the tribal areas of Tarai as a paradise for loaning during the first three decades of Post-Independence period. They were extremely unscrupulous and the rate of interest charged by them was exorbitant. They were not merely interested in charging excessive interests on loans advanced by them, as has been pointed out earlier, but had a much more dangerous intention of grabbing tribal land by tempting them to obtain easy money from them on loans. It is disturbing to find more than half of the tribals were not able to repay the loan and had to borrow again to make their repayment.

There were two ways for obtaining loan for repayment. In the first mode the tribals took loan from one money lender to repay another and in the other the same money lender changed the pronote. In these transfers all sorts of malpractices were indulged in with the result that the borrower could hardly pay the interest. There was always a divergence between the loans actually taken and loans shown on papers. The tribals who then had land aplenty with no idea of its value, did not realize the repercussions of parting off with a portion of their land to the land grabbers. In the beginning it is said that there were instances of tribals bartering away their land for even a bottle of liquor.

The loan was taken mostly for agriculture and purchase of animals. Among the non-agricultural requirements for which loans were taken, the foremost place is occupied for marriage ceremonies as well as for festivals. The State Government has however taken a number of measures to regulate unscrupulous money lending including the formation of Cooperation Credit and Cooperative Thrifts Societies. But the cooperative framework is still weak and has yet to make its presence felt.

The tribals claim that when they heard of the Partition in 1947 and the sufferings of the refugees, they received them with open arms when they were rehabilitated here and gave them food to eat. Together with this they welcomed the other settlers also like the Jats, the freedom fighters, agricultural graduates, released army personnel and others, little realizing that the new settlers would forcibly occupy their land. Thus they are also victim of their own generosity.

Various efforts to check land alienation have failed absolutely because of politics and other factors. The popular leaders today get strong ballot and financial support as well as physically strong and energetic men to help the cause of their election, while these tribal communities have none to offer or no capacity to negotiate their offer of ballots. The Tharus and Buxas have no leader or strong organization which can fight for their rights or look after their welfare and alienation of land; the biggest bane of deforestation. Tribal conventions, traditions and patterns being largely rigid, inflexible and deep rooted, offer strong resistance to change. Illiteracy, their guileless nature, lack of political consciousness and social development have prevented the tribals from understanding the shrewdness of the kulaks in snaring them into usury.

Finally the tribal elders have failed to organize them under a leadership of their own community, partly owing to their personal interests and partly because of a weak financial base. Politicians of the ruling party have rightly assessed the divisions within the tribal groups and they obviously favour the elements who have deprived the tribals of the land, because they have nothing to gain by espousing the cause of tribals and much to benefit from befriending their tormentors. That makes the lot of the Tarai tribals hopeless and steeped in indebtedness.

Before 1947, the tribals led almost a secluded life. The administration had also adopted an attitude of not infringing into their privacy. The Kham Superintendent, who was considered as the King of Tarai, dealt with them through the Padhan and avoided direct contact.

The tribals hardly moved out of their village except to the market and fairs. On rare occasions they visited other villages, either to attend a nuptial ceremony or a funeral. Apart from the forest officials and people they came in contact during the village fairs and market, the Padhan was their main source of information and contact.The tribals lived a peaceful life and enjoyed considerable freedom in choosing their place of settlement and cultivation.

The habitat of the tribals was comparatively inaccessible by the nature of its location on the one hand and a malarious climate on the other. The other factors which discouraged the immigrants from disturbing the tribals was the myth of their sorcery and witchcraft. Complete absence of mines and minerals in this region also prevented contact with outsiders as we find in the tribal areas of some other places. As there was no problem of population pressure on land as is encountered in other tribal areas, the tribes of Tarai were not forced to migrate in search of employment. Another striking feature was that tribal life in Tarai was not affected by war economy. Further, unlike other tribals areas, the Christian missionaries have not been very active here. It might have been due to the dense forests infested by wild ferocious animals. Very inhospitable malarial climate was the other reason. The presence of dacoits was also a deterrent.

Ensconced amidst forests, the tribals of Tarai were leading a life of peace and tranquility. But this equanimity was rudely disturbed with the coming of Independence. For these tribals, changes have taken place at a terrible pace since 1947 and they are taken by surprise and overwhelmed with the new developments which are mainly due to external forces and factors. The sweeping changes have caused economic conflicts and tension.

The tribals who had little contact with the outside world suddenly found themselves exposed to different communities like refugees from East and West Pakistan, land grabbers, new Government officials serving in departments unheard of before 1947, money lenders and others with conflicting interests, different values and attitudes.The contact with the new settlers which was sudden and all embracing has caused a great socio-economic tension creating a dislocation in their cultural matrix.

The inroads of money economy has perpetuated the assertion of individual authority, consequent upon which joint family is giving way to nuclear families. A sizeable number of people now prefer to cultivate their own land independently, spend their income on their own family and live as a separate unit. The fragmentation of land holdings has taken place and the number of landless labourers is increasing .

A vital problem which the tribals are now facing is the disintegration of their culture. The rich tradition of folk music and dance which manifests the aesthetic value of the tribals is waning. Their growing contact with the new settlers and coming within the reach of the electronic media has played havoc with their cultural, social and ethical values.It is having a wrong impact on their personal as well as social life. Crime, which was unknown previously, has seeped in and cases of theft and murder have been reported. Even then the tribals have still preserved their old virtues of honesty, simplicity and hospitality. With the growth of new consciousness the younger generation has developed a sense of apathy towards their oral traditions, with the result that tribal songs and dances are being replaced by film music and dances.

Imposition of ideas by Indian 'sadhus' (mendicants), Christian missionaries,reformers, do-gooders, social workers and even Government officials are having a negative effect on their basic cultural values, which makes them feel small and perplexed regarding their indigenous culture. The insistence upon abandonment of old customs and rites under the pressure of Hindu contact has brought the custom of dietary restrictions and taboos. Further the pride in claiming a higher social status, wearing of the sacred thread and conforming to the tenets of Hinduism in some form or the other are all indicative of a change that is coming over the tribals. By inviting the Brahmins in various ceremonies like birth, marriage and death etc., under the influence of Hinduism, the tribes have to incur unnecessary expenditure.

Deforestation has also affected the status of the tribal women who enjoy a higher status than their male counterpart. Amongst the Tharus and Buxas as mentioned earlier, there is a tradition that their women are of royal descent and they came to Tarai in the medieval period with their retinue of servants to escape the onslaught of Mughal brutality. With the passage of time they married their servants but even after marriage they retained their superiority. However now there is an unmistakable evidence of men folk trying to dominate them on the ground of safeguarding their honour from aggressive settlers The younger generation is active in trying to curb their freedom by imposing a ban on their going to weekly markets and fairs. In this they have been considerably influenced by the social set up of the neighbouring communities, where women have a subordinate role.They are also egged on by the nontribals who ridicule them by stating that they are dominated by their women. The women-folk however have reacted to the infringement upon their rights and have openly defied the ban imposed on them. As men do not have much control over their women owing to their inferior status, the situation has fomented trouble in the tribal community which has resulted in family bickerings and has marred marital happiness.

Deforestation has depleted those shrubs and trees which bear edible fruit and some of which were used as medicines by the tribals in the past. They are jamun (Syzygium cumini), guler (Leg erstroomic indica), tendu (Disospyros tomentosa), phalsa (Grewia sapida), bel (Aegle marmelos), bahera (Terminalia belerica), pula (Kydia calcyina), bakli (Anogeissus litifolia), gutel (Trewie nuliflora), gojina (Ficus numphii), and amaltas (Cassia fistula).

It has also reduced the number of livestock. Tree leaves were used as fodder, but they have been wantonly cut creating problems for forage. Headman Prem Singh of Buxa village

Beriya Daulat laments that with dwindling of fodder trees, grass blanks have also vanished affecting the cattle population. In the past the Buxa villages at and average had 150 animals which included cows, buffaloes and bullocks. But now most of the families do not have more than four animals. Amongst the fodder trees which have dwindled at a rapid pace are sain (Terminalia tomentosa), bakli (Anogeissus litifolia), pipal (Ficus religiosa), pula (Kydia calcyina), bahera (Terminalia belerica) and gojina (Ficus numphii). This is another setback the Tarai tribals have received during the recent past.

It can be concluded that the biggest problem which the tribals are facing with the rapid development of agriculture and destruction of forest is land alienation. Today we have a strange phenomenon of tribal backwardness in a highly developed area. To an extent the over growing prosperity of the area is at the cost of tribal interests. In allotting land to the new settlers, the interests and requirements of the original inhabitants, the tribals were not taken into account. It is pathetic indeed that the area development activities should create problems for the original inhabitants. Again the mockery is that the urgency of the situation was not realized till the problem became chronic and out of control. To alleviate the grievances of the tribals, their land, which has been fraudulently usurped by non-tribals, should be handed back to them, even though it might be a Herculean task to implement this measure. Restoration of their land would provide them protection from exploitation and give them a feeling of security which is lacking at the moment. The other urgent measure required is the consolidation of land holdings in both the Buxa and Tharu areas. This besides raising its productivity would also help in restoring their land.

The problem of encroachment in Tarai has been studied by Government officials, yet for the Tarai Land Committee, 1968 the problem of land alienation has not been its focal point of examination. It is suggested that a high power committee be set up to study all the aspects of land alienation.

In view of the fact that the tribal indebtedness is closely

linked with land, it would be necessary to enact a law to meet the needs of land owning indebted tribal families. As a matter of fact in sensitive tribal areas private money lending should be banned. The Government has already taken steps to ban the transfer of land from tribals to non-tribals to regulate money lending, but this has to be backed by a strong executive action. For the moment however, their debt upto a particular date can be waived off and for this a proper debt redemption programme can be launched.

It is gratifying that owing to the ban on transfer of tribal land,the Buxas and Tharus are owners of land on record, but actually this assets has been detrimental to their interests. The income levels where major part of state subsidies and credits are permissible are so low that owing to land holdings for name sake on papers, they can hardly take advantage of these. Moreover the tribals are not shrewd enough to win favours of the Government officials by manipulating papers or greasing their palms, nor do they like to be in their clutches since they have had bitter experiences in the past when unscrupulous employees of the State bluffed them, primarily because they were illiterate. The process though reduced to a great extent now has not been checked completely.

Another specific problem of the tribals is their habit of excessive drinking which has been further aggravated by the excise policy of the Government. A sizeable part of their income is spent on liquor. The dealers are aware of this weakness and sell them on credit and charge prohibitive rates of interest. Owing to the excise policy of the Government, illicit distillation of liquor has increased enormously and the worst affected are the tribals, since liquor is a necessary accompaniment of their all social functions. The tribals are spendthrift and prone to alcoholism. In the prevailing situation, keeping in view their traditional background, the tribals should be permitted to brew liquor for their personal use as well as for social functions.

The extent of factor utilization and cropping activity is invariably low in tribal enterprise as compared to their counterparts, the new settlers. Yieldwise, their assets, land, implements, livestock etc. have less impact on productivity. They do not seem to be inclined to set up subsidiary occupations, high yielding crops and cottage industries. They overspend in meeting social expenditure and hardly care to boost their income by greater use of labour, land capital and finding an access to better markets.

Low pace of technological change in production seems to be a major factor in explaining their low incomes as compared to the land. It is an undisputed fact that inquisitiveness and preparedness to accept anything useful which may filter to them as an advice or suggestion, is largely missing. This tendency can change if greater inter-community interaction and competition is created. Education and increase in inter-community social work, consciousness and confidence can change the present state. Tribal Development Federation should have played a greater role in this context, but it has failed miserably. The universities of Pantnagar and Kumaon, must work towards this social development and technical knowledge. The two universities located in the area could have taken up field surveys of the tribal areas and their problems, thus highlighting their pathetic condition and also suggest a way out. The tribes in this respect also are ignored.

The tribals who still have good sized land holdings, should be encouraged to take agriculture on scientific lines. They should be given a package of improved agricultural practices, including irrigation,training in crop management on animal husbandry, good seeds, fertilizers, implements, insecticides and pesticides. They should also be encouraged to take up social forestry. Families which have small or marginal holdings as well as landless labourers should be given assistance and trained in animal husbandry, poultry farming and cottage industries.

Further for capacity building, small multipurpose cooperative societies with exclusive tribal membership should be organized, so that they are managed by the tribals themselves. These societies should meet the credit, agricultural inputs, essential commodities and marketing facilities of the tribals.

To remove economic imbalance in Tarai, the development of tribals at a rapid pace is the need of the hour. A special cell should be created which would constitute of Government officials, social workers and experts who have worked on different aspects of tribal life. It is essential that those people and organizations who are interested in tribal welfare programmes should be involved.

Today illiteracy is the main bane of the tribals. The rate of drop-outs at each stage from class one onwards is very high. To eradicate illiteracy, schools specifically for the tribals should be opened. The Servants of India Society is doing laudable work in propagating education amongst the tribals; but at the Government level the implementation of schemes is very tardy. The timely distribution of scholarships, money, books and notebooks is lacking. The solution to a great extent lies in the rapid educational progress of the tribals.

Protection, regeneration and collection of minor forest produce should be optimized. The tribals should be helped to process them, so as to earn higher income from sale. For this institutional arrangements be made for its marketing. Together with this formation of forest villages at par with revenue villages be taken up. It will help the tribals to process usufruct produce. The tribal economy be considered within the parameters of the forest policies of the State and Central Governments. To make this beneficial to the tribals they should be encouraged to play the role of the guardians of the forests. This can be possible by making them aware of the sustainable and vibrant forests being in their own interest. Such an enlightened approach pre-supposes two conditions. Firstly the foresters should be sympathetic to the tribal aspirations and should be capable of counselling them preferably. Secondly, through education and proper extension methods the tribals should be encouraged to look to the forests as their source of sustenance and hence their self-interest in the protection of the forests.

The population of the tribals is more or less constant. At

present it is so for the negative forces of being in an inhospitable malarial climate with little medical facilities as well as poverty. With betterment in their condition they should be taught the norm of limited families.

To conclude it is obvious from the study that the tribals of this area are victims of the greed of the neo-settlers and the Government officials are in league with them. Even after the State Government having issued orders to alleviate their grievances, this nexus has made them ineffective with the result that they continue to suffer miserably at their hands. A feeling of discontent is pervading amongst them which is evident to any researcher. Lest this discontentment is exploited by fissiparious tendencies, urgent remedial measures must be taken. It is notable that at times anti-social elements, like the terrorists in recent past, have made the tribesmen their messengers. If the tribals continue to be exploited and harassed the Tarai may be an incipient Naxal area on the foot-hill of the Himalaya. The sooner the Government realises the urgency the better not only for the tribals, but also for the whole nation.

3
Gujjars- the Forest Dwellers

Gujjars are followers of three religions, viz. Hinduism, Sikhism and Islam. That makes the past history of this pastoral tribe of India fascinating. It bespeaks of their being nomadic, which took them to various places in the country and made them to adopt more than one religion. Their being nomadic was necessitated for being 'Go-Chars' as they were called in Gujarat and Kathiawar, supposed to be their original home. As they were cow grazers the appellation 'Go-Chars' stuck to them, which has now become 'Gujjar'. The historian W. Crooke is of the opinion that the tribe derives its name from the Sanskrit word 'Gujara' after which their original home Gujarat was named. During the course of time the Gujjars found rearing up buffaloes more profitable, due to their higher milk yield, they have now stopped breeding cows and almost exclusively own buffaloes.

The Gujjars claim to be the descendants of Nand of Gokul, who according to mythology was the foster father of Lord Krishna, the reincarnation of God Vishnu. Nand also bred cows and was a leader of his community. Nothing else is known about the origin of Gujjars. Their early history is rather obscure. V.A. Smith is of the view that the Gujjars were foreign immigrants, "closely associated with and possibly allied in blood to the White Huns". The nomadic tribe, known as Huns was divided into two main streams which in the ancient days were spread across the valleys of Volga and Oxus.The Huns, who went to Volga Valley, spread in Eastern Europe and inhabited the land between the rivers Volga and Danube. The section of the Huns which had settled in Oxus Valley was called Ephtalites or White Huns. Hordes of these White Huns attacked the Kushan kingdom of Kabul and entered into India during the fifth century A.D. They ultimately overthrew the legendary Gupta Empire. Their leader Toramana established his rule in Malawa, prior to 500 A.D. He died in 510 A.D. and was succeeded by his son Mihirgula. He proved to be the greatest Hun ruler of India. His capital was Sakla, the modern Sialkot now in Pakistan. He died around 540 A.D. After his death, there was a rapid decline in the power of the White Huns. Even then petty Hun chiefs continued to rule small territories in North Western India, upto the seventh century A.D. Gradually the White Huns were taken into the folds of Hinduism.

The earliest reference of a separate Gujjar Kingdom is mentioned in the fifth century A.D. It was in Rajasthan, with Bhimal or Srimal as its capital. The Gujjar Pratihara King of Bhimal later conquered Kannauj and became the paramount power in Northern India. From Bhimal, they also made inroads into Gujarat and established the minor kingdom of Bharoach or Baroach. The eminent king Raja Bhoj and other kings of Kannauj dynasty, who ruled in the ninth, tenth and eleventh centuries, accordingly to V.A. Smith were all Gujjars.

It may be possible that the Gujjars are the scions of the White Huns. A.G. Bingley identifies the Gujjars with the

Kushan or Yuchi or To-chari, a tribe of Indo-Scythian stock; whereas D. Ibbetson and M.A. Sherring are of the view that the Gujjars are of Rajput descent. But Baden Powell does not agree with this view and has stated that they have a distinct tribal origin and in the course of time migrated with the Rajput and others. As reported by Crooke, the Gujjars were initially Hindus and converted to Islam at different times. But a legend, prevalent among the Gujjars of Avadh, holds Timur responsible for mass conversion of Gujjars when he ransacked Delhi. According to another tradition, the Gujjars were forced to embrace Islam much later during the period of Aurangzeb.

To begin with they inhabited the western part of India and later migrated and spread all over North-Western India. The main settlements of the Muslim Gujjars in India are in Jammu and Kashimir, Himachal Pradesh and Uttar Pradesh. It was only during the British period that Muslim Gujjars of Jammu entered Kashmir where they were encouraged to settle down by the erstwhile Maharajas. The Gujjars of Kashmir live on the fringes of the forests of the Kashmir Valley in winters, but with the coming of summer and melting of snow in the mountains, they move up with the buffaloes to the heights of the mountains.

Most of the Gujjars of Himachal Pradesh have also come from Jammu. Amir Hasan is of the view that, "....As a matter of fact, they are widely known as Jammu Gujjars." According to a legend current among the Jammu Gujjars of Himachal Pradesh, about 300 years ago, the marriage of the ruler of Sirmaur in Himachal Pradesh was settled with the daughter of the Raja of Jammu. The bride insisted that she would go to Sirmaur only when her Gujjars also accompanied her. The ruler of Sirmaur had to agree and thus the Gujjars made their entry into Himachal Pradesh in the form of dowry. Amir Hasan opines that from Himachal Pradesh the Muslim Gujjars further spread to the north-western portions of Uttar Pradesh. The forest officials claim that the Gujjars from Himachal Pradesh must have come to Uttar Pradesh about a hundred years ago.

Gujjars of Uttar Pradesh/Sub-Himalayan Tarai :

The Muslim Gujjars of the Sub-Himalayan Tarai are a hapless lot. They have remained an obscure group and as such have failed to procure for themselves the rights and privileges their counterparts in other states have succeeded in ensuring for themselves. Even though they are steeped in poverty, illiteracy and backwardness, they have neither been included in the list of Scheduled Tribes nor that of the Backward Castes; whereas their brethren in Himachal Pradesh enjoy the privileges given to Scheduled Tribes and in Jammu Kashmir as Backward Classes.

They came to Tarai and Bhabhar or Sub-Himalayan Tarai some 90 years back. Today their main settlements in Tarai and Bhabhar are Tarai Central, Tarai Eastern and Tarai Western Forest Divisions as well as Haldwani and Ramnagar Forest Divisions. According to tradition, cattle breeding is their main source of livelihood, which needs fodder aplenty and the same having been in short supply and therefore costlier in Himachal, they shifted over to Tarai and Bhabhar where they found it in sufficient quantity those days along with water. Probably nomadism could have been another factor which brought them here and on witnessing the abundance of grazing land, they made Sub-Himalayan Tarai as their winter abode. Because of their nomadic habits in the past, they used to migrate to the hills in Munsiyari, Tehri and Uttarkashi during summers and came down to Tarai and Bhabhar during winters to graze their animals in the forests. But since 1962, when China attacked India, the Gujjars of Tarai and Bhabhar have discontinued their summer trek to the hills, though within Tarai and Bhabhar they are still mobile, where their movement is guided by better grazing facilities for their cattle.

The Gujjars are forest dwellers, for them forests are their livelihood, their very existence and it is significant that the Gujjars of Tarai and Bhabhar are called 'Van Gujjars' or Forest Gujjars. The number of Gujjars families in this area is about 600. For generations they have led a pastoral nomadic life depending almost entirely upon the herd of buffaloes for subsistence and sustenance.

Material Culture :

The Gujjars are simple and guileless people. It is difficult to find atleast among the Muslims of Uttar Pradesh, a more exclusive and closed group than the Gujjars of Tarai. In view of their nomadic life in the past and habitation in the thick of forest, they do not usually intermix with other Muslim communities in the area. They have made no efforts to retain their link with the Hindu Gujjars of Western Uttar Pradesh and have also lost contact with their brethren living in Jammu- Kashmir. With the Gujjars of Himachal Pradesh they still have marital connections though such unions are on the decrease.

Being a nomadic tribe their material assets are very limited. Their main possessions are their buffaloes and a house to live in, which is temporary and built on forest land. The dwelling of a Gujjar is called 'dera'. These 'deras' are built on small clearings in the midst of thick forest and are absolutely isolated. In Tarai five or six 'deras' are clumped together and at times they are separated from each other by a distance of one to four kilometers. Usually the Gujjar dwellings are near water sources and where water is not easily available, the Gujjars have sunk hand pumps.

Their homes are very neatly designed, clean and efficiently maintained. The Gujjars live in thatched huts which are quite large in size. They are square at the base and the roofs which are conical in shape are made of thatch supported by strong 'ballies' or wooden poles. Some houses have mud walls on the sides. The affluent Gujjars construct an extra thatched hut which is used as a sitting room. A large number of cots are placed in this hut.

Most of the Gujjar huts have no walls. In some huts mud walls are used, but here also the thatched roofs are supported by the wooden poles. The animal sheds are separated from the residential quarters and the thatched roofs of these sheds are supported by a frame made of wooden poles placed both vertically and horizontally, so that the wild animals cannot enter the sheds at night.

The residential huts are quite spacious and multipurpose. They are used for cooking food, storage and sleeping . Partition walls made of mud are erected for convenience. The floor area of these huts can vary from 4.3x4.3 m to 12.8x12.8 m. 'Pucca' houses are found only towards Chorgaliya side, near Haldwani, where a few Gujjars have acquired land and are leading a settled life as agriculturists. But these are exceptional cases. The Gujjars by and large lead a nomadic and forest life. As no 'pucca' house can be constructed on forest land, the Gujjars are compelled to reside in huts.

It takes 10 to 15 days to build a 'dera'. People work collectively in constructing it and do not receive any payment for its construction. This denotes a strong community feeling among the Gujjars. A Gujjar habitation in Tarai does no give the impression of a village as is seen in rural India, because mostly the Gujjar dwellings are not clustered together. Not more than six or seven families usually live at one spot. The dwellings are scattered over a large area in such a manner that water and grazing facilities can be evenly utilized and there are no infringements on each other's grazing area. This again shows the role played by the strong social feelings in a Sub-Himalayan Tarai Gujjar community.

The Gujjars have an aesthetic sense too. They are fond of decorating their houses and belongings like trunks with floral motifs and geometrical designs. In some dwellings decorative patterns are made with the help of colour pigments. The houses are regularly cleaned and plastered with a mixture of mud and dung. There are no toilet facilities in Gujjar houses, though in some settlements a small portion is assigned in the main hut for bathing purposes for ladies. Men take bath in the open.

Socio-Cultural Profile :

The Muslim Gujjars of Tarai are Sunni by faith. According

to Amir Hasan, a large number of Indian Muslims are converts from Hinduism. To distinguish between these converts and descendants of Muslims of foreign origin who had migrated and settled in India, the term 'ajlaf' and 'ashraf' respectively have been coined. The ashrafs or Muslims of foreign origin enjoy a higher social status than the ajlafs or the converts. There is a tendency among the ajlafs to identify themselves with the ashrafs by making a determined bid to discard their Hindu origin and by undergoing a thorough process of Islamization*

The Gujjars come within the category of ajlafs, but on survey it was observed that they do no suffer from any complex of being inferior to the ashrafs. They have made no attempts to ashrafize themselves and have retained their separate identity.

Despite their conversion to Islam, the Gujjars have maintained many rituals and practices of their Hindu ancestors. They have retained the 'Gotra' ** system, though they are not clear about the genesis of their Gotras, except that it refers to their Hindu ancestry. Their important Gotras are Kasana, Lodha, Padhana, Bagri, Dinda, Dhetra, Chabra, Pathan, Kasani, Bhainsi, Chauhan, Kushiwal, Baniya, Pessuwal, Chechi, Checha, Khatana, Chopra and Kalas. These Gotras are however not analogous with the Hindu Gotras and can be identified more with the Hindu castes or sub-castes. There is no evidence to show that one caste is superior to another caste and as such

---

* *Islamization is a process of purification from non-Islamic practices.*

** ***Gotra System:*** *" The original meaning of gotra is a 'cowshed' or a 'herd of cows'; in the Atharva Veda the word first appears with the meaning of a 'clan' which it has retained with a special connotation ...... Gotra as it existed in historical times was primarily a brahmanu institution... All brahmins were believed to have descended from one rishi or legendary seer after whom the Gotras were named. The religious literature generally speaks of seven or eight primeval Gotras, those of Kashyap, Vasistha, Bhrigu, Gautama, Bharadwaja, Atri and Vishwamitra. The eighth Gotra that of Agastya, is named after the sage*

there is no caste hierarchy amongst the Gujjars. The people of same Gotras are called 'biradar'. The predominant Gotras are Kasana, Lodha and Padhana. The Gujjars are very particular and possessive about their Gotras. It was stated that if a woman eloped with someone during her pregnacy and remarried, the father of the child would do everything to retrieve the child of his Gotra after tracing her. The Gotra of a male child remains unchanged even on adoptation and a girl has to be married in a Gotra different from her parental Gotra.

The Gujjar families in Tarai are mostly nuclear and the separation of married son from their parental families can be attributed to the exigencies of nomadism, economic situation and the vagaries of forest life. Even though following the Chinese aggression of 1962 they were not permitted to enter the Alpine meadows in the border districts, within Tarai however, nomadism is still practised in search of better forests and grazing facilities. For a tribe which loves nomadism and is mobile, joint living at times can be cumbersome. Moreover the forest officials usually deal with the head of the family, who on behalf of his family members is entitled to receive certain concessions and facilities mostly grazing from the Forest Department. Therefore, greater the number of families more the facilities received from the Forest Department and hence more the divisions in the family.

The economic situation is also responsible owing to which the Gujjars find it expedient to separate their married sons from them. The lesser the size of the family, the lesser would be the size of the herd of animals and lesser the problems of

---

who is said to have taken the Vedic religion beyond the Vindhyas, and who is a sort of patron saint of the Dravidians. His name may have been added to those of the original seven as the south became progressively Aryanized. These primeval Gotras were multiplied in later times by the inclusion of the name of many other ancient sages. The chief importance of Gotra was in connexion with marriage, which was forbidden to persons of the same Gotra". (Basham, A.L.-The Wonder that was India PP 153-154).

grazing. Family dissensions and uneven distribution of household chores between women is also a cause of family split. But as compared to other communities in rural India, family bickerings are not very pronounced and a sole cause for married sons to have a separate establishment.

A striking feature of the Gujjar families which was observed during the survey was that the number of females as compared to the male population is less. The female-male ratio amongst the Gujjars of Tarai is 1 to 1.4. The birth and mortality rates amongst the Gujjars are high. A woman may give birth to 10-15 children, even cases of 20 were reported. Out of these eight to 10 and sometimes even less may survive. Being pastoralists they need more helping hands and hence they prefer to have more children in their family. The male child is always preferred, however unlike other Indian communities the birth of a female child is not considered a set back, since she is an economic asset as a helping hand. The Gujjars are against family planning owing to their religious beliefs.

The Gujjar society is patriarchal. The father is the head of the family, who is called 'Buzurg' or 'Mukhia'. He is also known as 'numberdar'. All important decisions regarding family matters are to be taken by him. The mother being the female head or 'numberdarni' of the family wields considerable respect and influence and has a say in family matters, but in social and economic matters the Mukhia consults the male members of the family only.

A Gujjar woman cannot be considered equal in status to her counterpart. The eldest son occupies an important position in the family and is considered next to the Mukhia. The women folk may not take part in biradari matters, but in family affairs their presence is conspicuous and their advice cannot be ignored owing to the fact that they are more hard working than the male members. Unlike other Muslim women they do not observe purdah and enjoy more freedom and a higher status in the family as compared to other Muslim sects. The Gujjar woman has no right to inheritance, which is the sole prerogative of the male. However, a Gujjar male is entirely responsible for the maintenance of the wife and family.

Social Organization :

The Gujjars are a well-knit society. Among them religion and social norms have a restraining effect on their behaviour, which prevent internecine feuds amongst them. Discipline is further maintained by bonds of kinship. The Gujjars try to resolve their own problems and avoid any outside interference. In order to settle inter family disputes, to lay down norms of behaviour and to find solutions for problems affecting the community as a whole, the Gujjars have their panchayat or a committee of elders. The panchayat is constituted only if there is a cluster of settlements. Even isolated settlements associate themselves with the nearest panchayat. The head of the panchayat is called 'Pradhan'. The contentious issues mostly brought to the panchayat for resolution are pertaining to grazing, encroachment, living space, boundary dispute, lopping of trees from other's territory, drinking water, marriage, divorce, elopements and abductions. Widow remarriage, payment of overdue debts, decision of gift money to be paid at different weddings by the 'biradri', inheritance and division of property is also made through the panchayats. If a Gujjar is caught indulging in drinking or gambling, committing robbery or theft, he is punished by the panchayat and fined. In the past if any Gujjar was caught mixing water in milk, he was fined or ex-communicated. The rate of selling milk to the baniya is also decided by the panchayat.

Gradually the effectiveness of the panchayats is on the wane and their decisions are being challenged in the court. But in matters of marriage, the panchayat still reigns supreme. If a married or unmarried woman elopes with someone, the couple is ostracized and can be admitted to the biradri only after the panchayat takes a decision which in case of a married woman enjoins upon the paramour to pay a heavy penalty to the husband which can amount to a thousand of rupees. In matters of heart the Gujjars are very liberal and when in love they can spend a fortune. If the girl is unmarried, the paramour gives a girl of his family in return to a bachelor of the aggrieved family or a penalty is paid in cash as decided by the panchayat.

In the past if a Gujjar flouted the rules of the panchayat or he failed to respect its verdict, he was immediately declared outcast. He was not invited in any social ceremony of the community, whether it was a marriage or funeral. Later on when he would make an effort to return to the biradri, the panchayat would clamp certain restrictions on him and impose a pecuniary fine before taking him back into the folds of the biradri. The fine was accepted as a donation by the panchayat.

Economic Condition :

The economy of the Gujjars is in a shambles. A survey of some settlements conducted by this writer in 1992 corroborates the view point. Given below are a few examples of this study :

Garappu Aath Number Khatta :

In this settlement there are 12 families. Nine families in this settlement are breeding buffaloes and three cows. The average production of milk,from both buffaloes and cows, is 300 litres per day. The milk is supplied to the businessmen in Haldwani whose workers known as 'kahars' collect the milk daily from the settlements itself. The rate at which they were selling milk to the baniya or the city businessmen during the time of survey was five and a half rupees per litre for buffalo milk and cow milk was being supplied for four and a half rupees per litre. From Diwali to Holi there will be one rate and Holi to Diwali the rate will be different. The rates depend on the fluctuations in Haldwani market.

The Gujjars in this Khatta are now interested in leading a settled life either as agriculturists or they want to do dairying; but none of them possess agricultural land, nor they have enough money to start dairying. They state that since forests were in abundance in the past and fodder was aplenty they didn't switch over to agriculture. Moreover they are in the clutches of the baniyas who exploit them and would not relieve them easily. Every Gujjar here is mired in debt of the baniya to whom they sell their milk. The loan varies from two thousand to sixty thousand rupees. This indebtedness is for the last three to four generations. The loan that they have taken from the baniyas forbids them from starting milk cooperative societies.

The Lalkuan Milk Union tried to organize them in a cooperative society, but could not succeed owing to indebtedness and ignorance on the part of the Gujjars as well. Only one Gujjar in this settlement can read and write. His name is Ali Dad and he came here at the age of 14 as a herdsman. Later he became a cattle owner and at the moment he owns 12 buffaloes. He is not sure whether the establishment of a milk cooperative society in their settlement would really improve their financial status. Moreover he said that the Lalkuan Milk Union would not be able to collect milk from their deras during rainy season, because the mode of transport used by the Union is trucks whereas during rains their settlement is approachable by cycles only. The Milk Union purchases milk on the basis of fat content for which the Gujjars are not prepared, though Ali Dad or the other Gujjars could not give an explanation for it. The Gujjars are aware to an extent that the baniya exploits them, but they are happy that he provides them a loan whenever and wherever they want it which the Lalkuan Milk Union will not be in a position to do. As also during emergency he provides them with medical facilities. But they do not seem to be aware of the manipulations which the baniya does while entering the amount taken by them as loan.

Gulam Nabi, an elderly Gujjar said that within the last two decades their economic condition has plummeted down. About 10 years back he owned 90 buffaloes, but now he has only eight and the main reasons which he attributed to this were paucity of fodder and the restrictions imposed on them to take their cattle to higher altitudes for grazing.

The Gujjars claim that the forest officials harass them and for lopping even a single branch they have been fined upto

Rs.100. They have to give 'Haq Pani' to the forest officials in the form of butter or ghee annually. This has become a tradition and is considered as a right of the forest officials. During the marriage ceremonies of forest officials it is considered a privilege for the Gujjars to supply them milk, gratis. Grazing is a big problem owing to the paucity of grass in this settlement. Additionally farmers from neighbouring areas also leave their cattle to graze in those tracts which were the traditional grazing lands of the Gujjars. There have been incidents when their cattle were lifted by farmers or professional cattle lifters, but they do not report the matter to the police. Since they do not have money to bribe them, the policemen do not take cognizance of their complaints, on the contrary they harass them. The high-handedness of the police was reported by several Gujjar settlers. Owing to the shortage of fodder during summer season ten buffaloes died here last year. The other causes which can be attributed to the shortage of fodder are forest plantations as well as nibbling of forests by agriculture. The grazing tax that the settlers here are paying is Rs. 8 for 10 buffaloes annually to the Forest Department.

Baur Khatta :

There are three Gujjar families here and they are living in this settlement for the last 20 years. The first family is of Hazi Nur Alam. There are 25 buffaloes owned by the family. The average yield of milk throughout the year is 20 litres per day. He is supplying milk to the baniya Chiranji Lal in Haldwani and will continue to supply milk to him life long, since he has to pay a loan of Rs. 60,000 to him.

The second family is of Gulam Hussain. Gulam Hussain has 35 buffaloes and the average yield of milk is 25 litres per day. He is also supplying milk to Chiranji Lal and his predicament is similar. He has also taken a loan of Rs. 30,000 from Chiranji Lal.

The third family is of Gulam Rasul. He has 15 buffaloes and the average yield of milk for the year is 13 litres per day. He is supplying milk to Chiranji Lal from whom he has taken a loan of Rs. 20,000.

Apart from Haq Pani, all the three families breed a cock each for the forest guards. There are no medical, educational or veterinary facilities in close proximity to this Gujjar settlement. No one in the three families is educated and their children are also not attending school.

Rai Khatta (Barhani Range) :

This is a registered Khatta in the records of the Forest Department and is 101 years old. At present only five families are residing here but before 1968 there were more than thirty families. Most of the families have shifted to other areas in Tarai an Bhabhar in search of better pastures and fuel with the result that this Khatta has shrunk more than half of its original size. The total population of the settlement is 30 and the number of animals is 75 out of which 70 are buffaloes and five bulls. The average yield of milk is 30 litres per day throughout the year. They are supplying milk to the baniya Chiranji Lal in Haldwani. The rate at which they supply milk is Rs. 5.50 per litre upto Diwali and Rs. 6 per litre after Diwali. The financial condition of the residents here is slightly better as compared to other Gujjars, because they are cultivating on forest land and their holding at an average is about 0.6 ha. They have not taken any loan from the baniya, but they prefer to supply him milk rather than the Milk Producers Union at Lalkuan because the Milk Union does not buy milk from them on those occasions when it turns sour, where as the baniya is prepared to bear this loss.

Pateliya Khatta :

This Khatta is registered in the forest records. There are three families residing here, one of Gulam Rasusl, the other of Muhammed Ali and the third of Hassan Din. Gulam Rasul supplies milk to Chiranji Lal at the rate of Rs. 5.50 per litre. He is not keen to supply milk to the Milk Union because the Union purchases milk on the basis of fat content. Moreover, the inaccessibility of the Khatta during rainy season also discourages him to supply milk to them. Finally Chiranji Lal has helped him in hard times and a Gujjar never forgets a favour. Chiranji Lal supplies rations and other essential items to his family throughout the year.

Gulam Rasul is of the view that in the Khatta the grazing areas have been demarcated by the three families owing to which there are no bickerings and no unnecessary lopping of trees for fodder and fuel. Further they have not encroached upon forest land for agricultural purposes and are not harassed by the Forest Department. They do not provide Haq Pani to the forest officials as the other Gujjars do.

Insulated from the outside world for a long period, the Gujjars were apathetic towards any change initially. But their contact with the outside world in the recent past has infused in them a yearning for economic betterment, though there are some constraints. The same quantum of forest and grazing land has to bear the brunt of increasing human and cattle population. Moreover the life style and attitude of the Gujjars hallowed by traditions of their forbears has resulted in sociological constraints.The motivation for progressivism has in consequence to be strongly advocated. But the Uttar Pradesh Government is doing nothing in this direction. There is also a total absence of non-governmental organizations working on voluntary basis amongst the Gujjars of Tarai. A vexatious element in the present situation is the alleged discrimination in treatment by the Forest Department. Pursuit of an enlightened forest policy which takes into consideration the needs of the Gujjar population has to be followed.

Since the Gujjars are not self reliant, they need a helping hand to launch themselves on a state of take off and here Government, and non-governmental organizations both can be helpful. Since no non-governmental agency is working among them, the responsibility of official agencies is greater. It is essential that a supportive infrastructure will have to be created in the fields of veterinary services, live stock improvement, communication facilities together with education , health and water supply. The Gujjars are peeved at complete absence of these facilities in their settlements. Nurturing of panchayats and introduction of cooperatives can help in chanellizing their economic and social activities. It is also essential to revive their folk lore, folk music and dance which has been lost with the vicissitudes of time and in their long struggle for survival.

When the Gujjars came to Tarai and Bhabhar, there were abundant forests, whereas the number of their buffaloes was small. In 1921-22 e.g., the number of buffaloes of the Gujjars was 150 which increased to 628 in 1926-27. In 1936, the number of buffaloes belonging to the Gujjars increased from 1000 to 2000. This was found to be excessive and in 1946 the number was subsequently reduced to 800, vide Commissioner Kumaon's Order No. 2942/mi-78, dated July 10, 1946.

Previously there was little biotic pressure on the forest resources. According to the Forest Department, about 20 years back, there were about 150 Gujjar families in Tarai and Bhabhar with cattle numbering 2500. But today there are more than 400 families living in Tarai and Bhabhar and the number of their cattle has soared upto 16,000. The Gujjar families are scattered over the forests and every family claims grazing monopoly in forests around their dwellings, which has further added to the biotic pressure on the forests. Considering that a large number of Gujjar settlers live in forests and subsist on milk trade only, the situation has become extremely difficult for them to eke out a living. Initially when milk was in abundance, the Gujjars used to sell milk products like butter and ghee, but with the reduction in yield, they sell only milk today. Most of the Gujjars are steeped in indebtedness of businessmen to whom they sell their milk cheap. This reduction in their pecuniary status has come within the last two decades owing to the rapid shrinkage of forests and their inability to switch over to other professions. Lack of education has also prevented them from adapting themselves to the changing environment. There are no educational institutions in close proximity to the Gujjar dwellings. Only in exceptional cases a few Gujjar families have sent their children to school. However, no Gujjar has passed high school and there are only seven children who have studied upto class five.

During my survey I observed that some Gujjars have started cultivating small patches of forest land, but being extremely honest, a simple warning from the forest officials is enough to prevent them from encroaching upon or cultivating forest land unlike many other communities in Tarai and Bhabhar. However a few of the Gujjars are financially well off and have purchased land in Chorgalia.

In the past the Gujjars used to move to the hills during summers, thus giving rest to the forests in Tarai and Bhabhar for about six months. But since 1962, the Gujjars have stopped migrating to the hills with the result that the saplings do not get enough time to grow and owing to the dependence of Gujjars on these forests for such a long period, they have been damaged considerably. Previously when fodder was in abundance, the Gujjars used to comply with the regulations of lopping; but in recent years, on account of increase in the number of cattle and the decline in the grazing areas, the Gujjars have resorted to excessive lopping, branch cutting and even cutting of young shoots of trees. They are heavily penalized by some of the forest officials for their negligence and at times they have to bribe them with milk and chicken, which in Gujjar parlance is known as 'Haq Pani'.

It is true that the practices adopted by the Gujjars are damaging the forests which have to be protected in the larger interest of the country, but we should also accept the fact that the Gujjars are a tribe and that they have practised nomadism for a long period and their main occupation is buffaloe breeding. Thus dairy farming must form the focal point of any economic development project for the Gujjars. The following recommendations can be made on the basis of field survey:

(i) The Forest Department should either undertake a scheme for fodder development in the vicinity of Gujjar settlements or land should be allotted to the Gujjars both for agricultural purposes and fodder. Most of the

Gujjars in Tarai and Bhabhar, unlike their brethren in other parts of India are interested in agriculture. So a scheme should be prepared for their permanent settlement in Tarai and Bhabhar. It is suggested that those Gujjars, who are desirous of getting land for fodder raising, may be allotted land in plantations free of cost for first five years and those opting for agriculture should be allotted land on half rates. It is hoped that given such incentives, the Gujjars will raise enough fodder for their buffaloes and gradually start stall feeding them.

The idea of complete ban on grazing inside the forests in not a viable proposition until the Gujjars are given permanent settlements. In the meantime fodder areas can be developed for their animals by the Forest Department. In the past in the Tarai and Bhabhar there used to be 'Chaurs' or grass blanks in the forests where animals used to graze without damaging the forests. Owing to deforestation and increase in biotic pressure these Chaurs have vanished. However like these glades, fodder areas could be developed inside the forests or on the fringe areas and this fodder development should become an integral part of the Gujjar developmental schemes.

(ii) A programme for introduction of improved varieties of buffaloes and upgradation through artificial insemination or cross breeding should be worked out. Together with this the number of animals should be restricted. It is beneficial for the Gujjars to have only good milch buffaloes, but they are not going to go by this advice immediately, as the numerical strength of cattle is regarded as a status symbol among them, especially for marital alliances. Stall feeding should also be popularized and shortage of fodder can be met to an extent by:

(a) Having only pedigree cattle.

(b) Limiting the uneconomical cattle.

(c) Feeding the cattle on green fodder and other nutritive feeds.

Castration of local degraded he-buffaloes should be resorted to limit the number of uneconomical cattle. Such cattle should be segregated from others and gradually disposed off. Purchase of these buffaloes should also be stopped.

(iii) It is noticed that pedigree cattle brought from outside start losing their milch capability and are susceptible to local diseases like river flu, foot and mouth, render pest, mistitis and haemorrhagic septicemea. To counter this problem it is advisable that besides purchase of better breed cattle, efforts to upgrade the local breed should also be made. For this purpose cross breeding should be undertaken. This can be achieved by using better breed male buffaloes for breeding the local buffaloes. In the initial stages preferably good cross-breed male buffaloes should be used and switching on to pure bred animals should be done in the later stages. Thus at minimal cost a large number of buffaloes can be upgraded resulting in good milk yield. This experiment has already been successful at Vikasnagar in Dehradun district, Ranikhet and Almora. The cross-breeding in Tarai can deliver the desired result only when matched with simultaneous animal nutritional programme, so that the required balanced feed and fodder is made available to the cross bred animal from the very beginning. By raising the standard of feeding, the production of indigenous animals can be increased to a large extent and thereby also preventing deterioration in their good qualities.

Establishment of a separate organization for development of pasture and grassland is needed, so that systematic improvement of pasture and grass can be undertaken with latest techniques available in the country and abroad. This will not only benefit the forest dwellers, but will also maintain the ecological balance in the region. In the beginning some areas, where plenty of fodder is available during rainy season, may be selected and fenced for fodder growing. This fodder may be collected before flowering season and bailed in the form of hay and stored in the neighbouring settlements. The Gujjars living in close proximity may be supplied this fodder on subsidized rate on the condition that they will not graze their animals in the forests and will participate voluntarily in the programme. The Gujjar women in particular should be motivated to participate in this programme to make it a success.

Regulation of grazing is also to be introduced in the region. It is already being practised very successfully in several high altitude communities,such as those in Sikkim in, Kameng, the Bhotias of Uttar Pradesh and the high land communities of Himachal Pradesh. Rotational grazing will have to be worked out by the Gujjars in consultation with departmental experts of the Forest and Animal Husbandry Department, keeping in view the carrying capacity of the tract taken for experimenting. Subsidies for this purpose may be considered and a five year rotation should be adopted to allow for regeneration of grass.

Regulation of grazing should be combined with regeneration or replantation of degraded forests. The replanting programme should concentrate on fodder trees and on quick growing fuel species. Fodder forests produce a considerable higher sustainable yield per hectare of fodder than the grassland, and it also produces green fodder at seasons when there is no grass available. Varieties of fodder trees will have to be identified, nurseries for multiplication established in each eco-developmental unit and a massive programme for plantation launched. The Gujjars should be taken into confidence and be made responsible for planting and maintenance, but technical guidance would have to be provided and the saplings distributed free for an initial period of five years, so as to complete the first rotational cycle. Besides, this community rights should be maintained in those Gujjar settlements which are in close proximity under the above mentioned measure of development.

(iv) A cooperative scheme should be preferred and executed for:

(a) Animal feed.

(b) Purchase of milk cattle.

(c) Processing of milk.

(d) Marketing of milk and milk products.

(e) Credit needs.

(f) Consumer needs.

(v) Animal Husbandry and Cooperative Departments should prepare schemes for improvement of animal breed and raising fodder crops. They should also provide technical advice, including the latest dairy technology, financial assistance and better breed of animals for Gujjars.

(vi) The Gujjars, who have established a permanent settlement on their own in the forest, their habitats should be connected by roads by the Forest Department. This will help development of dairying on cooperative basis amongst them, as vehicles of the Cooperative Federation will be able to collect milk from them during all seasons. At present they are being subjected to exploitation by the middlemen, because of the lack of transporting facilities.

(vii) The Gujjar women constitute an important segment of the population and work more than their male counterparts. But they are extremely backward, hence vocational-cum-literacy classes should be started for young girls and women. They have also to know a lot about personal hygiene and here the village level workers can play an important role by working with them and educating them.

(viii) Schools and Primary Health Centres should be opened in close proximity of Gujjar habitats.

(ix) The main problem is to wean away the Gujjars from nomadism, which is detrimental to the regeneration of forests. They should be grouped together in milk cooperatives and settlements congenial to their particular social and cultural needs. Together with providing them means of livelihood, their cultural heritage should also be preserved.

(x) The Gujjars are suffering in their capacity for milk production owing to the inadequacy of water supply for drinking and washing etc. In all the Gujjar settlements which I surveyed there was only one source of water, a hand pump. No settlements had more than one hand pump. In the past the Gujjars were migratory, but now in the Sub-Himalayan Tarai they are more or less sedentry. Therefore it is essential that adequate water should be provide to them or they should be permitted to sink more hand-pumps in their area.

(xi) No utilization of faecal material of the livestock population of the Gujjars is being done hitherto. This cattle dung can be used for compost or for bio-gas or even for burning as fuel in the nearby villages. The Gujjars can make some extraearning by selling the compost as manure and dry cowdung as fuel in the nearby villages.

(xii) Introduction of cottage industries based on forest usufructs among them will also add considerably to their earning.Additionally it will make them interested in the vibrant and thriving forests. This will help in limiting the destruction of forests to a great extent.

(xiii) Latest fuel efficient and smokeless 'Chulhas' should be popularized among them by free or subsidised distribution of such ovens to the Gujjars. This will minimize the necessity of cutting trees for fuel wood. Further they should get fuelwood free of cost, which can be in the form of fallen and dried wood.

(xiv) The Gujjars should be taken into confidence and actively involved in preparing a comprehensive programme for their development.

(xv) Finally the Gujjars of Sub-Himalayan Tarai should be enlisted as a Scheduled Tribe so that steeped in poverty and ignorance as they are, they can reap the benefits of the provisions under tribal development. Unlike their brethren in other states, they have not been included hitherto as Scheduled Tribes in Uttar Pradesh.

Article 342 of the Constitution provides that the President may with respect to any State, Union Territory specify the tribes or tribal communities which shall be deemed to be Scheduled Tribes in relation to that State or Union Territory. Interestingly but sadly the anthropologists, sociologists, social workers, administrators and others who have been involved with the tribes and their problems either on theoretical plane or on practical grounds are still not on the same wave length regarding the concept and definition of tribes. From 1917 to the 1931 census, for instance the nomenclature referring to tribes underwent successive modifications such as aborginals or depressed classes. After Independence they were standardized as 'Adivasis' and Scheduled Tribes, but this standardization did not remove all ambiguity. The Gujjars of Uttar Pradesh are a victim of this ambiguity though the concept and definition of a tribe have certainly narrowed down to an appreciable extent now. It is imperative that the Gujjars of Tarai should be redeemed from the shackles of definitions and ambiguity and should be enlisted as a Scheduled Tribe keeping in view their forest dwellings, their geographical isolation, economic backwardness, common culture, common ancestry and their least desire to change.

4
The Gothias

The Gothias are forest dwellers and their settlements are known as 'Khattas' or 'Goths'. Khattas or Goths are spread all over the Tarai and Bhabhar areas in Kumaon. The 'Khattas' had come into existence since time immemorial. It seems that the people residing in the hills descended to these areas with their cattle in winter months, primarily to escape from the severe cold of the winters and also for earning their livelihood. They were known as 'Ghamtappus' or baskers in the sun. Since Tarai and Bhabhar provided good grazing grounds for the cattle, the hillmen prepared ghee and 'khoya' during the winters to earn their livelihood. Later during the British period they also worked as agricultural and forest labourers. In course of time some of the settlements assumed the shape of permanency, whereas some were inhabited temporarily. These settlements accordingly have been recognized in the Forest

Department records as 'Permanent' or 'Temporary'.

It is difficult to say anything authentically about the origin and beginning of this annual cycle of migration. However, a few of the inhabitants of the 'Goths' maintain that even prior to the rule of the Chand dynasty in Kumaon, this seasonal traffic of the hillmen from the hills to Tarai and Bhabhar and back had been in vogue; though there is no archival support to this claim. However it is an undisputed fact that this migration has been pretty old, for example in the document of the Tarai and Bhabhar Forest Department of the year 1890, there is mention of the conditions on which they were allowed to settle in the forest. Again there is a reference of these Khattas in the documents relating to grazing for the year 1909. "There are several cattle stations in the Bhabhar forest that belong to hillmen who do not cultivate in the Bhabhar. The owners may be purely professional cattle breeders, or men coming down from the hills with their families and cattle for the cold weather, in order to find work and thus increase their scanty incomes; these latter are locally called 'Ghamtappus'. This is a very old practice and must have come down from time immemorial. The professionals breed and sell cattle, make ghee and butter. The Ghamtappus work in the Bhabhar villages, reserved forests, on the canals, or collect the minor forest products required by the down-country buyers. The cattle stations thus formed are either temporary for a few months in the year or may be permanent and occupied throughout the year. The former contain cows and bullocks with a few buffaloes and ponies, and generally belong to Ghamtappus who come down in November and return in April, the latter are full of buffaloes, and belong to the professional class of cattle owners. These latter may further be located in some Bhabhar villages during the rains. Returns of these various classes of cattle stations would be interesting. Free materials are provided to them for sheds etc. The sheds built are massive and re-erected every year. No restrictions are imposed, the owners grazing as many cattle as they like and settling wherever they like". The same year the British Government gave grazing rights to these villagers and also the right to collect fodder and fuel from the forests.

The migrants came primarily from Baramandal, Pali Pachhaun, Kali Kumaon and Faldakot areas of the present Almora and Pithoragarh districts. Only the residents of high altitude and medium altitude villages from these areas came down to the plains. Under productivity of land, almost negligible agricultural activity and shortage of fodder during winter months as also economic backwardness were the main reasons behind this seasonal shifting. Further there was no permanency about this practice in the past, neither all the families of a village, nor did the families which migrated once came every year. At the same time a whole family necessarily did not shift, though there are examples of families having two establishments, both in the hills and in Tarai and Bhabhar This resulted in fluctuations in the number of cattle from year to year.

It seems that it was during the British period that the administration induced local people and provided immense facilities for grazing and cattle breeding in these Khattas. The bounty of nature bestowed to these areas during the period were rich luxuriant grass and fodder leaves which were available for feeding the cattle all the year round. Big firms of national repute, such as M/S Edward Keventer, M/S Health Chemicals, were attracted to these Khattas and made them primary sources of their milk supply. This gave impetus to the local milk industry in the interior of the forests and a large number of people earned their bread through this industry.

Although the British administration took a generous view by providing facilities to these cattle owners, they also had a selfish motive behind this. During those days these forests were very dense and provided refuge to dacoits and criminals. General Sir Henry Ramsay, the then Commissioner of Kumaon in his report of May 1884 on Bhabhar has mentioned that, "When I first came to Kumaon large bands of dacoits kept the Bhabhar in a state of terror. Moreover jungle life was solitary, roads were least maintained and infested with wild animals.

The country was in a disturbed condition and these forests could have provided ideal hideout for rebels and activists. To have a control over these factors, it was necessary to establish camps at suitable places". These Khattas served this purpose very well and with a few facilities, the British administrators settled a part of the population there, which ultimately helped them to keep a vigil and have a firm control over these valuable forests. There were no rules and regulations as regards the settlement of Khattas and no fixed area was allotted to any Khatta, which made them free to bestow their bounty on settlers at will and thus make them feel indebted and therefore loyal.

Since it was a selfish motive on the part of the British administration, the developmental part of the Khattas dwellers remained neglected. No grazing schemes or cattle breeding schemes were ever introduced in these Khattas. There were no roads to take out the produce from the forests for the use of the general public. Owing to uncontrolled and over grazing, the rich grass-lands were destroyed and better species of fodder grasses became extinct. The ravages of wild animals also destroyed the pastures. Epidemics were brought in by stray cattle, as no planned breeding schemes were ever introduced. This led to a deterioration in cattle wealth. Moreover with the dawn of Independence, a large tract of the forests of Tarai and Bhabhar was brought under cultivation and consequently some Khattas have become extinct. At present in Tarai and Bhabhar there are 84 Khattas spread over an area of about 2000 square kilometers. Out of these 33 are permanent Khattas and 51 are temporary. According to the data provided by the Forest Department for the year 1973 the number of families in the permanent Khattas was 551, the cattle population was 10,539 out of which 5,165 are milch cattle. In the temporary Khattas, the number of families was 1,113, the cattle population was 6,381 out of which 1,497 was milch cattle.

No survey was conducted by the Forest Department after 1973. The scenario has changed absolutely in the Khattas now. The details of the survey conducted by me are given below.

Bindu Khatta :

It is 6 km from Lalkuan, the nearest township. In 1948, 129 families were registered by the Government. At present according to the Forest Department the number of registered families in Bindu Khatta is only 175, though actually 3000 to 3500 families are actually staying there. This encroachment started between 1970 to 1982 and today the total forest area encroached upon in Bindu Khatta is about 4050 ha. The encroachers are peasants, contractors and retired personnel from different departments like revenue, army, forest, roadways and railways. There are now seven villages in Bindu Khatta apart from the settlement of the original 129 families. Since 1985, the new settlers have started ten registered milk cooperative societies. Before 1970 there was thick khair (Acacia catechu) forest in Bindu Khatta, but now the area has been wantonly deforested and some new settlers are said to be involved in illegal timber trade also.

Before 1948, people in Bindu Khatta used to migrate to the hills during summers, but with the formation of the Lalkuan Milk Society in the same year, the practice was discontinued. Of the original 129 families, 125 are from Naini Tal district, and four from Almora district. The condition of these settlers is miserable. Lack of education prevents them from taking white collared jobs while their poor financial condition does not permit them to start new enterprises. Only eleven people amongst them are employed, six are working in the nearby Century Paper Mill in Lalkuan, as security guards and the rest five as labourers. There are five teachers from this Khatta. Two of them are employed in Lalkuan Primary School, one in Primary School Ghornala, one in Primary School Bindu Khatta and one in Junior High School Bindu Khatta.

The main grouse of the original settlers is that in 1976 land was to be allotted to every family at the rate of 1 acre (0.40 ha.) for residential purposes and 2.50 acres, (1ha.) for growing fodder. But in the meantime the process of encroachment started and land could not be allotted to them. Before, 1970, forests were aplenty and grazing was no problem, but now with the grabbing of land by the new settlers and the setting up of the Century Paper Mill, forests and grazing lands both have vanished. Deforestation has also destroyed their cottage industry. Previously people from the Khatta used to weave mats from 'bindu' and 'padera' grasses, but now the grasses are not available. The establishment of the Century Paper Mill is also having a negative effect on the health of the Khatta residents. Most of them are suffering from breathing problems.

There are no medical or veterinary facilities, except that some veterinary assistance is provided by the Cooperative Milk Society at Lalkuan. There is one Primary School and one Junior High School in Bindu Khatta. The Primary School is run in thatched huts and in the Junior High School there are two small rooms which were constructed by donations made by the settlers. There are no proper roads in the Khatta and during the rains owing to slush and water, Bindu Khatta is almost cut off from the outside world.

These grievances of the Bindu Khatta settlers have also culminated in violent demonstrations to quell which the police had to resort to firing. The detail of these demonstrations form part of the chapter on agriculture, as this dissent has agrarian overtones.

Khamari Khatta :

The Khatta is 6.50 km from Lalkuan and its area is 20 ha. It is registered and in 1973 according to the Forest Department there were 10 families and 144 animals. Today there are 16 families in this Khatta. Their main vocation is agriculture and dairying, but not even a single family owns more than one ha of land. There is a 'khoya bhatti' in the village. The people in this Khatta in particular have realized the importance of family planning. Whereas previously people used to run to the forest on witnessing a family planning worker.

The people in the Khatta are still living in a primitive stage. Amongst the 16 families, only one person is in service. He is a soldier in the armed forces. There are no medical and veterinary facilities. In the Khatta there is privately owned Primary School managed by some Debki Nandan. There are 40 students in this Primary School The problem of grazing is very acute in the Khatta and this has directly affected the milk yield. In 1947-48 the yield of milk in the Khatta was 40 canes per day. Now it has come down to 4.5 canes* per day.

Baur Khatta :

Located at a distance of 12km from Lalkuan, this Khatta is mentioned even in the forest records of 1883. The area of the Khatta is 61.5 ha. In 1973 there were 39 families and 901 animals. But today the number has come down to 36 families, out of which 31 are from Almora district and five are from Nepal. The Nepalese came here as herdsmen and later became cattle owners.

The main vocation of the Khatta is agriculture and cattle breeding. It is shocking that though it is one of the oldest Khatta, there is no school, no medical and veterinary facilities. There are no proper roads and no one has studied beyond class nine. The main reason for the drop out is poverty and illiteracy which have prevented them form launching other enterprises or even securing them a job.

Saanp Kathani :

It is eight km from Lalkuan and is exactly 102 years old. In this Khatta, there are people both from the hills and plains but mostly from the hills. There is one Nepalese settler also. In 1955 there were 30 families in this Khatta who were trading in milk. In 1973 their number came down to 11. But now there are 14 families out of which 13 are cattle owners and one is rearing goats. They are agriculturists also and the average land-holding is about 1.13 ha. Upto 1955, average number of animals with each family were 90, but owing to paucity of fodder now the number has started dwindling. Previously the

* One cane is equivalent to 40 to 42 litres.

Khatta dwellers had a 16.4 ha. blank in the forest which was used for grazing purposes, but owing to internal dissensions, this pasture land has been confiscated by the Forest Department. The Khatta is registered.

There are no schools in the Khatta, no roads, no medical and veterinary facilities. There is one bull attendant of the Animal Husbandry Department there and the only help he can extend is that of injecting the animals. The main problem of the Khatta is of drinking water. In the Khatta the main source of potable water is a hand pump and a rivulet which dries up during summers. The people have applied to the Forest Department for boring a tube well, but hitherto they have not been given permission.

Raikhal Khatta :

It is 22 km from Lalkuan. According to the forest records in 1973 there were 42 families in the Khatta. Today there are 69 families out of which 57 are from the hills, four are Nepalese and eight families are of Gujjars. In this Khatta also the small farmers of the neighbouring areas have been included as residents of the Khatta in the Milk Society records of Lalkuan. The Khatta is registered but is being nibbled by agricultural land.

The 57 families from the hills own 350 buffaloes and 500 cows. The average yield of milk throughout the year is 325 litres per day. The Neplese came here as herdsmen, but now they own 20 buffaloes and 35 cows. The average yield of milk is thirty litres per day. The eight Gujjar families are settled in the Khatta since 1962.

The Gujjars supply milk to middlemen in Haldwani. They prefer to give milk to the middlemen and not to the Cooperative Society, because they can get loan from the middle-men whenever required. Some of the Gujjars are aware that they are being exploited by the middlemen, but still they prefer them as compared to the Cooperative Milk Society. The rate at which they supply milk is Rs. 5.50 to Rs. 6 per litre. The

Nepalese and the hill people supply milk to the Milk Cooperative Society in Lalkuan as well as to the middlemen. Some milk is also supplied to the two 'Khoya Bhattis' in the Khatta.

In the Khatta there is one Primary School upto Class V which is housed in thatched huts. There are no medical or veterinary facilities and no proper roads. During the rainy season the Khatta dwellers have a tough time as the roads are full of slush and are infested with horse flies.

Beria Khatta :

It is 4 km from Bailparao the nearest township and is not registered. There are three families in the Khatta. The first family is of Puran Singh. He is a graduate and has been staying there since the last 30 years. The next family is of Mohan Singh. His father Swarup Singh came here 60 years back. The third family is of Anup Ram. He has been residing there with his wife and two sons since last six years.

Kuagadar Khatta :

The Khatta is registered by the Forest Department. It is in the Baur Forest Range of Tarai Bhabhar Forest division. According to the Forest Department, in 1973 there were nine families in this Khatta and they owned 198 animals. But now the number of families have gone up to 16 and the animals to 610.

Dan Singh Bohara Bisht and Pan Singh Negi have 'Khoya Bhattis' in the Khatta. The Khatta dwellers supply milk to them as well as to middlemen in Haldwani. In the Khatta there are no educational medical or veterinary facilities.

Nigaltya Khatta :

It is 10 km from Lalkuan in the Barhani range of Tarai-Bhabhar Forest Division and is a registered Khatta. In 1973 there were 34 families in the Khatta and 1119 animals according to the records of the Forest Department. But now there are only 30 cattle breeders out of which only three have kept their families there. Since there is an acute shortage of fodder owing to deforestation and new eucalyptus plantations, the number of animals has now dwindled to 422 buffaloes and 210 cows. The average production of milk is 400 litres per day throughout the year which is supplied to 'Khoya Bhattis' and middle men. The cattle owners have small agricultural plots also in which they grow fodder for their cattle and cereals. The residents of this Khatta owing to shortage of fodder and fuel have realized the importance of forests and are against illicit felling of trees.

Khassi Bhoj :

It is six km from Lalkuan in thick forest. The Khatta is registered and in 1973 according to the records of the Forest Department, there were eight families and 203 animals. Today there are 11 families and 239 animals out of which 223 are buffaloes and 16 cows. The average yield of milk per family is about 21 litres throughout the year and they supply this milk to middlemen in Haldwani.

Almost all Khatta dwellers complain that they have no medical, educational or veterinary facilities. In a few of them there is also drinking water scarcity. As the Khattas are not connected with roads, they cannot supply milk to the Milk Union and as such are being exploited by middlemen.

The Inhabitants of the Khattas

The inhabitants of the 'Khattas' of Tarai and Bhabhar are primarily the residents of the hill areas of Kumaon mostly from Baramandal, Pali Pachhaun, Kali Kumaon and Faldakot areas, as has been mentioned earlier. These areas are not very fertile, only 15 percent of the land being cultivated. Out of this too, irrigation facility is available in one per cent area only. Except for limited area on the foothills and valleys, the land is not productive. This leaves a majority of the inhabitants either landless or with small land holdings.

Consequent upon rise in human as well as animal population in these areas, there has been excessive grazing and shrinkage in the forest land, which in turn has led to soil erosion and degradation. It has adversely affected the economy of the people. The area lacks in industrial employment opportunities also. After sowing the 'rabi' crop, the peasants have little work to do in their fields. At the same time owing to snowfall in higher altitudes there is extreme cold and no grazing facilities. That made the inhabitants to descend down to these 'Khattas'.

Breeding of cattle and selling milk and its products is the main avocation of these people; some of them used to reside in these 'Khattas' all the year round; whereas the rest used to leave for the hills in the beginning of the rainy season with their cattle and return with the onset of winter. In view of the ever increasing difficulty of grazing in the hills along with better opportunities of mild trade in Tarai and Bhabhar area, many of them have started residing permanently in these 'Khattas'. This is also for plenty of water being available for the cattle in these areas. Most of such people own land and houses in the hills as also in Tarai and Bhabhar. A few of them are the original settlers of these villages and are called 'sirgiroh'. But comparatively they are very few in number.

There are also people who get bamboo, 'sandan', 'gethi' etc. and trees on concessional rates from the Forest Department and sell products like wooden utensils, baskets, mats etc. to the nearby villages to supplement their income. Inhabitants of 'Goths'and 'Khattas' near towns also sell fuelwood gathered from the forests. This work is mostly done by women.

In the past a few of the comparatively affluent residents from these Khattas, who hail from Kali Kumaon, came to the Tanakpur and Khatima areas in Tarai and Bhabhar to carry trade on barter basis. The practice is still in vogue though on a very small scale. They brought hill produce, e.g. chillies, potatoes, pulses, ghee etc. and in exchange got paddy from the purchasers like Tharus and local farmers, and on return sold them to the people in the hills. Also there were a few who loaned money to Tharus at a higher interest rate and purchased foodstuffs from them in lieu of interest. To prevent this exploitation of the Tharus by the Kali Kumaonis the British had started a Cooperative Credit Banking Scheme for the tribals in the late nineteenth century.

The Customs and Traditions :

The people from the hills, who have settled in the 'Khattas', have maintained their religious customs and traditions. Every 'Khatta' has its own appropriate festival, and the ceremonies associated with it gives expression to the needs of the people during that season. In the upper reaches of Kumaon, the ruggedness of the terrain and the forbidding natural environment of the Himalaya has had its deep impression on the various customs and has profoundly shaped the outlook of its people. The people of the Khattas have retained these customs and traditions.

The Tradition of Jagar :

The people in Khattas have faith on 'Jagar' or the invoking of demi Gods to ward off all evil. The literal meaning of 'Jagar' is 'Jagarn' or the invoking of demi Gods in which the folk singer, 'Jagaria' sings panegyrical verses in their praise. The accompanying musical instruments are 'hurka' or a small drum, 'thali' metallic plate and 'dhole' big drum. The psychedelic tune, the rhythm of the music and the beat of the drum creates a charged atmosphere in which some men and at times women also get into a frenzy and start dancing vigorously. It is said that in this stage of ecstasy a particular individual in the group gets possessed by the invoked demi Gods and answers the queries of the assembled crowd. The queries are normally regarding ailments and the general welfare of the people.

Jagar can be held throughout the year for any number of days by individual families pertaining to personal problems. But mostly it is organized for twenty two nights at a stretch and is called 'Baise' derived from the Hindi numerical twenty two. In 'Baise' the whole community is involved and every individual family contributes for the ceremony in kind and dines together during that period. In Jagar' the singer is called' Jagaria' and' the dancer 'Dangaria'. The important demi Gods for whom 'Jagar' is held in the Khattas are Golla, Gangnath and Nar Singh.

Golla :

Lord Golla was the son of Halrai, the feudal lord of the principality of Dhumagarh in the present Pithoragarh district. Golla was born from the eighth wife and was his only male progeny. It is said that after marrying seven wives when he could not father a son, Halrai became very sad and requested the court astrologer to predict his future. The astrologer told him that a son would be born to him from his eighth wife. One day Halrai went to the forest for a hunt and after perambulating on horse back for several hours he became very thirsty. To quench his thirst he went to a nearby hut where a beautiful girl Kalika met him. He was so attracted by her beauty that he requested her to marry him. She agreed and soon the nuptial ceremony was solemnized. Both then went to Halrai's fief and started living happily. But the seven wives were extremely jealous of Kalika and were looking for a chance to harm her. Soon they got the opportunity. Halrai was out hunting one day when a son was born to Kalika. The seven wives hatched a conspiracy. They tied a cloth around the mother's eyes during the delivery on the pretext of warding off the evil eye and later told her that she had given birth to a 'sil batta' or grinding stones. The newly born child on the other hand was put in a small wooden box and then thrown in the river Gori. Fortunately a fisherman found the box while fishing. The fisherman opened it and was delighted to see the child. He was issueless and adopted the child as a gift of god. According to the tradition of the Khattas, since the child was retrieved from the river Gori, he was named as Goriya. With the passage of time Goriya became Gorla and later Golla. When Halrai returned home, he was told that his wife had given birth to a 'sil batta'. He was so infuriated that he abandoned her.

When Golla came of age, the treachery was revealed to him by his adoptive father. Golla wanted to avenge the injustice meted out to his mother and was looking for an opportune moment. It is said that one day he took a wooden horse to a spring where the seven wives of Halrai had come with their entourage. He then put the horse's mouth into the spring and started coaxing it to drink water. On witnessing the sight, the seven wives started laughing and commented, "Hey crazy man how can a wooden horse drink water". Golla retorted that if a woman could give birth to a 'sil batta' then a wooden horse could also drink water. The news of the incident spread like a forest fire and Halrai also came to know about it.He was then convinced that his seven wives had conspired against Kalika. As a punishment he had them killed. Golla was then made the lord of the fief; his mother's prestige was also restored and she was called back to the palace.

Dhumagarh was one of the important principalities of Kumaon which was being ruled by the Chand dynasty, and the chieftain Golla. It is believed that he was the general of the Chand army. He was a brave warrior and had led the Kumaoni army to several victories. He was also an ace horse rider and his mount was a white steed. In one of the battles probably, against the Gurkhas he was killed in action. Since he had laid his life for the people, he was elevated to the status of a demi god and the Kumaonis started worshipping him.

Today he is regarded as a symbol of gallantry by the people of Kumaon and also as a God of justice. People from the villages who have been subjected to humiliation and injustice go to his temple and plead their case. They also appeal to him in a written form with the details of their case and hang the letters in the temple and await their turn for justice being meted out to them. The temple of Golla was at first built in Champawat, the original capital of the Chand dynasty. In close proximity to the temple there is a field where on certain nights it is believed that Lord Golla can be seen riding his white steed and the sound of the galloping horse can also be heard. When Chands transferred their capital to Almora during the sixteenth century (1560 A.D.) a temple of Lord Golla was also built at a place called Chitai in close proximity to the new capital. Subsequently one of the courtiers of Chands, the Maḥars settled down in Mehra Gaon near Bhim Tal and established a temple of Golla at Vinayak and then at Ghorakhal near Bhowali. Today there are several temples of Lord Golla in Kumaon and he is worshipped by many Kumaonis as a family deity.

Gangnath :

Lord Gangnath is another deity who is held in high esteem by the residents of the Khattas. According to tradition, Gangnath was born in a feudal family. He was the son of Udeychan or Vivechan, the Lord of the principality of Doti in Nepal. He had a solar lineage. When Gangnath was born, his father requested the court astrologer to prepare his son's horoscope and also to foresee his future. The astrologer forecasted that the boy was blessed with all virtues except that by the time he was twelve years old he would renounce the world. At the predicted age it was believed that he would marry Bhana or a Brahmin girl named Bhana and subsequently renounce the world. To prove the forecast wrong, Udeychan decided that he would marry his son with a princess of his choice and then change her name to Bhana Bamini. Later, on the advice of the courtiers he married his son seven times before he reached the age of twelve. But destiny could not be changed and at the age of twelve Gangnath actually fell in love with Bhana. She was from a Joshi family and was a resident of the village Danya Kurkauli near Almora. It is said that Gangnath saw his love for the first time in a dream. Later he went to the village to meet her on horseback and donned the garb of a mendicant so that he could not be recognized. When he arrived at the village, Bhana saw him from the window. It is stated that she was awaiting him and immediately hauled him to her room with a rope. After this incident they used to meet regularly. But their clandestine meetings were soon exposed and the Joshi clan with the help of Kala Jhakaruwa, the black smith of the village murdered the young lovers. After their death, Gangnath became a ghost and haunted the Joshis. Thus to appease him, the Joshis built a temple of Gangnath and started worshipping him. About Gangnath it is stated by the Khatta dwellers that he is the God of the downtrodden and like Golla undoes the injustice inflicted upon the people.

Nar Singh :

He is one of the nine reincarnations of Lord Vishnu and according to Hindu mythology he killed the demon Hirnakashyap. This demon had been blessed by Lord Siva that he could neither be killed by humans nor animals. It was not possible to finish him inside a house or in the open. Moreover he could not be killed in daylight or in darkness. He took advantage of this boon and tortured every form of life. But his son Prahlad was just the reverse. He was a staunch devotee of God owing to which he had aroused the ire of his father. In exasperation he tried to eliminate him but could not succeed. Ultimately when Hirnakashyap's tyranny had become intolerable, Lord Vishnu reincarnated as Nar Singh to protect Prahlad from his clutches. As Nar Singh, Lord Vishnu assumed a human form, but his head was that of a lion, he was neither man nor animal. Further to honour Lord Siva's blessing he killed Hirnakashyap on the threshold of the palace and the time he chose for eliminating him was sunset.

Problems of Khattas :

Consequent upon the rise in the price of land in Tarai as also the improved facilities for the sale of milk and its products, human as well as animal population have risen in Tarai. This has resulted in clash of interests of Khatta dwellers and the new settlers as well as these areas vis-a-vis forest conservation. In this connection it is notable that in the settlements of Tarai and Bhabhar Forest Division undertaken a few years back, these Goths and Khattas have not been regularized. It has been made quite clear in G.O. No. 15(3)/XIV-B66, dated 13.6.1969 that the inhabitants of the Goths have no claim over the forest land. This is the sad plight of the Khatta dwellers who have been coming to Tarai-Bhabhar since time immemorial, but have not been allotted land in this area though on the one hand there are people who have encroached upon forest land with impunity in the recent past through muscle power or political clout.

The population density being less during the early years after Independence, there was not much demand for forest produce and there was no restriction on grazing. But the situation changed drastically with the coming up of farms in the reserved forests, as there was a rapid shrinkage in the grazing areas. Additionally with the increase in population density in the tracts on the fringes of forests, the biotic pressure on the existing grazing lands further increased. Along with these to meet the developmental needs of the country as also of the forest-based industries, raising of new plantations became necessary.

The Goths or Khattas fall within these plantations. With the ever-expanding plantations, which necessitated clear felling followed by planting of saplings, areas available for grazing began to shrink. Clear felling also reduced the number of trees available for grazing. At the same time in new plantations, grazing is prohibited for atleast three to five years. Further owing to fencing of new planted areas, the movement of cattle became restricted and the surrounding grazing areas of the Khattas were also reduced.

The demand for milk in Tarai and contiguous area is ever on the increase, whereas the present supply cannot cope up with the demand. It has made this trade lucrative, which has been more so due to the establishment of the Cooperative Milk Society in Lalkuan. A few of the affluent people residing in the nearby villages and townships have started keeping their milch cattle in the Khattas under the charge of their employees. This has also added to the grazing problem of the Khatta dwellers. The following are the problems and demands of the Khatta dwellers in the present situation on the basis of the field study conducted by me:

1. As grass does not grow under eucalyptus,their plantations have caused difficulty in grazing.
2. Plantations should not be developed around Khattas and the areas where plantations so far have not been raised, they may be excluded from such plantations.
3. Plantation activities have uprooted many families in the Khattas and they have been subjected to great hardships. The Government on the one hand is settling landless and others in Tarai and Bhabhar, and on the other old inhabitants of the Khattas are being put to considerable hardship.
4. If the grazing areas of these Khattas are restricted, they will have to be resettled elsewhere and new pasture lands to be found for them, which is very difficult.
5. As the milk producers do not own any land, they can neither produce food for themselves, nor raise fodder for their cattle. Every herdsmen in the Khattas should therefore be allotted half acre (0.2 ha) of land for growing fodder of good quality for their cattle. This land can be given to them on lease.
6. Every family be allotted on permanent basis 7.50 acres (3ha.) of land for agriculture.
7. Atleast half acre (0.2 ha.) of land be allotted to them on permanent basis for animal residence.
8. As the herdsmen are not allowed to construct permanent structures, they as also their cattle reside in highly unhygienic conditions. Frequently they become victim of forest fires also, which almost ruins them and forces them to lead a life of perpetual poverty and squalor. Considering this the Forest Department should allow them construction of permanent structures for themselves as also their cattle.
9. The roads leading to Khattas are in a bad shape and full of pot holes. This puts the residents to considerable

trouble and it is difficult for milk vans to ply on them. During the rainy season, the roads are full of slush and the ditches overflow with water owing to which it is very difficult to negotiate them. Moreover during the rainy season some of the Khattas are cut off from the rest of the world for several days. The Forest Department should construct good approach roads to these Khattas.

10. Drinking water poses a great problem to the residents and their cattle, particularly because the Forest Department does not permit them to sink tubewells in the Khattas. Every Khatta, the residents feel, should be provided with a tubewell.

11. The Forest Department auctions milk 'bhattis'* annually which is detrimental to milk cooperatives and encourages middlemen. The Forest Department should not auction the 'bhattis' and cream separators in the Khattas. The residents are already members of the Milk Producers' Federation or propose to be one and they should be permitted to manage them.

12. Every Khatta should be allotted common land for community purposes like shepherds' residence, milk room, school, hospitals, play ground etc.

13. The Forest Department realizes road tax from the Milk Federation vehicles on their visits to the Khattas for milk collection. This tax is ultimately realized from Khatta dwellers as they are members of the cooperative organization. Cooperative organizations should thus be exempted from this tax.

14. The Khattas have no postal, medical, grocery etc. facilities and they should be provided these.

15. The residents of the Khattas should be provided with materials like grass for their thatches.

---

* *Apparatus meant for boiling milk.*

The officials of the Forest Department on the other hand feel that most of the demands of the Khatta dwellers are not justified. The National Forest Policy has to be kept in view while providing facilities to the Khatta dwellers. It enjoins that two-thirds of the land in the hills should be under forests. Cheap grazing facilities as desired by the forest dwellers result in a vicious circle of drawbacks. It means uncontrolled rise in the number of cattle which leads to reduced grazing facility, fall in the quality of cattle and breeding, requiring even more cattle to make good the decreased yield from the cattle. The belief that the wealth of a Khatta dweller is estimated by the number of cattle owned by him, is the root cause of the unhappy condition of our cattle. This has to be countered if improvement in this direction is desired. It is also necessary to save our forests, which is in the interest of the locals as also the whole nation. Proximity of Khattas to the forests should not allow its inhabitants to play with the interests of the whole nation, nor should they be benefited at the cost of national interests.

As against the National Policy objective of 66% land in the hills being under forests, the actual cover in the State of Uttar Pradesh is only 15%, and this too is ever shrinking due to various reasons. Besides, to create more jobs, as also to save foreign exchange, plantations have to be undertaken to provide raw material to the factories and for new projects. To curb the import of newsprint, wood pulp has to be provided to the new factories to ensure indigenous production. According to the Marketing Research Corporation of India, there are chances of exporting wood to the neighbouring Asian countries. This means that least forest land should be given for non forest purposes.

Even while being conscious of the urgency of forest conservation, the Forest Department has tried to accommodate the needs of the Khatta dwellers in its plan. The Kumaon Forest Fact Finding Committee, 1959, instituted to go into the problems of the Khattas recommended that:

(a) "At the time of demarcating an area for plantation as far as possible the Khattas be left as before, failing which they be allotted alternative sites.

(b) The Khatta dwellers should be given material for building huts liberally."

The Forest Department is of the view that there are no rules regarding the inhabitants of these Khattas, they come and settle there at will. The boundaries of the Khattas are also not fixed with the result that their areas are ever expanding and thus encroachment on the forest land is on the increase. The demands of the Khatta owners show that on the one hand there are the aspirations of the people residing on the land occupied illegally and on the other the demands of the National Forest Policy. After discussing the problems of the Khattas with officers of the Forest Department and the field staff, their view points and suggestions regarding the situation are being summed up below:

1. Khattas and Goth owners complain that the productivity of their cattle is very low as they lack proper pasture facilities. It is true that as against an ideal of 0.5 ha. pasture per animal, they have barely 0.22 ha. pasture land. To state that this is due to the plantation areas being closed for grazing is not valid, as even if those areas were left open for grazing, availability of pasture per cattle would have been only 0.26 ha. Also to say that due to eucalyptus plantations there has been shrinkage in the pasture facility, is not valid. Cattle are seen grazing in the eucalyptus plantations as soft green grass is always found in these plantations. Shrinkage in the grazing areas has come only due to the dissemination of lantana. This plant has spread in the Tarai-Bhabhar forests on such a large scale that it has restricted the grazing areas substantially. Eradication of this weed is necessary to prevent its incursion on pasture land.

2. The Khatta owners want half acre (0.2 ha.) of land per

family for growing fodder. Land can be allotted individually to all the families in different Khattas, if the proposition is economically viable.

3. The fodder problem can be solved only by adopting the following course of action:

(a) Rearing of only good breed cattle.

(b) Curtailing the number of unproductive cattle.

(c) Feeding cattle on green fodder and other mixtures.Stall feeding besides increasing the productivity of cattle will restrict damage to forests by them.

4. Experience shows that the pedigree cattle brought from outside fall victim to the diseases in Tarai and gradually lose their milk yield. As such it is advisable to upgrade the local cattle by the methods listed below:

(a) **Upbreeding of local cattle:** For this purpose good local cows should be cross-bred with exotic breeds like Jersey and Brown-Swiss. Initially local cows should be served with cross-bred local bulls having only 50% exotic inheritance. Progeny of such cross-breeding will show vast improvement in milk yield even in the first generation. Already such an effort is being made at Ranikhet and Almora in the Kumaon region.

(b) **Improvement of local buffaloes:** Similarly Murrah he-buffaloes may be used to upgrade local buffaloes. To make this effort a success, it is necessary that local scrub bulls should be castrated, as also disposing of such cattle and discouraging its purchase should be enforced.

5. The rate of grazing tax associated with its irregular realization is responsible for greater number of nondescript cattle. To reduce their number it is necessary that the rate of grazing of such cattle be increased, so that their maintenance becomes difficult and the Khatta dwellers are discouraged to breed them. This can also be achieved by allowing only six cattle to graze at

normal rates and by increasing the grazing tax for excess cattle. Imposing of higher grazing rate should be resorted to after three years of launching the breeding improvement campaign, as within this period the Khatta owners will start reaping the positive results of the campaign and would not have any difficulty in making the payment at higher rates. Moreover if a family has more than six good breed cattle, it will have a better income and as such would not be affected by the increase in grazing tax.

6. Dairying is the main avocation of the Khatta dwellers of Tarai. Every family in these Khattas owns 20 animals at and average out of which 10, i.e. only half are economical. Consequent on rearing only good cattle green fodder will have to be provided. Thus those families opting for more than six buffaloes will have to provide fodder for the excess buffaloes on their own.

7. Green fodder can be raised in the eucalyptus plantations between rows of trees. As eucalyptus trees are cut at a rotation of seven to eight years, plantation land for green fodder will not be difficult to provide. For this purpose every Khatta can be allotted two plots in eucalyptus plantations to enable them to raise green fodder on them with a rotation of four years.

8. In the areas lacking irrigation facilities in Tarai, lucern can be grown as fodder crop. It will give a yield of 600 to 700 quintals per ha per year from October to June. The areas having irrigation facilities may have an increased yield of 800 to 900 quintals in Tarai. During the rainy season, berseem can be sown as green fodder. Additionally during rains Napier and Sudan grasses can also be grown.

9. Green fodder produced in the revenue villages and farms can also be a good source of fodder to the cattle in Khattas, provided they are in close proximity to the villages and farms are linked to them by roads. Grow-

ing of green fodder is in no way less profitable than cash crops. If an offer of purchase of fodder is made to the villagers or the farm owners, they are likely to raise green fodder crops and this will be a dependable and perennial source of fodder to the residents in the Khattas. With increased productivity of cattle consequent on being fed on palatable greenage, they will be able to pay for it.

10. There are 33 permanent and 51 temporary Khattas in Tarai region of Kumaon. If land is given for permanent settlement, many of the families will not like to move back to the hills as per their seasonal move. Instead many families in the hills will like to come down for similar benefits. As these settlements are within the forests, they are already causing problems for the proper management of forests. They are the main source of encroachment, and their permanent settlement will further damage the floral as well as faunal population of these forests.

11. Approach roads are necessary for the Khattas. The Forest Department has not been able to do it so far, because of the paucity of funds, which if provided, the Forest Department is prepared to undertake not only the construction of such roads, but also of metalling them.

12. The residents of the Khattas desire facilities like schools, hospitals, tubewells etc., as they are necessary for the present day living. However, it is equally important to take into account the unhealthy condition of our forests and nothing should be done to damage them.

The Khattas are spread all over the forest, many of them situated deep inside. If the Khattas are allowed these facilities, they will soon develop into villages, which will also require land for community facilities. Thus the expanding villages will contribute further to the decadence of forests.

5

Agricultural Development and its impact on the marginalized population in Tarai

Agriculture is the prominent sector of the Indian economy. Nearly three-fourth of the Indian population resides in rural areas. Needless to say that the sole occupation and source of income of these people is agriculture. It is thus obvious that the better living standards of the rural people can be achieved by boosting up agricultural production through modern agricultural techniques. A desired level of agriculture production plays vital role in building up a strong economic structure of countries mainly based on agriculture. One of the main reason for the strong economic standard of developed countries is their achievement of a desired level of agricultural production. On the other hand developing countries have yet to achieve this standard to tone up their economic structure. In this context Punjab and the Sub-Himalayan Tarai of Kumaon are torch bearers to agriculturists in other parts of the country. In Tarai and Bhabhar sudden spurt in agricultural activities is due to the colonization and migration during the post Independence period.

Many a times during the British rule also, efforts were made to colonize the region for agricultural purposes . But all these efforts failed. The scourge of malaria and vagaries of climate thwarted these attempts at human habitation in the area. This region was then called the Andamans of U.P. It was for its most unhealthy malarial climate and also for the number of tigers it harboured. Continuous heavy rains created ditches, ponds and swamps, which became the breeding grounds for mosquitoes. Today owing to the planning of Pt. G.B. Pant, Chief Minister of U.P. , Bhawan Singh Bisht, the Superintendent of Tarai and Bhabhar in 1947, Major M.S. Sandhu, Deputy Director of Colonization and the herculean efforts of the settlers here, mostly Sikhs, this region is humming with activity now and has become one of the most prosperous agricultural belts in India. It is borne out by the data given below in respect of different crops raised here:

Total reported geographical area of Tarai and Bhabhar.		231,567ha.
Area under agriculture:	Rural	177,244 ha.
	Urban	3,804 ha.
	Total	181,048 ha.

The area of main food crops raised during Kharif and Rabi seasons are detailed below:

KHARIF :

Name of the crop	In irrigated area (ha.)	In unirrigated area (ha.)
Paddy	94,075	6600
Maize	12	235
Pulses	39	428
Sugar cane	40,340	4578
Turmeric, chilly,ginger	74	11
Soya bean	113	4696

RABI :

Name of the crop	In irrigated area (ha.)	In unirrigated area (ha.)
Wheat	110,695	1906
Barley	175	50
Peas	466	316
Masur	531	2883
Mustard	4217	2458

(Source : Collectorate, Naini Tal.)

A comparative data of the average production of some of the important food crops is being detailed.

Name of the food crop	Average	Production	in quintals/ha.	
	Tarai & Bhabhar	U.P.	Punjab	India
Rice	28.62	18.27	32.29	17.40
Wheat	28.97	21.71	37.15	22.81
Maize	10.74	13.20	17.87	15.18
Gram	10.02	8.79	7.45 7.12	
Soya Bean	20	12.96	- 10.15	
Sugar Cane 653.95	600	588.11	99.06	9

(Source : Collectorate, Naini Tal.)

The data provided by the states appears to be incorrect. This affects the credibility of the data provided by the Ministry of Agriculture, Government of India, as it is based on the information fed by the states. A glaring example of the inaccurate data provided by the state of U.P. is being cited. According to the statistical report, 'Agricultural Statistics at a Glance, March, 1993' of the Ministry of Agriculture, Government of India, the average production of wheat in U.P. is 21.71 quintals per ha., whereas on the report published by the Directorate of Agricultural Statistics of the U.P. Government, the average production of wheat in U.P. is 23.37 quintals per ha. The same difference can also be observed in other cereals given below :

Name of cereal	**Average Production, Quintal/ha. in U.P.**	
	According to U.P. Government.	**According to Government of India.**
Rice	17.18	18.27
Maize	11.02	13.26
Bajara	10.11	11.15
Millet	7.45	9.36

The productivity data in the Tarai and Bhabhar area provided by Naini Tal Collectorate also is not reliable and does not tally with the one provided by the Chief Development Officer, Naini Tal. The data which was collected on the basis of field study is however more accurate. It is being detailed below:

Kharif Crops, 1993	Productivity quintal/ha.
Rice	30.14
Maize	14.87
Soya bean	17.88

Rabi Crops, 1993	Productivity quintal/ha.
Wheat	30.87
Mustard	7.54
Gram	9.87
Peas	11.31
Masur	6.72

Wheat and paddy are the most important cereal crops and among cash crops, sugarcane is most important. Of the three major cereals, wheat is the most important. It is a rabi crop, sown during the period of October - December. The best soils for wheat are well drained loams and clay loam mixes. The presence of these and other agro-climatic conditions in the region are highly favourable to the cultivation of this crop. Progressive farmers from this area mostly grow high yielding varieties.

The next crop in order of importance is paddy, a kharif crop that is sown in the months of June - July. It grows best on clay loams and clay soils. Low lying clay soils are preferred for long duration varieties and lighter soils for quick maturing varieties. This crop thrives best under conditions of high temperature and humidity and as such its cultivation is favourable in Tarai. About three-fourth of the progressive farmers and two-third of the less progressive grow traditional paddy varieties as observed during the survey. The new high yielding varieties were grown by two-third of the progressive farmers, but by less than one in twelve of the less progressive farmers.

Among cash crops, sugarcane is most important not only in Tarai, but the whole of Uttar Pradesh. It grows best on medium heavy soil, but can also be raised on lighter soil with irrigation and on heavy clay soil with irrigation and drainage. The growth period for cane is usually ten months, about twice as long for cereal crops. The sugarcane crop typically runs through both the major kharif and rabi seasons, and occupies plots on which otherwise atleast two other crops could be grown. There is the widespread practice in U.P. of cultivating a second crop of cane from the first plant, called ratoon. This requires cutting cane back after the first harvest, following which the second growth takes almost as long as the first, but is appreciably less in yield per ha. Sugarcane is the most important cash crop of Tarai, especially in Rudrapur block and is grown by well over 60 percent of the progressive farmers and about half of the less progressive. The small cultivators sow it in relatively small areas and it can be explained by their devoting a larger proportion of the sown areas to food crops for meeting family consumption needs and to high yielding variety wheat. There are six sugar mills in the area, almost all of which have come up after the farmers having taken to sugarcane cultivation as cash crop. The addition to the number of sugar mills in Tarai has given a boost to sugrcane cultivation in the area.

It was found out in the survey that the general extent of agro-climatic and related differences between the two zones, Tarai, where there is abundance of water and Bhabhar which is dry, differentiate farmers. It was observed that small farmers and less progressive farmers were about the same, whether located in Tarai or Bhabhar. But the locational condition clearly distinguished the large progressive farmers in Tarai from Bhabhar.

The farmers with large holdings in Tarai are more receptive to new changes in technology as compared to in Bhabhar. Moreover the farmers are more enterprising and have the capability to diversify. Information obtained on aspects of agriculture of large progressive farmers also revealed differences between the blocks of Rudrapur, Kashipur and Bazpur in Tarai. The farmers in Kashipur and Rudrapur are showing a tendency to diversify to industries like cardboard, rice mills etc.

On the basis of land holdings the farmers in Tarai and Bhabhar fall into no less than five categories :

1. Marginal farmers who have less than one ha. of land.
2. Small farmers who have one to two ha. of land.
3. Semi-medium farmers who own two to four ha. of land.
4. Medium farmers whose holdings are four to ten ha.
5. Big farmers who possess more than ten ha. of land.

The big farmers are located mostly in Tarai area. The majority of them are Jat Sikhs who have migrated from West Punjab, now in Pakistan. There are a few Punjabi families who too have large holdings. They have also migrated from West Punjab. The Jat Sikhs are more hard working and progressive as compared to other farmers as they came from agricultural families and have been successful in colonizing this region into a prosperous agricultural belt. The medium farmers who are less progressive are also mostly from Punjab. In Kashipur and Rudrapur there are some big farmers who came from U.P. some of them are Jats. Rudrapur and Kashipur being situated on the trunk road and rail routes, settlements in these blocks took place earlier than Bazpur and other blocks. This largely accounts for the presence of farmers in Rudrapur and Kashipur who were born nearby or elsewhere in U.P. In Bazpur block there are some Jat families who own large farms. They too have an agricultural background. Some hill people like the Raja Sahib of Kashipur also have large holdings but they are not as progressive and receptive to now ideas as Jat Sikhs are to the changes in agricultural technology.

Additionally there are agricultural graduates, released army personnel and freedom fighters who were allotted land in Tarai. They too have not been able to achieve the affluence of the Sikhs. The worst condition is of the Bengalis who came from East Pakistan, now Bangladesh and were settled here after the partition. Similar is the condition of the Tharu and

Buxa tribals, the autocthons of the area.

In Tarai agricultural land has been leased out directly by the Government to the farmers, and the sale or fragmentation of land is prohibited by law. While this measure has been able to check fragmentation of land, it could not totally stop its transfer. It is remarkable that 70 percent of large farmers and more than 77 percent of the medium and small farmers augment their earning by renting in additional land. Previously they used to raise crops in forest plantations also, but the practice has been discontinued owing to terrorism in Tarai. Now the U.P. Forest Corporation is raising crops in plantations. This has directly affected the income of small and medium farmers who used to supplement their earnings by taking plantations on lease for a fixed period for agricultural purposes. They raised crops between rows of saplings in the forest plantations.

Application of new technology :

The extent to which new technology in agriculture is being applied and the length of time farmers have adopted it adds sharpness to the present dimensions of progressive agriculture. The data given below of the number of agricultural implements in 1987 as compared to those in 1972 is a vivid example of the receptive attitude of farmers in Tarai to new technology :

Agricultural implements	Number in 1972	Number in 1987
Harrows & cultivators	5469	13231
Thrashers	3275	6642
Sprayers	991	332
Seed drills	348	3662
Tractors	3715	7297

Source: Environmental Status Report, 1992 : SHERPA (Society for Himalayan Environmental Rehabilitation and People's Action, Lucknow.)

The increase in consumption of chemical fertilizers during last few years present a clear picture of today's progressive agricultural scenario. Whereas the total consumption of fertilizers in Tarai-Bhabhar during the year 1976-77 was 1,91,100 quintals only, which rose to 6,85,400 quintals during 1988-99,thus registering 3.5 fold increase. Fertilizers used during the kharib season, 1993 alone accounted for 4,34,400 quintals. Taking into account that the same was used during the Rabi season also, about 8,00,000 quintals fertilizer was used during the year.

Apart from the above mentioned, nitrogen, phosphorous and potash fertilizers, 14,800 quintals of zinc sulphate was distributed to the farmers during the kharib season in 1993 and 18,100, quintals for the rabi season. Together with this insecticides, pesticides, fungicides, herbicides etc are being distributed to the farmers at subsidized rates.

To give a boost to agricultural production the Government is distributing seeds to the farmers at subsidized rates. The amount of seeds distributed to the farmers in Tarai and Bhabhar during kharib in 1992 was 5694.89 quintals, which rose to 7389.00 quintals during 1993. Seeds given to the farmers on subsidized rates during the rabi season, 1993, amounted to 6591.00 quintals. For the rabi season in 1994, 7470.00 quintals of seed were proposed for enhancing the production of agriculture.

For agricultural purposes loans are also being advanced by commercial and cooperative banks to the farmers. The loans advanced to the farmers of the 10 blocks in the area during kharib season 1993 amounted to Rs. 1839.75 lakhs. The target for distribution of loan to these blocks for rabi season was Rs. 4072.00 lakhs.

To keep pace with the agricultural production in Tarai and Bhabhar there has been an increase in irrigation facilities since 1980. The main source of irrigation in Tarai and Bhabhar at present are :

S.N.	Source of irrigation	Tarai & Bhabhar
1.	Canals in kms	1546
2.	Government tube wells (number)	275
3.	Masonry wells	332
4.	Rahat	122
5.	Pump sets	3032
6.	Boring pump sets	22354
7.	Privately owned tube wells	8538
8.	Water tanks	362
9.	Minor canals in kms	778

(Source : Statistical Patrika, Naini Tal, 1990.)

Some enterprising farmers in Tarai and Bhabhar have diversified their activities and have started horticulture, poultry etc.to supplement their income.

Horticulture :

Fillip to fruit trees plantation in Tarai was given by the then U.P. Government Farm, wherein such plantation was laid in its Haldi block in early fifties. This encouraged the farmers also to take up horticulture. With the inception of a few fruit processing units in Tarai, the plantation has received further boost. The main fruit grown by the farmers are mango, guava, lemon, bananas, papaya and leechi. The area under horticulture in different blocks in Tarai and Bhabhar is detailed below:

S.N.	Block	Area (ha.)	Production (quintals)	Productivity (quintals)
1.	Haldwani	1150	38500	33.40
2.	Ramnagar	1320	49600	37.50
3.	Kotabagh	980	35400	36.10
4.	Rudrapur	870	28100	32.20
5.	Kashipur	735	26550	33.80
6.	Khatima	450	15500	34.40
7.	Sitarganj	410	14300	34.80
8.	Bazpur	715	24400	34.10
9.	Gadarpur	450	24500	54.40
10.	Jaspur	582	21150	36.30

(Source : District Horticulture Office, Naini Tal.)

Latest data on the total production and productivity of the main fruit is as follows:

S.N.	Fruit	Area (ha.)	Production (quintals)	Producitivity (quintals
1.	Mango	4950	16,80,000	339.00
2.	Leechi	1050	20,000	19.0

Vegetables :

With the colonization of this area a few towns have come up here. This has developed a ready market for vegetable produce. Though vegetable farming needs intensive operations, it fetches good money and that too throughout the year. Some farmers grow vegetables to increase their income. In this context Haldwani block has taken the lead. The data is provided below.

S.N.	Block	Area (ha.)	Production (quintals)	Producitivity (quintals)
1.	Haldwani	1260	1,00800	80
2.	Ramnagar	580	96400	80
3.	Kotabagh	280	22400	80
4.	Rudrapur	750	60000	80
5.	Kashipur	210	16800	80
6.	Khatima	250	21000	84.0
7.	Sitarganj	280	22400	80
8.	Bazpur	330	26400	80
9.	Gadarpur	695	40150	57.7
10.	Jaspur	613	31000	50.5

(Source : SHERPA Environmental Status Report.)

The main vegetables grown are peas, radish, cauliflower, cabbage, lady finger, jack fruit and onions. Potatoes are also grown by some farmers, mostly in Bazpur, in 221 ha. in Kashipur, in 169 ha. and in Haldwani, in nine ha. Increase in tourist traffic also has made vegetable cultivation a profit making proposition.

Poultry :

Poultry farming has become an important source in the last two decades for generating extra income for the farmers. It is more popular in Haldwani and Kashipur tahsils. The details of the total number of birds is given below in the next page.

S.N.	Name of Tahsil	Poultry Birds	Other Birds	Total
1.	Haldwani	63996	-	63996
2.	Kaladhungi	4359	4	4363
3.	Kashipur	93222	76	93298

4.	Bazpur	11222	22	11244
5.	Gadarpur	5513	787	7300
6.	Kichha	16633	200	16883
7.	Ramnagar	6348	6	6354
8.	Khatima	31736	102	3183
9.	Sitarganj	22029	3133	25162

(Source : Animal Husbandry Department, Naini Tal.)

Fisheries :

India is the seventh largest producer of fish in the world, though the consumption here is less than 3 kg per person, whereas in Japan the average consumption is 27.7, Denmark 21.6, Sweden 20.5 and U.S.A. 25 kg per person.

Pisciculture is not popular amongst the farmers in Tarai, though some farmers are indirectly involved in this vocation. Fishes are raised in dams by the Fisheries Department and are subsequently auctioned. Fishes are bred in Tarai in the waters of Nanak Sagar, Begul, Tumaria, Baur and Bhauran dams whose area is 12051 ha. In 1992-93 the production of fish was 5363.81 quintals which fetched Rs. 3,80,000 through Government auction.

In Tarai there are several dry lakes which can be used for pisciculture. The Fisheries Department has identified 468 such dry lakes. However the department has not been able to motivate the farmers to adopt pisciculture as an additional source of income, though in Tarai the big farmers can take it up on large scale.

The significant progress attained by the farmers here is owing to their herculean efforts as well as the assistance extended by the Government.Besides carrying extensive field survey of the whole Tarai-Bhabhar area, the author undertook detailed survey of Bazpur Block as a sample of whole Tarai. It was found out that most of the progressive farmers there use new technology; more than 95% apply high yielding variety seeds, more than 97% use chemical fertilizers and more than

70% own independent irrigation facility. More than 45% of the less progressive farmers own tractors and power thrashers. Among the less progressive farmers more than 55% are using high yielding variety seeds, 78% chemical fertilizers and about 28% have their own irrigation equipment.

It may reasonably be expected that one trait of a progressive farmer, regardless of size or holding is that he is quick to take advantage of the new agricultural technology as soon as any element of it becomes generally available at the cost he can afford.

The long term priorities of non-agricultural nature among the progressive farmers, especially the Sikhs, are the education of their children, both boys and girls in best public schools or missionary institutions in hill stations and subsequently to settle them abroad. The next priority is to own some allied industry or have shares in business. The less progressive farmers emulate the progressive farmers and they are also imparting the best possible education to their children. Both the progressive and less progressive farmers are obsessed with the idea of educating their children in English medium institutions in hill stations and in the recent past it has also become a status symbol amongst them. As regards the industries and shares in business, the less progressive farmers neither have the required capital, nor the enterprise to diversify as compared to progressive farmers. The less progressive farmers unlike the progressive ones are not crazy to send their children abroad.Their priorities are to send them in civil services or technical jobs like medical and engineering. Defence services, especially amongst the Jat Sikhs which were at one time on top in their list of priority have lost their charm now. It has paled into insignificance as compared to civil services and technical jobs. It can thus he stated that there is a strong inclination to accept new technology and a determination to build up new assets on their farms among the farmers. However their priorities in the non-agricultural sector reveal the strong commitment of the farmers to maintain a balance between a bright future of their scions and the welfare of their farms.

Another important aspect which was taken into consideration was agricultural labour which accounts for nearly one half of the agricultural working expenditure in the average of both progressive and less progressive farmers. The farm labour force includes all agricultural workers, male and female in the age group ranging roughly between 14 to 60, working members of the farmers' family as well as other permanent or causal labourers.

With respect to agricultural labourers, the big farmers differ in two important ways from the medium and small farmers. Firstly their average number of family members working on the farm is appreciably lower. The main reason which can be attributed to this is to insure better education to their children.

Secondly the big farm owners have more permanent workers and less causal worker than less progressive or medium and small farmers. Progressive farmers want a maximum permanent labour force appropriate to the scale of their farm operations for two main reasons. One is to have hand skills useful in applying new technology for example in operating and maintaining new technical procedures in irrigation, cultivation or fertilizing. The second reason is to insure a steady labour force through periods of peak farm operations when causal labour may be scarce or more costly.

Besides cash payments, permanent workers are given residential quarters and food stuffs. Farmers were not able to give reliable estimates on the payment and the number of hours their permanent or causal labourers worked. However per ha. expenditure on causal labourers is greater than on permanent workers by all types of farmers in all sizes, groups or holdings.

The agricultural labour situation in Tarai differs from practically all parts of U.P. The basic reason is that the Tarai belt has been cleared and colonized in the recent past. Thus most workers came to the area to find expanding farm employment in market and service centres, in processing of food, crops or animal products, equipment repair and construction activity in public works and in private sector. The problem in Tarai has been more often one of labour shortage and not of over supply.

The labour wages in Tarai have rocketted high in the last eight years owing to terrorism, so have costs of food and other essentials. Now-a-days the agricultural workers there insists on cash payment, a great change from being paid in kind, such as foodstuffs as was the practice in not distant past. It is estimated that labour payment is by far the largest share of the total farms operating expenditure, about 52 percent for the progressive farmers and 45 percent for the less progressive group.

The comparative affluence of the Tarai farmer is based on the high water table and humus content of the soil. Till the time that Tarai was covered with dense forest the water table was very high. It was because of the surface run-off of water being prevented and its being absorbed by the soil. With the deforestation prior to colonization this water retention capacity of the soil has been drastically reduced, which has resulted in gradual going down of the water table. It is owing to this factor that whereas in the initial stages even without irrigation facility the land produced good crop, now irrigation is essential.

To prevent further deterioration, social forestry should be taken up as a movement. Acting on the old adage that 'nothing succeeds like success' social forestry should be made profitable by starting wood and forest usufruct based industries in the area. To make forestry popular a maximum of such industries should be in the cottage and small-scale level. Along with it the farmers should be encouraged to take up agro-forestry. This besides making the fullest possible use of the farm land will add to the income of the farmers as also restore the green cover of the area.

To revive, though only to some extent, the green cover in the area farmers may also take up horticulture. With the boom in recent years in the tourist traffic in the nearby hill stations of Tarai there is a ready market. Another fillip to it can be given by the Government or the cooperative societies by providing marketing facilities in the areas where the Tarai and Bhabhar fruit can fetch better price. Even though during the recent years many industrial units have come up in the area, the fruit processing units are non-existent there. To make horticulture farming a success, fruit preserving and processing units will be of immense help.

Owing to heavy dosage of chemical fertilizers, the soil texture in the area is losing its water retention capacity As the chemical fertilizer dressings reduce humus content in the soil, its moisture retention capacity is limited. To prevent further deterioration in this regard chemical fertilizers should be replaced with manures and cakes. Green manuring besides adding to the earnings of the farmers will add to the humus and thus improve soil texture. This should be made a part of the crop rotation in the area. Crop rotation should also aim at maximum possible use of the manures applied to the fields.

The Pantnagar Agriculture University, which is in the heart-land of Tarai also has contributed considerably in making agriculture a big success in the area. This was made possible due to the basic research at this University in developing better varieties of crops in the initial stage of its institution. Pantnagar seed at a time was knows for its quality all over India. During recent years the tempo of research of this University has gone down. It will immediately affect the agriculture in the area. If the Tarai and Bhabhar area is to continue its fame as a granary of India, the tempo of research work at the Pantnagar Agriculture University will have to be revived

The details of the success story of agriculture in Tarai and Bhabhar have a few negative aspects also. First and foremost the prosperity of some of the landed farmers is based on coercion. The extent of coercion resorted to by the big farm holders is evident from the fact that whereas the Tharu and Buxa tribals, aborgines of the area prior to the colonization of Tarai owned vast chunks of land, today they have been reduced to a state of abject poverty. Some of the new settlers used their money and muscle power to dislodge the poor tribals from their land with the result that the land owners of yesterday have become landless labourers in their own land. This is injustice, which should be removed.

That the local officials fully connive at this loot of the land, is evident from the fact that they did not act against such perpetrators of injustice. Though according to the Land Ceilling Act, a family can retain only a maximum of 7.38 ha. of land, a large number of farmers own land exceeding 400 ha. Obviously the money power has made a laughing stock of the Act in the area. To ensure equitable distribution of land, the Land Ceilling Act should be enforced strictly though some agricultural experts and farmers do not agree with this view point. They strongly feel that small land holdings cannot be maintained as viable units. Moreover the land allotted to the landless failed to sustain them. With the result that it again slipped to their hands in the form of a commodity the best use of which was under the circumstances seemed to be selling it off.

Peasant Unrest :

Tarai which is plagued with agrarian problems unfolds a saga of conflicts between the peasants, the land holders and the Government. In this region there are about 575 huge farms some of which are centres of exploitation and human misery. One of the biggest is the Parag Farm*, which is about 2050 ha. in area in Government records. This farm was taken on lease in 1932 for a period of 99 years by a gentleman from Agra, Prayag Narain. Out of the total land leased to him, 25% of it was allotted for the construction of a factory, roads and for the residence of labourers. According to the condition of the lease, the land is still rent free. The scions of Prayag Narain have

---

* *About Parag Farm and Khurpia, some facts have been cited from the unpublished Ph.D. thesis, 'Nagar Palika Shashan Ke Rajniti, Kumaon Tarai Kshetra Ka Ek Adhyayan', by Krishna Kumar Srivastava, Kumaon University, 1984*

minted money from the land, but the condition of the labourers even after 1947 has not improved. In 1958 the labourers launched an agitation in Dhimari block, but it was of no avail. The Land Ceilling Act was passed in 1960-62, but Parag Farm did not come within the purview of this Act. Again on July 1, 1969, the Zamindari Abolition Act and the Land Reforms Act were enacted, but Parag Farm remained unaffected though 100 villages in Tarai and Bhabhar came within their range.

About the Parag Farm it is stated by the people staying in and around the area, that the farm area is 2129.13 ha. in revenue records, but the actual area through infringement is about 7790 ha. It may be an exaggerated view, but the fact remains that encroachment on Government land has been made. In the farm there were 450 temporary labourers and 350 permanent. On 16th September, 1980, a 'Kabja Abhiyan', that is land grabbing movement was launched by the landless labourers. The movement was a total fiasco and one of the labourers was killed.

In close proximity to the Parag Farm is the Khurpia Farm. This farm according to the inmates of the farm itself is nct in the land records of the Government. In 1971 a labour union was formed in this farm to alleviate the condition of the labourers, but it did not succeed.

In May 1981 a joint labour union was formed by the workers of the Parag and Khurpia Farms. The land lords have adopted various measures to quell the activities of the union and they have succeeded. However the union which is dominated by the CPM has been able to improve the working condition of the labourers to some extent, but as regards dissemination of political consciousness it has failed miserably.

The G.B. Pant Agricultural University, Pantnager has also a vast expanse of land allocated to it, 6560 ha. in area. In 1978 the labourers in Pantnagar went on strike. They had two main demands viz. increase of wages and distribution of land to the labourers which came under the Ceiling Act. The agitators were crushed ruthlessly.They were fired at and beaten up mercilessly.

It is said that the corpses were burnt in a sugarcane field, which is in close proximity to the spot where the firing ensued More than 40 labourers died in the firing spree. The exact number cannot be estimated because a genuine muster roll was not maintained by the university authorities. After the firing incident some teachers and students came to the forefront and agitated against the establishment and the gory killings. But the movement soon boiled down to a cast war and resulted in utter failure. The students were polarized on cast basis by those officials who sided the administration for its misdeeds. The repercussions of the caste bickerings are pronounced even today. This has been responsible for stifling the academic environment of the university.

Another burning problem is of the landless agriculturists of taungya villages. The taungya forestry system as defined by nineteenth century foresters is, "a method of plantation forestry which uses one means of production, shifting cultivation to promote another, commercial timber extraction, and takes its name from the Burmese word for shifting cultivation taungya or hill cultivation or hired cultivation or system or taungya arboriculture". The development of taungya forestry in nineteenth century colonial Burma was a pioneering attempt to promote sustainable teak production. Subsequently adopted elsewhere, it has become an important technique in the science of agroforestry.

Once the marketable timber has been extracted, cultivators burn the residual forest and, at the first rains raise crops for their personal use. Subsequently they plant tree seedlings as also raise food crops in and as long between the seedlings till the time they can be produced in the field, which mostly used to be for five yearo. It is the duty of the cultivators to tend the growing trees. When the taungya is no longer suitable for food production, cultivators abandon the field and move to a new area in close proximity and repeat the same cycle.

Taungya cultivation was started in Sub-Himalayan Tarai in 1932 in the sal (Shorea robusta) forests which are considered to be fit for taungya. The special objects of management were:

1. To convert these forests gradually into uniform forests.
2. To attain the normal forest by obtaining a normal series of age classes by artificial means.
3. Consistent with the objects (1) and (2) to obtain the greatest possible sustained yield of large timber without overfelling, to meet the general demands of the market.

The silvicultural system adopted was conversion to uniform with artificial regeneration combined with control selection fellings and cautious thinnings in unallotted periodic blocks.

As the object of management was the conversion of the existing forest into uniform forest, the question of future rotation was less important than the conversion period. In view of the complete absence of regeneration for so many years and the sporadic dying of sal, the conversion period was fixed at 100 years by which time it was expected that a 38.2 cm crop would be obtained. The selection limit for selection fellings in unallotted periodic blocks was fixed at 50.2 cm at chest height.

Taungya cultivation was discontinued in the Sub-Himalayan Tarai in 1955 and since then the problem of settlement of these cultivators has posed a serious problem.Kota Range in Ramnagar Forest Division has three villages of taungya cultivators viz. Rampur, Leti and Chopra which were established in 1932. These villages were settled primarily to undertake taungya cultivation. There were 130 families in the villages and the inmates worked as casual forest labourers also. They had been allotted 0.22 ha. to 1.32 ha. of land, per family for their personal use as ' mafi' land. In the initial stages they rendered satisfactory service, but after 1947 they started demanding 'mafi' land to be converted into 'hissedari' land.

According to the Forest Department, from 1947 to 1955 these cultivators worked perfunctorily in the plantations, but after 1955 they totally seized to work and renewed their demand for allotment of land. Taking into consideration their demand, the Forest Department referred the matter to the State Government, G.O.No. U.P. 1204/148, dated 11.11.1960, with a rider that if their demand is met with it would set up a wrong precedence. Subsequently the State Government ordered the eviction of taungya cultivators from the forest land. The Forest Department initiated steps to vacate the land in light of orders of the State Government, but the move was strongly resisted by the taungya cultivators. As a sequel the department deferred the action temporarily.

The matter was referred to the State Government again and this time it reacted in a sympathetic manner. As per the G.O. No. 9250/148-116/34/6, dated 17.3.1963, the Government ordered that:

1. The taungya cultivators must not be allowed to raise permanent, 'pucca' dwellings within the forest area.
2. They should be persuaded to opt for some other area outside the forest for cultivation or for taungya.
3. If they are reluctant to conform to the orders of the Government for taungya cultivation to shift to some other area then proceedings should be initiated against them for eviction.

The aforesaid terms and conditions were also not acceptable to the taungyas. Therefore departmental action to evict them was initiated. Different charges were levelled against each cultivator and eviction orders were moved in the office of the 'Sarvajanik Adhikari' (Public Officer) in the Kashipur Court. Subsequent to this, the taungya cultivators initiated correspondence with the State Government. As a result the cases under process in the court of the Sarvajanik Adhikari were restrained under G.O. No. 3270/19-B-116/34/61, dated 13.6.1963. Concomitantly the Conservator of Forest in the headquarters at Lucknow sent information to await till further orders from the Government. Following which these measures were undertaken, vide G.O.No. 6583/14-B-116/61 dated 30.10.1963 by the Government:

1. Taungya cultivators should be allowed to retain possession of the land allotted to them subject to their vacating the encroachment.
2. They should be allotted land for five years on lease on the condition that it would be renewed after every five years on the termination of the date of lease.
3. The leased land allotted to the cultivators will be non-transferable and strictly in the name of the original allottee.
4. The lease conditions will be acceptabls to the taungyas and those who have been leased forest land it would enjoin implication that they will assist the Forest Department as and when contingency arises in matters of plantations, forest fire control and other exigencies.

According to the orders of the Government the taungya cultivators were expressedly asked if the conditions as laid down were acceptable to them. They refused to accept these conditions and subsequently a revised agreement was sent by the Assistant Secretary Forest (K) Government of U.P., vide letter No. 3655/14/-B-116/34/61, dated 1.9.1966. The terms of the agreement were rejected again, since condition (8) was subsequently appended against the original agreement. The taungya cultivators had the following objections regarding the revised agreement :

1. Regarding condition (1) their plea was that instead of lease they should be made a permanent land holder.
2. The cultivators were not willing to accept the status of 'mausimi haq' (seasonal right holder) as referred to in condition (4).
3. According to condition (8), allotment of 'patta' was made under Government Grants Act of 1895, which the cultivators were reluctant to accept.

The department accordingly apprised the Government of the reluctance of the cultivators in accepting the terms and conditions of the Government. Subsequently the Government in September, 1971 instructed to enforce the orders issued by it in the year 1963 and to complete the formalities of allotting land within a stipulated period failing which the defaulters would be dispossessed of their land. It was further stated that the relatives of some of the actual allottees were cultivating land in different villages. Their numbers were,twelve in Rampur, seven in Leti and ten in Chopra. They should also be considered along with others for allotment.

To this day the situation is no where near a solution. A solution has been only a topic of correspondence between the Forest Department and the Uttar Pradesh Government. Even after nearly a decade of deliberations nothing has come out of it. While the Forest Department on its part is not ready to cede the forest land for agriculture, the Government also does not want to set a precedence and thus open up Pandora's box. If today it is taungya cultivators, the next day the Goth owners are sure to be there and after conceding their demands, refusing the same to the Gujjars will be impossible. It will mean virtual disappearance of the Tarai forest.

In this controversy a moot point is that the taungya cultivators made their appearance in the Tarai forests not on their own, but only on the behest of the Forest Department. They have been there for the last six decades. Just as for the Indians in Fiji now for some Rabuka having emerged, it is impossible to come back to India; similarly it will be unjust to ask the taungya cultivators to leave the forest and fend for themselves. These cultivators are in a miserable plight, they have been reduced to a state of abject poverty and are finding it difficult to fend for themselves. The condition of women is worst. They have to negotiate long distances in search of fodder and fuel which has increased their working hours and has a direct affect on their health.

The main grouse of the taungya cultivators is that the land which they have been cultivating for several years has not been transferred in their names hitherto. Their contention is that the Forest Department is prepared to lease them land since 1973, whereas taungya cultivation had started in Tarai since 1932. Further land revenue is to be charged at the present market rate which the poor cultivators cannot afford to pay. Moreover land lease is not transferable and after the father's demise it cannot be transferred in the son's name.

Their other demands are medical and veterinary facilities, opening of an Intermediate College, construction of roads and drinking water as well as irrigation facilities. As deforestation has a direct effect on the women folk and their health, the cultivators strongly feel that they should be given old age and widow's pension as admissible to other citizens.

The Forest Department and the U.P. Government are morally bound to resettle them. They cannot be compared to the Goth owners and the Gujjars. The more the delay in settling the problem, the more complex it becomes. With the reputation gained by India of having resettled a vast number of refugees from the West and the then East Pakistan in the aftermath of Independence, given a will it should not be difficult to provide them a basis for their livelihood.

In the context of the present day political scenario a solution is imperative. As per the report of the Forest Department in continuation to the District Magistrate, Naini Tal's confidential letter No. Memo/14-R.C. Kham, dated 18.3.1980 there were 130 families in the three taungya cultivator villages and 368 encroacher families. Almost all of them belong to the Scheduled Castes and landless. As such they have to be rehabilitated. The sooner the U.P. Government puts into action its decision to settle them on the land acquired under the land ceiling law the better.

Dissent Foments in Bindu Khatta :

In addition to the problem of the taungya cultivators another problem which has plagued Tarai and Bhabhar is that of the Gothias or residents of Khattas. The Gothias are forest dwellers. Khattas or Goths are spread all over the Tarai and Bhabhar region of Kumaon Himalaya. The Khattas had come into existence since time immemorial. People in the hills used to descend to Tarai and Bhabhar during the winters, primarily to escape from the severe cold and also to graze their cattle. In course of time some of the settlements assumed the shape of permanency,whereas some were inhabited temporarily. These settlements accordingly have been recognized in the Forest Department as temporary or permanent. At present in Tarai and Bhabhar there are 84 Khattas spread over an area of about 2000 square kilometers. Out of these 33 are permanent Khattas and 51 temporary. The settlements of these forest dwellers has not been regularized as yet and they are considered as encroachers by the Government. Bindu Khatta is one of the Khattas where the people are courageous enough to ventilate their ire. This has brought them in direct confrontation with the State Government. Other Khattas are also facing innumerable hardships, but the residents of Bindu Khatta are more vocal in manifesting their resentment. Even though the ordinance of the U.P. Government prohibits illegal occupation of land, the people in and the adjoining areas of Tarai and Bhabhar are not deterred by it. Today this region is one of the most prosperous agricultural belts of India and in the last three decades the price of land has escalated very high. Subsequent to the spurt of economic activities, there has been a mad rush to settle down in Tarai and Bhabhar. People from all walks of life have swarmed to this region since 1962. The new residents of Bindu Khatta have also been inspired by this spurt of land rush.

In Bindu Khatta there are two categories of residents viz. the original settlers and those who came here after 1970. In 1975, the U.P. Government decided to allot land to every family in Bindu Khatta at the rate of 0.41 ha. for residential purposes and 1.025 ha. for growing fodder. The scheme was on the anvil that the news of it spread like prairie fire. Hopes for allotment of land started soaring and people thronged Bindu Khatta with the intent of owing land. Among the aspirants there were relations of old settlers also who had been invited by them. But owing to the chaos caused by the mad scramble, the scheme could not be implemented and the lofty statements made by the authorities and politicians proved to be empty rhetorics. However, most of the people who had come to Bindu Khatta did not return. Concomitantly they formed an organization known as 'Harit-Shwet Krantikari Parishad', and grabbed land for residential and agricultural purposes. Some of the local politicians interested in vote bank politics contrived with the encroachers. Others who enjoyed the patronage of politicians in power encouraged the guileless people from the hills to settle down in Bindu Khatta and extorted money on the pretext of giving them protection. Retired army personnel, Scheduled Castes and peasants from the villages of Almora, Pithoragarh and Chamoli districts fell in their trap. A sizeable number of settlers from the hills sold their land in the native villages and migrated to Bindu Khatta.

These settlers from the hills are in a piquant situation. On the one hand they have invested all their earnings in Bindu Khatta and on the other they are living with the fear of being ousted from there. The local bigwigs, who have befooled the poor people from the hills, have themselves occupied more than 6.15 ha. of land each. There are 23 such ring leaders and to muster political support these leaders have named two settlements in Bindu Khatta as Sanjay Nagar and Tewari Nagar after the late youth leader Sanjay Gandhi and the eminent politician Narain Dutt Tewari respectively.

The Divisional Forest Officer in a letter dated 8th September, 1980, No. 763/4-2, to the Conservator of Western Circle has clearly stated that politicians were instrumental in land grabbing in Bindu Khatta and owing to their political clout, the department was unable to take any action against them. The politicians are aware that the land encroached upon cannot be regularized, but to retain their leadership they are delaying the process of take over. The politicians who have connections in the power centres of Lucknow and Delhi are befooling the Khatta dwellers and have adopted every sort of tactics to support their view point. They have stooped down to the level of fanning feelings of casteism and regionalism.

A few amongst the new settlers in Bindu Khatta are landless. Then there are those who have grabbed land first and later ensnared retired army personnel and peasants from the hills to invest their savings in Bindu Khatta. Additionally there are businessmen, contractors as well as some Government officials, who have occupied land under false names.

From time to time the new settlers have agitated and voiced their feelings against the U.P. Government. Their main demand is regularization of land grabbed by them. But it seems that the U.P. Government is not going to wilt under pressure and its policy is clearly indicated by the ordinance of 1969, which states that even people who have been staying in Goths for more than 100 years have no legal right over the land occupied by them.

The main grouse of the new settlers in Bindu Khatta is that the big farmers in Tarai own more land than is permitted to them under the land ceiling rules, but the Government has taken no action against them. This is inspite of the fact that some of the big farmers have encroached upon tribal land.

There seems to be an element of truth in their argument. To evade ceiling laws, most of the big farmers have bought land in the names of their relations, servants, fictious name and at times even in the names of their pets. An important political leader in the recent past had allegedly registered 63.50 ha of land in the names of his pet dogs. There are several examples when in collusion with the officials of the Revenue Department, land was prevented from coming within the purview of ceilling laws in the name of cow sheds, orchards, pasture land, stables, fodder farms, dairy and agricultural research centres. During the field study it was observed that in several farms most of the units against which exemption under ceiling laws was claimed did not exist. An analogous case of one of the agricultural companies of Tarai is being cited below.

The total land in the name of a company in Tarai is 566.77 ha. A delay was caused intentionally in disposing off the ceiling case of this company and the final decision was given on Ist

August, 1967. In the decision, 475.87 ha. of land was exempted from ceiling on the following grounds :

Exemption sought for		Area in ha.
1.	Orchard	78.95
2.	Roads in the farms	36.29
3.	Sewra rivulet and streams	53.28
4.	Settlement	16.82
5.	Fodder farm	184.50
6.	Cremation ground & pond for breeding fishes	3.53
7.	Area transferred to school	102.50
	Total	**475.87**

Thus out of 566.77 ha. of land only 90.9 ha. was declared as extra. In the course of field study by this writer, most of these items were non-existent in the farm.

Tribal land as stated earlier has forcibly been grabbed by some of the big farmers .It was done more often than not with the connivance of the revenue and police officials. Land grabbing was also done with unscrupulous money lending by some 'banias' (local traders), some 'banjaras' (roving traders who trade mostly in cereals) and a few of those new settlers who could not use muscle power. They snared the tribals into usury and took possession of their land and crop through deceit.

It is significant that besides tribal land, the trespassers did not spare even the Government land, which they recklessly occupied owing to the nonchalant attitude of the authorities or in connivance with them. In a belated bid to correct the entries and to accept the reality of the situation,the Government adopted a policy of regularization of trespassed land vide G.O. No. 1-35(12)66, dated July 6,1967 of the U.P. Government. But this compromising attitude of the Government has encouraged the criminal elements to encroach further upon forest and tribal land.

However, the faulty ceiling laws and illegal occupation of tribal and Government land by some of the new settlers does not exonerate the people of Bindu Khatta from encroaching upon forest land. But it has certainly encouraged them to emulate those big farmers who are guilty of grabbing land. The politicians are also responsible for misguiding them. They are aware of the vote bank and to win over the residents of Bindu Khatta they beguile them with false hope of regularizing the trespassed land during elections. It is intriguing that the political leaders who have been instrumental in regularizing illegal occupation of forest land in the past have hoodwinked the residents of Bindu Khatta though somehow they have managed to prolong the case and have succeeded in keeping the issue alive.

The policy of the Government regarding Bindu Khatta is dubious and ultimately the sufferers are the forest officials and the residents of Bindu Khatta. The Government is not keen to solve the problem. From time to time the residents of Bindu Khatta have agitated, but their movements were ruthlessly crushed by the Government.

The contradiction in Government's policy is evidenced by the Naini Tal District Collector's letter which was sent by him to the Forest Department during the 1980 elections. In the letter No. Memo/Encroachment, dated May 8, 1980, the District Collector instructed the Forest Department that the huts of the encroachers should not be demolished on any condition during the Assembly Elections. The Forest Secretary of the U.P. Government had also given similar instructions to the Forest Department of Tarai during the election period.

The dilatory attitude of the Government and its ambigious policy has brought the officials of the Forest Department and the residents of Bindu Khatta in direct confrontation. In a display of opposition there have been excesses from both the sides. In 1992 a Sub-Inspector of the U.P. Police was murdered in Bindu Khatta. In the past also there have been similar incidents when both the Forest Department and the residents of Bindu Khatta have adopted brutal tactics. On February 5, 1983, two landless labourers of Bindu Khatta were wounded allegedly by the forest guards. It might have been done at the behest of some senior officials, because no action was taken against the forest guards.

Similarly on another occasion, the Divisional Forest Officer, Tarai East, ordered his subordinate staff on 19.3.1992 to evict the encroachers from Khamiya Block East. To carry his orders, the Range Officer, together with 18 forest and five police officials reached the site. On witnessing them the residents of Khamiya Block got infuriated and encircled the officials. They raised slogans against the Forest Department and concomitantly surrounded them from all sides. The officials tried to placate them, but they were in a belligerent mood and in a fit of frenzy damaged the truck and destroyed all the documents. Subsequently they were assaulted by the demonstrators. Some of the officials sustained serious injuries and the rest fled the scene. No action was however taken against the agitators.

To make a solution possible the politician who revels in double talk has to be tackled first. He has to be convinced first on the necessity of afforesting not only the forest land, but also the degraded farmland together with the village commons. He has to be motivated to provide the society a lead in this respect. He will do so only when he is convinced that afforestation which also supports cottage industries can lead to improvement in the economic condition of his constituents.

Such an awareness campaign should be directed towards the forest dwellers also. Till the time they are prevailed upon to leave their existing settlements they have to be motivated to look towards the forests as there wherewithal and as such make them the lover of trees and guardians of our forest wealth.

This besides suitable publicity campaign amongst them also requires our foresters and authorities to take a humane and sympathetic attitude towards the people inhabiting the Khattas and Goths. This can be done by accepting their legitimate demands, like giving a fillip to the cooperative movement amongst them. This besides improving their economic condition, will make them more receptive to the view point of the foresters. Forest officials can utilize a viable cooperative movement to wean them away from the avocations damaging the forests and instead take up more remunerative professions causing lesser damage to forest wealth. Encouraging dairying among them, which can be profitable only if better quality cattle are reared and stall fed. They can be allowed to raise fodder crops in the plantation area, which will also be beneficial to plantations.

Similarly through cooperatives they can be provided gainful employment through usufruct produce like collection of seeds, bamboo etc. Befriended thus these settlers can turn into unpaid guardians of forest wealth. They can be persuaded to prevent incursion by new settlers. Once the foresters are able to win over the hearts of these settlers they may heed their advice on limiting their families also. Thus if the foresters are able to help the settlers taste better quality of life with improved economic condition, the idea of planned parenthood may be a success among them, which will lead to lessened biotic pressure on forests.

By exposing the Khatta dwellers to better quality of life, they themselves will shift near to human habitations. They can be helped to settle on the outer fringe of forests. This will be an entirely new deal to these settlers, which will also mean mitigating the source of so many ill happenings in our forests.

6

Milk Cooperative Movement in Tarai

Milk industry in Tarai has its beginning in the 'Khattas' and 'Goths', where the 'Ghamtappus' (baskers in sun) used to repair during winters. They belonged to the hill areas of Almora and Naini Tal districts as mentioned earlier. As the climate during winters in that part of the country used to be cold and there being little work in the fields during that season, they used to descend to the Khatta and Goth habitations and then return to their villages with the onset of summer. The practice of this seasonal shift has been in existence since very old, so have the Khattas and Goths.

Shifting of cattle along with the families was also called for economic considerations. Milch cattle in the severe cold climate of the Kumaon hills, if continued to be in that inhospitable climate, used to lose in milk yield. It was for two reasons. Firstly, there was little green fodder. The financial condition of the people in that area not being well, they were not able to supplement this deficiency with nutritious feed. Secondly, what ever energy the animal had, was utilized in protecting it from cold. These two factors resulted in lesser milk yield as also shortened lactation period. Lactation period once shortened tends to be habitual and thus a loss in quality of the animal. To avoid this prospect shifting of the cattle to green fodder areas was necessary. This shift was also beneficial for dry cattle. Being in warmer climate along with feeding on green fodder made them healthy. This besides earlier conception also helped in improving their quality.

As the 'Ghamtappus' resided in the Khattas and Goths for over a couple of months, they needed the means to earn bread for themselves for at least that duration. Their milch cattle provided them one of the primary means to that end. If there was a market nearby, they used to sell milk there. The milk saved from selling was used for preparing 'ghee' or 'khoya', which could be sold later on.

Thus the Khatta and Goth settlers not only made milk a means of their subsistence, but also provided their neighbours an important supply. This had been going on for quite long,may be even one or two centuries, that the Jammu Gujjars arrived in Tarai about one hundred years back-with their cattle, which almost wholly consisted of buffaloes. To begin with they came to Tarai as nomads. Tarai was on their way to the meadows on the slopes of the Himalaya just below the snow-line. Spending the summer and rainy months there they descended with the approaching winter. Their sojourn in the Himalayan slopes came to an end with our deteriorating relations with China in early sixties. With it came the end of their seasonal visits to Himalaya and the start of their being in the Tarai the year round.

The appearance of this community on the scene heralded the start of milk industry in Tarai. As the milk from their buffaloes was the only means of subsistence of the Gujjars, there was milk production in considerable amount. This meant sale and purchase of milk as also involvement of sizeable number of people in the trade, thus making it a virtual industry.

For various factors the industry has been kicking and thriving. Naini Tal has been a place of tourist interest. As it is situated at height of 1938 meters and has a salubrious climate, tourists used to visit this place even prior to India attaining freedom. During those days the provincial capital also used to shift to Naini Tal in the summer months. To meet the requirement of this floating population during summer months, there was added demand of milk. As chance would have it the lactation cycle of the Gujjar buffaloes was such that they were in milching condition during summers and rains and dry during winters. Thus the Gujjars were able to meet this seasonal demand. That besides giving them ready market also provided a sound base to this industry.

Even though per force of circumstances milk industry had come into being in Tarai, it had two drawbacks. Firstly, to satisfy the felt need of the floating population as also marketing the surplus milk in the Khattas and Gujjar deras,' milk trader habitats came into being. As usual the trader was fleecing the money both from the milk producer and customer. Besides purchasing milk from the Gujjars and the Khatta inhabitants, the trader started to work as money-lender also. He spread his network so deftly that in no time the poor and illiterate Gujjars as well as the Khatta dwellers were completely at his mercy. Their cattle as well as personal effects were mortgaged to the trader. As such he used to fix the purchase rate of milk at will. Thus at the hand of the middleman the milk producer was being exploited. Secondly, operating on individual, and as such on unorganized basis, he was not able on his own to market the milk in far off places like Naini Tal and Bhowali.

With significant accretion in the Government personnel and the tourists following the country attaining Independence in 1947, a solution to the milk supply problem became urgent. In 1948 U.P.(then United Provinces now Uttar Pradesh) Government sanctioned a scheme with the twin objective of the economic welfare of the milk producers and augmenting the milk supply to hill region during summers. To free the milk producers from the clutches of the traders the Government advanced the Khatta dwellers interest free loan, which amounted to Rs. 2,65,000 during the first two years of launching the scheme. To improve the milk supply in the hill region, milk producers were required to organise themselves in Cooperatives Societies, which in turn formed the Lalkuan Cooperative Milk Supply Union, Haldwani. The Gujjars did not take interest in this scheme. The Union used to collect milk from the members of the societies and sell it to the customers through its outlets at various places in Tarai and the hills. Data based on the two letters dated 8.10.1968 and 3.1.1970 to the U.P. Government (though slightly varying) regarding the early milk cooperative societies formed is given below :

Name of Khatta	Registration number and date	Approximate number of cattle owners		Approximate number of milch cattle		Distance from Lalkuan
		8.10.68	3.1.70	8.10.68	3.1.70	
Saanp Kathani	No. 536 22-4-1949	30	20	1000	661	5 kms.
Bindu Khatta	No. 527 24-31949	90	83	2000	995	5 kms.
Baur Khatta	No. 494 21-2-1948	60	52	1500	204	10 kms.
Dauli	No. 1085 29-12-1951	22	20	800	913	10 kms.
Raikhal	No. 534	20	13	800	393	20 kms.

These five milk cooperative societies formed the nucleus of the Lalkuan Cooperative Milk Supply Union. Subsequently societies from other Khattas viz. Punjabi Chaur, Luniaganj, Khassi Bhoj, Banskhera and Bhura also joined the Union. To make the Union a success by ensuring cooperation of the Government departments the Board of Management of the Union was headed by the Superintendent, Tarai and Bhabhar.

He remained ex-officio Chairman from 1948 to 52, when the post was made elected and as such went to a non-official person. Additionally the Government made a grant of Rs. 313,000 to enable the Union to establish a dairy. It also provided the Union service of a Technical Manager.

This back up from the official side not only made sure that the milk cooperative was founded on a sound basis, but also that the private milk traders were prevented from harming the movement. In consonance with the spirit, the Forest Department did not allow these traders to have their khoya bhattis in the Khattas having milk cooperative society. The Forest Department continued this helpful attitude in other matters also. It is notable that these Khattas were within forest area on forest land.

The helpful attitude of the Forest Department however changed with the induction of a non-official as Chairman of the Union. The department instead of preventing traders to install their khoya bhattis in the Khattas having milk cooperative societies promoted and selected the practice of allowing the khoya bhattis to the highest bidder. It forced the milk producers to sell milk to the bhattis on the terms of the owners. The department also did not allow the Khatta owners to sell the manure of their cattle as also the hide of dead animals. This besides harming the milk co-operative movement, prevented the cattle owners from supplementing their income by selling manure and cattle-hide. It also meant a national waste.

The Milk Union in 1964 approached the Government to change its attitude:

1. As the production cost of milk in the Khattas is lower than the other milk suppliers, the Lalkuan Milk Union could supply milk cheaper to the public; the Government should therefore be considerate to its demands.

2. It was evident that the Tarai-Bhabhar forests had the capacity to grow good quality nutritious grass, but as thousands of bales of grass were burnt and destroyed every year, it was going waste. It could be put to good

use by making it available to the Khatta cattle, which besides increasing milk yield would also help improve cattle breed. It would not only meet the requirement of improved breed cattle of the Khattas, but also provide them to the whole State at cheaper rates.

3. In the hill areas milk producers every year purchase thousands of cattle, but are forced to sell them cheap to butchers after lactation, as they do not have sufficient grass to support dry cattle. It is a big national loss. The Union offered to start salvage farms to breed such cattle, if the grass wasted every year was made available to the Societies.

4. As the Forest Department did not allow the Khatta owners to sell the manure produced there, a huge quantity of the same was wasted every year. Whereas on the one hand the State was investing huge sum of money in import of fertilizers or in establishing fertilizer factories to augment food production and thus make a success of the 'grow more food campaign', on the other hand, good quality organic manure was being allowed to go waste. The Union therefore desired reversal of policy in this regard, which would additionally augment the income of the Society as also generating more employment.

5. As in the case of manure, the Forest Department did not allow the Khatta owners to sell the remains of their dead cattle. This un-cooperative and unreasonable attitude of the Department besides preventing the milk man from earning from the mortal remains of their cattle, also resulted in national waste. The Union wanted this attitude to be changed.

Additionally the Khatta owners since the very inception of the Khattas were living in huts. So were their cattle. They wanted permission to construct pucca houses for themselves and sheds for their cattle. The Khattas, being in the forests, were connected to outside world with bridle paths only. During rainy season a few of the Khattas become inaccessible. They wanted connecting roads. They were bereft of medical and veterinary facilities also.

The Forest Department as also the Government did not pay any heed to even these reasonable demands of the Khatta dwellers. Despite several representations their pleas were not attended to. The unhelpful attitude of the forest officials becomes more apparent for their ordering the closure of the Milk Union cream separators at Dolly, Raikhal and other Khattas. During rainy season when Gaula river was in spate the Khatta milk-men could not reach the Cooperative Milk Union collection centres. At such times the cream separators were of much help, as the milk-men could preserve milk in the form of cream.

The forest officers even after several representations at different levels did not comply with the request, saying that the permission to install cream separators had already been given to the highest bidder and that as such to allow the Milk Union cream separators in the Khattas would be illegal. To this the Union and the Khatta dwellers replied that to escape the clutches of the middle-men the Government had encouraged the milk producers to join cooperatives, whereas allowing a private party to run cream separators would go against this policy of the Government. Secondly, how could the forest authorities compel the milk-men to sell milk to the owner of the cream separators ?

But, for the reasons best known to the forest authorities, they remained impervious to these arguments. They continued to create problems for the Khatta dwellers. Due to indiscriminate and unplanned forest plantations in the Khatta areas the grazing area for the Khatta cattle was ever declining. With the result that they often strayed into the plantation area, where the forest officials were ever on the look out to nab them. This made the Khatta people to pay penal fines.

A further set-back to the milk industry came in the form of the Uttar Pradesh Government's decision not to shift to

Naini Tal during summers from 1960 onwards. This decrease in demand for milk products was compensated gradually with the increase in the number of tourists and the defence personnel after 1962.

As the Lalkuan Milk Union and the Khatta dwellers continued to represent to the Government on their problems, the U.P. Government, on April 9, 1973 appointed Vijay Bahadur Singh, Assistant Conservator of Forest to go into the problems of the Khattas. He submitted the report on September 30, 1973. It is yet to see the light of the day, what to say of taking any action on its recommendations.

The Milk Union continues to espouse the cause of the milk producers in the Khattas. Its efforts have not only prevented extinction of a few Khattas, but have also rejuvenated milk cooperatives in Baur Khatta, Ghornala, Bindu Khera, Shisham Bhujia, Khuria, Dolly, Bhura, Saanp Kathani, Khassi Bhoj, Pipal Parao and Chuha Khatta.

The Lalkuan Milk Union, known as the Naini Tal Milk Producers' Cooperative Union Ltd., Lalkuan since 1991, has made the arrangement of collection of milk from the Khattas with its own transport and supplies it to different areas in Naini Tal district. It provides veterinary and animal husbandry services to the Khattas in the form of first aid, vaccination, general diagnosis, artificial insemination and emergency services. Camps are held in Khattas once in a month to guide the dwellers regarding dairying. The Union also distributes cattle feed and seasonal fodder seeds to them at subsidized rates and demonstrates to them the process of sowing of new species of fodder seeds.

Dr. Kamal Singh, an employee of the Milk Producers' Union, has succeeded in embryo transfer and is now in the process of implementing this scheme in the Khattas. For this achievement the Union is known all over India. One of the Milk Union officials informed this writer that it was one of the oldest milk cooperative ventures in the country and was renowned in India for its expertise. Even the Anand Dairy, Gujrat, a leader in dairying industry in the country, sent its experts to Lalkuan. But for the unhelpful attitude of the U.P. Forest Department it could have remained in the forefront of the cooperative dairying industry in the country. However, the Union did not let down milk cooperatives in the Khattas and they continue to thrive as given in the table below on data of developmental activities available in September 1992:

S. No.	Name of Khatta coopt.	Coopts. membership	Milk in litre month	Sale fodder in kg	Primary cases	Emergency treatment	Fodder seeds distb.	Vet Campaigns
1	Bindu Khera	178	6846.8	500	-	4	15	-
2	Ghora Nal	82	3192.0	-	-	-	5	-
3	Shastri Nagar	53	3840.3	-	-	-	25	-
4	Tewari Nagar	72	3367.8	-	-	-	15	-
5	Haldu Dhar	86	4836.2	125	-	-	-	-
6	Shisham Bhujia	62	2892.1	-	-	-	-	-
7	Sarojini Nagar	73	1771.6	-	-	-	5	
8	Vikas Nagar I	84	2567.3	-	22	4	25	-
9	Subash Nagar	38	1744.1	-	35	2	20	-
10	Rajeev Nagar	39	905.3	-	-	-	10	
11	Khuria	75	2600.8	-	-	-	5	-
12	Shanti NagarII	48	1728.1	-	-	1	50	-
13	Rawat Nagar II	32	1611.6	-	-	-	15	-
14	Saanp kathani	96	5537.	5 300	-	-	-	-
15	Baur Khatta	56	5665.0	-	-	-	10	-
16	Sanjar Nagay	131	5455.9	100	-	3	10	32

17	Indra Nagar	113	3393.3	25	25	-	-	90	
18	Rajeev NagarI	95	6656.9	250	-	1	15	46	
19	Raikhal	89	5973.8	-	-	-	-	-	
20	Tunikhal	49	4039.5	650	-		5	15	-
21	Dolly	25	802.0	-	10	1	5	-	
22	Chuha Khatta	33	2657.5	-	57	-	-	-	
23	Pipul Parao	40	3064.0	-	18	-	-	-	
24	Bhura	35	1263.4	-	-	-	2	10	
25	Rawat Nagar	I91	3198.0	75	-	-	-	-	
26	Vikas Nagar II	12	1111.8	100	-	-	-	-	

The Lalkuan Cooperative Dairy Milk Union founded on October 28, 1948 and registered under the Cooperative Societies Act on 16-2-1949 had the twin objectives of saving the Khatta milk producers from the indebtedness of the middlemen and meeting the milk requirement of the residents and tourists. At the time of its its inception it functioned from a rented building in Bhotia Padao, Haldwani. With the establishment of a dairy at Haldwani in 1955-56 it was known as Lalkuan Cooperative Milk Supply Union Ltd., which was changed to Lalkuan Milk Producers' Cooperative Union Ltd. in 1980 and was finally named as Naini Tal Milk Producers Cooperative Union Ltd.

This brought in significant change in the functioning of this Union. It became the focal point of milk cooperatives in the whole district. With the assistance of the State Government and the Haldwani Municipal Board the Union was housed in Mangal Padao. The Union started organizing milk cooperative societies in the hill and Tarai-Bhabhar areas. With the expansion in activities of milk collection and processing, marketing facilities also had to be expanded. This resulted in establishing a 10,000 litres a day capacity dairy at Lalkuan in 1970. With a view to help economic uplift of the rural areas as also to meet the ever increasing requirement of milk and milk products a plan was prepared in the year 1984-85. Resultant upon the expansion in its activities the capacity of the Lalkuan Dairy has been raised from 10,000 litres a day to 20,000 litres in 1992-93.

Currently (November 1993) the Union is engaged in multifarious activities to ensure vast milk cooperatives movement not only in Naini Tal district, but also in the other hill districts of the State. A 10,000 quintal capacity animal feed production unit is under construction at Rudrapur. It will be sufficient to meet the requirement of balanced feed for the cattle of the whole district and also spare some for other districts.

Khatima area in Kumaon Tarai is besides being fertile, and above 86 percent of its population comprises scheduled castes and tribes, marginal and landless farmers. With a view to provide them employment as also to improve their economic condition a foot-hill dairy has been installed there with a chilling capacity of 10,000 litres per day. It will benefit not only the local milk producers, but also milk producers from the neighbouring districts of Pithoragarh, Pilibhit and Bareilly. To ensure similar development in the hill areas of the district, the capacity of the Chilled Milk Centre, Bhowali has been increased from the existing 1,000 litres a day to 5,000 litres. To benefit the milk producers' societies in Bajpur-Kashipur areas a 20,000 litre per day capacity chilling centre has been installed at Bajpur.

The Union provides veterinary aid for sick animals. It has arrangements for vaccination against contagious diseases. Sometimes cattle develop infertility following diseases. The Union holds camps to treat such animals. Improvement in the breed of cattle is necessary for better production. With this end in view the Milk Union has established artificial insemination, natural insemination and embryo transplant centres in the area of its operation.

At present there are artificial insemination facilities with frozen semen in 25 Cooperative Societies. Because of this facility per month about 180 fertilizations take place with the semen of Murrah, Jersey, Holstein, Freizen etc. pedigree breed bulls. Natural insemination is still popular in the rural areas of the district. To cater to such milk producers, 47 bulls have been distributed among its societies. They are supposed to fertilize 300 cattle per month. As stated earlier one of its employee Dr. Kamal Singh succeeded in embryo transplant. Encouraged with his achievement the Milk Union sought assistance from the Naini Tal Dairy Development Board, Department of Bio-Technology, Provincial Cooperative Development Federation and the U.P. Dairy Development Board to established Embryo Transplantation State Sub-Centre, Lalkuan. The Centre in operation since October 1990 has already gained eminence in the whole country. The bulls born out of this technology are in demand in the region.

Besides upgradation of the breed the Milk Union is also trying to make available balanced feed to its members. 359 marked cattle feed is being supplied to the milk producers in 50 and 25 kg. packings. Along with it the farmers are being supplied seeds of better fodder. Perennial fodder crops are being encouraged in hills, while in Tarai-Bhabhar seasonal crops are being propagated. Thus efforts are being made to provide green fodder almost the year round. It is appreciated that women have to play a more important role in rearing milch cattle, the Union is making efforts to apprise them of the better and latest technology in this regard. With this end in view they are taken in groups to visit Pantnagar Agriculture University and other centres engaged in research on fodder. During the year 1993-94 more then 1050 women were taken on such exposure tours.

These initiatives of the Milk Union have brought in almost every segment of the population of the district within the fold of the milk cooperatives. Already the farmers of 30 percent villages are involved in this movement. The comparative figures given below of the last decade speak well of the progress:

S.No.	Item	Position of the year 1983-84	Position of the year 1993-94(Oct.93)	Increase %
1.	Milk Cooperative Societies	42	316	752%
2.	Membership	2173	16476	758%
3.	Average milk production (daily litres)	2049	18724	914%
4.	Daily average sale in urban areas (litres)	1832	15944	838%

There are two landmarks in the milk cooperative movement in the district. It started during the year 1948-49 and was given a significant boost after its reorganization in the year 1983-84. The all round progress achieved is illustrated by the data below:

S.No.	Item	1948-49	1983-84	1992-93
1.	Number of societies	7	42	295
2.	Membership-Backward Classes		143	1840
	Scheduled Castes		291	2412
	Women		57	2659
	General		1682	8521
	Total member		**2173**	**15502**

The movementt besides improving the general condition of its members, has also generated employment. Relevant figures for the last decade are being given below:

S.No.	Item	1983-84	1992-93	Increase %
1.	**Direct Employment**			
	At Milk Union level	81	112	138
	At Milk Societies level	42	408	971
	Miscellaneous	-	29	-
2.	**Indirect Employment**			
	Milk producers	2173	15502	713
	Milk transport	9	64	711
	Sales Agents	21	172	819

In terms of fical matters also the Milk Union has registered similar progress during the same decade, which is evident from the data below:

1.	**Capital of the Milk Union**			
	Authorized Capital (Rs. in lakhs)	27.46	130.34	376
	Working Capital (Rs. in Lakhs)	49.21	256.17	521
2.	Interval Value of Shares(Per Rs.)	0.90	2.04	227
3.	Fixed Assets (Rs. in Lakhs)	38.04	151.51	398
4.	Share Capital (Rs. in Lakhs)	27.61	62.29	226

The phenomenal progress in milk industry in the districts of Naini Tal and Udham Singh Nagar to a considerable extent was due to Pantnagar University situated in Tarai. Commenting on this Prof. H.C. Joshi of College of Veterinary Sciences, G.B. Pant University, Pantnagar says, "The constitution of G.B. Pant University of Agriculture and Technology, Pantnagar is quite significant in developing model dairy units around Pantnagar where one can see the fruits of 'white revolution'. This all is attributed to the transfer of technology in the form of efficient veterinary extension service."

The presence of Khattas within or in the close proximity of forests could also be utilized to make milk industry in this area a bigger success. As given earlier these Khattas in the initial stage formed the base of the Cooperative Milk Movement in Tarai and Bhabhar area of district Naini Tal. The way these Khattas and the Cooperative Milk Union were requesting the Forest Department to provide them necessary facilities to put the milk cooperative societies on sounder footing, has been brought out above.

How the Forest Department responded to the demands of the Khatta dwellers is evident from an incident in early July 1968. Having received several rebuffs in the hands of the Forest Department the Milk Union approached N.D.Tewari, who had led the Milk Cooperative Movement successfully in the initial stages and had by that time risen on national political scene, to intervene on their behalf with the Forest Department officers. He spoke to the Divisional Forest Officer, Haldwani, who asked him to advise the Milk Union and the Khatta dwellers to put up their request in writing. They wrote accordingly on 2-7-1968 and also saw him in a deputation on 4-7-1968. The D.F.O. instead of honouring his assurance to N.D. Tewari flatly told them that he had already sold out the permission to operate cream separators in Khattas to the highest bidder. This was virtually befooling the Khatta dwellers. Considering that the Cooperative Milk Movement was started in Naini Tal Tarai with the encouragement of the State Government and the Forest Department not objecting to the Khatta milk societies running their own cream separators, this attitude was very reversal of that policy.

If the forest officials thought that with that sort of shabby treatment as also the harassment they subjected the milk societies to, would compel them to leave the Khattas and thus their traditional encroachment on forest land, they should have been sorely disappointed. The Khatta dwellers stay put where they were. In the bargain the foresters have only earned their wrath, which has manifested in a few violent dissents.

Whereas a contented Khatta dweller could have turned out to be a protector of forest, this attitude has turned them into perpetrators of forest. This is brought out by their ever trying to nibble at the forest land.

Given an understanding and sympathetic attitude on the part of the foresters the Khatta dwellers, who started their habitation in Tarai as milk producers, could have been weaned away from agriculture on forest land. To make the ownership of milch cattle more profitable to them, they should have been given impetus to increase their milk yield. As this could be possible only by owning better breed cattle, they would have dispensed with their uneconomic cattle. This would result in lesser biotic pressure on forest resources, forests would have been saved to some extent. As better breed cattle are mostly stall fed and fed also on concentrates which increase milk yield, forest resources could have been preserved further more.

Capacity to produce more milk would have made the lives of the Khatta dwellers comfortable with the result that they would have been attracted to smaller family norm. As poorer the family, the more the requirement of bread earning hands, i.e. children and on the contrary happier the family lesser the requirement of bread earners, result being limited family. This would have further lessened biotic pressure on forests, thus turning the Khatta dwellers the unpaid protectors of forests. Their basic requirement of fuel, fodder and small timber could have been met with usufruct use only.

Thus with their negative attitude our foresters missed an opportunity to turn the Khatta dwellers into their friends and as such protectors of forests. Dr. R.S. Tolia, Milk Commissioner, U.P. and Kamal Nautiyal and Nandita Joshi, both Managers, Provincial Cooperative Dairy Federation , U.P. in their article contributed to the souvenir brought out on the occasion of the First All India Dairy Conference, Almora, U.P. in 1992 have lamented this attitude of the Forest Department. They note that the first Symposium of the Provincial Cooperative Dairy Federation, U.P. held at Haldwani in October 1962 had recommended appointment of a special officer by the Forest Department to liaison with the Milk Union and to cooperate with the Khattas in increasing their milk yield by provision of better fodder and grazing facilities. Hitherto no action has been taken in this direction.

Besides the Khattas there are nomadic Gujjars in Tarai-Bhabhar areas, who subsist almost wholly on milk yield from their buffaloes. As the Gujjars do not reside at a place for long, so far they have not been brought within the cooperative fold. It is only of late that efforts are being made by the Rajaji National Park authorities to persuade the Gujjars to give up their nomadic character, settle down permanently at the sites developed by the Government and carry on milk business with better results.

Even though the result of the Gujjar Development Scheme initiated by the Dairy Development Department is luke warm, it is a step in the right direction. Yet no such move has been initiated in Kumaon Tarai. Though nomadism is in the blood of the Gujjars, every one is attracted towards the alternative of a better living and so are the Gujjars of this area. Already a few among them have settled permanently, but to enable almost all of them to do so an enlightened attitude is reauired on the part of our foresters.

The aforesaid makes it clear that the milk production capacity of the Khattas and Gujjars is yet to be developed fully. If the two are given proper incentives Kumaon Tarai still has the potentiality to be in the fore-front of milk industry in the country. The Tarai foresters should also understand that with their present attitude they only compound the intricate situation further, which results in only continued destruction of forest resources. A change in their attitude will not only be beneficial to the forest dwellers, but also save forests and give a big boost to milk industry.

7

Industries usher in new way of life in Tarai-Bhabhar

The post-Independence era has brought in a sea change in the Tarai and Bhabhar region of the Central Himalaya. This has primarily been possible due to coming up of new settlements in the area which has resulted in steep rise in the population.

The land to settle such a large number of families was made available after deforesting a large chunk of Tarai by the Uttar Pradesh Government. The new settlers, a lot of whom came from erstwhile West Pakistan, very soon made a great success of their new acquisition, with the result that the area in a few years turned out to be the food granary of the whole country. This made the farmers to diversify their produce and in addition to the cereal crops they also went in for the cash crops like sugarcane. The change in the pattern of agriculture heralded in the coming up of agriculture based industries in the area.

This gave fillip to agro-based industries in the Tarai-Bhabhar. Already some rice and flour mills were functioning in the area, though only on cottage and small scale basis. Abundance in food production as also new found affluence of the new settlers resulted in establishment of other industrial units on larger scale. Cooperative movement as also the incentive provided by the Government to the entrepreneurs gave further boost to the industries based on agricultural produce.

With increasing grain production as per the law of demand and supply, the prices showed downward trend, which the farmer thought to be incommensurate with the labour he had to put in. Already for a long time he used to cultivate sugarcane to meet his domestic demand of jaggery, sugarcane and molasses, which he used to produce on cottage industries scale. Ofcourse he used this produce also for sale in the local bazars. With better yield he could spare fields for production of cash crops like sugarcane, so as to get better return from his farm. This trend was also helped by coming up of six sugar factories in the area.

Out of the six sugar factories, three are in the cooperative sector, which denotes the awareness of the farmers to guard their interests.

This has ensured a thriving sugar industry in this are. Proper health of this industry has also been assured for setting up of Messrs India Glycol Ltd, Kashipur, as it utilizes the by-product of these factories, which is beneficial to the sugar factories as also to Messrs Glycol India.So far it is perhaps the first of its kind in whole of India. It uses molasses as raw material, which is available in abundance as by-product of these sugar factories.

Success of these industrial enterprises gave further boost to industries in the area. This was also for three additional factors. The neo-rich farmers on the one hand had money to spare for industrial ventures and on the other wanted to earn even more. Secondly, shortage of printing paper in the country was proving to be a big drain of the scantly foreign exchange resources of the country. The situation was worsening further due to ever expanding demand for news-print. To ease the situation the Government gave incentives for setting up paper mills in this area. Thirdly, it was made possible due to easy availability of raw material in the area for the industry. The farmers having taken up surgarcane farming, baggas was available in significant quantity. Raw material was also available from the adjoining forests. To augment the raw material supply the farmers are also taking up agro-forestry. While big farmers are raising eucalyptus plantations, the smaller ones are planting trees on the boundary of their fields or any other space available.

Notwithstanding proximity to the Tarai forests as also the farmers ever more taking to the agro-forestry, wood-industry has not made much head-way in the area. This is evident from only one plywood factory having come up here. Messrs S.N.T. Plywood, Gadarpur established at a cost of Rs. 0.62 cores has 200 employees. Additionally furniture industry is making headway in Haldwani. But neither the wood nor the furniture industry could make much progress in Tarai, which is probably for the fact of the plywood industry being well established in Sitapur, on the outer fringe of Tarai, and the furniture industry being monopolised by nearby Bareilly since long.

Of late there has been further diversification in the industries in Tarai. This has been made possible for two factors. Firstly, the neo-rich of the Tarai, who had been looking for more lucrative avenues to make money, have started non-agro based industries also. This besides their comparative affluence was made possible for expanded training facilities as also concessions provided by the Government for setting up industries in the hills and industrially backward districts of the country. Secondly, setting up of a few industrial estates, wherein a host of facilities are provided to entrepreneurs has given further boost to the industries in the area.

Khadi and Village Industries Board has played an important role in training of local people to enable them to engage themselves in various industrial activities. Regional Training Centre, Kaladhungi imparts training in various cottage industry trades. These trades include spinning, weaving, bee-keeping, carpentry, fruit preservation etc. The Lok Vastra Unit at Haripura, Jaspur provides training in spinning, weaving, dyeing and printing of clothes. The Government polytechnic at Naini Tal has also played an important role in the coming up of industries in Tarai. Also the Industrial Training Centre of the Jan Vidyapeetha, Haldwani imparts three or six months' training to the youth in different trades. These include electronics, electrician, watch repairing, automobile repairing, tailoring, carpentry, hosiery, handloom etc.

In addition to these training institutes, entrepreneur development camps of two days to six weeks duration have been held at the development block level also. Besides the extension service officials of the Government, other agencies like the Small Scale Industries Service Institute, Entrepreneurship Development Institute and banks also have been associated with these camps.

Apart from providing training facilities the Government also provides financial incentives to the desirous entrepreneurs of district Naini Tal and Tarai, These are :

1. The Central Capital Interest Subsidy to the tuneof 25% on fixed capital investment on land, building and machinery which is given upto maximum of Rs. 25 lakhs to units established after March 1983. The subsidy is also allowed on more than 10% expansion and modernization.
2. 75% of the expenditure on transport of raw material to factories and finished goods from there to the nearest broad gauge railway station viz., Moradabad, Rampur and Bareilly is admissible as Central Transport Subsidy.
3. New industrial units set up after September 1982 were given exemption for seven years from the levy of

central as well as state sales tax on sale or purchase of finished goods and raw materials.

4. Subsidy on purchase of generating sets is allowed at the rate of Rs. 500 per KVA to large and medium units and at the rate of Rs. 1000 to small scale units.
5. Financial assistance is provided by the Pradeshik Industrial and Investment Corporation, Uttar Pradesh (PICUP) and the Uttar Pradesh Finance Corporation (UPFC) at concessional rate of interest varying from 11% to 14%.
6. New units are exempted from power cuts for five years and are not required to pay minimum consumption guarantee during the first year of getting connection.
7. The Government provides 75% subsidy on expenses incurred on the preparation of feasibility reports of the consultant approved by the PICUP.
8. In special cases margin money loans are given by the District Industries Centre to meet upto 50% of the margin money subject to a maximum of Rs. 3 lakhs.
9. The units exporting 100%of their products are admissible to special 10% capital subsidy.
10. New industrial units are exempted from payment of octroi on machines and building materials transported to and from the factory for five years.

Additionally there are some incentives, which are given as per the size of the industrial unit. The incentives are :

A. Large and Medium Sector Units:

1. New qualified entrepreneurs are provided seed capital loans upto Rs. 15 lakhs by PICUP towards promoters' contribution in respect of projects costing upto Rs. 3 crores each.
2. Units starting production after January 1985 can avail

the facility of deferment of payment of sales tax, collected on the sale of their products, to the Government in lieu of sales tax exemption. The sales tax collections are remitted to the State Government after seven years.

3. Technical entrepreneurs growing into medium sector industrialists and experienced entrepreneurs intending to take over medium sector units, closed or sick units are provided interest free loans by the Risk Capital Foundation, New Delhi upto Rs. 15 lakhs, Rs. 25 lakhs or Rs. 30 lakhs per unit when there is one promoter or two promoters or more than three promoters respectively of each unit.

4. Special Capital Subsidy is provided upto 15% to prestige units, each promoting ten or more ancillary units in the state.

B. Small Scale, Tiny and Artisan Units :

1. The U.P.Government assists the handloom weavers and their cooperatives by supplying yarn, marketing their products and modernizing their looms.

2. The U.P. Khadi and Village Industries Board provides concessional finance and marketing facilities to industrial cooperatives, institutions and rural industries under its fold.

3. Educated unemployed youth in 18 to 35 years age group, having studied at least upto High School with annual income upto Rs. 10,000 are given loans upto Rs. 35,000 on concessional terms for establishing industrial, service or business units.

Besides providing these facilities Uttar Pradesh Government is helping entrepreneurs by developing industrial sites. Medium or big industries are allotted land in Industrial Areas wherein construction is undertaken by the allotees as per their requirement. On the other hand there are Industrial Estates where the prospective entrepreneur is allotted sheds or plots as per his requirement.

A Small Industrial Estate was handed over to the Harijan and Social Welfare Department for management. Additionally there was a move to have one Mini-Industrial Estate each in the Haldwani, Sitarganj, Khatima, Rudrapur, Jaspur, Bajpur and Ramnagar blocks.

Apart from this a Hosiery Complex was developed at Kashipur. Of the 14 sheds in the complex six were allotted to entrepreneurs; whereas two were in possession of the Uttar Pradesh Finance Corporation. Of the six allotted sheds one is being used as the office of M/S Kumaon-Garhwal Chamber of Commerce and Industries. Surprisingly all the five hosiery units, supposed to have started since 1983, were closed. Not only that there was also sizeable money outstanding against them, Rs. 201,725.60 as premium installments and Rs. 52,965.62 as interest, thus making a total of Rs. 254,691.22.

It is no doubt a sorry state of affairs, for which the industrialists have their own alibi, ventilated by the Kumaon-Garhwal Chamber of Commerce and Industry, U.P. at a meeting of the Regional Level Seminar of the Udyog Bandhu (Fraternity of Industrialists) on August 21, 1993. It presented its view points on sick units per below:

1. Terrorism :

Tarai was a hot-bed of terrorist activities of the Punjab militants for quite some time. The problem on the one hand scared away the labourers and on the other made the industrialists to fill the coffers of the terrorists often on gun point. This made functioning of industrial units uneconomic as also hazardous. It resulted in many units being shifted out of Tarai and a few being closed.

2. Transport Subsidy :

(i) This subsidy was not available to all industrial units. It was only in 1991 that the rice and pulses mills were brought under this provision. Entrepreneurs have been representing for inclusion of the seed units and flour mills in the area. Inspite of strong pleas the request was yet to be granted.

(ii) Initially 75% of transport charges were sanctioned as transport subsidy at the rate of 56 paise per kilometre. Even though there has been steep rise in transport charge consequent upon the hike in the rate of fuels, the subsidy rate has been reduced to 48 paise per kilometre, which is unreasonable. In view of this the entrepreneurs have been representing for restitution of previous rate.

3. Power Supply :

(i) Frequent power rostering as also fluctuation in voltage is adversely affecting the production of the industrial units and is also damaging the highly sophisticated equipment. Lack of uninterrupted power supply results in considerable wastage of raw material in the industries of continuous nature. To avoid these losses continuous power supply at proper voltage should be ensured.

(ii) Against the power connections sanctioned to the industries security deposits are with the Uttar Pradesh Electricity Board. Interest becomes due to against them. But the same is neither paid, nor its is adjusted in the electricity bills. At the same time the money deposited with the authorities for temporary power connections also is not refunded after disconnection of the power supply against these connections. The entrepreneurs feel that removal such anomalies is necessary.

4. Bank Facilities:

(i) Even though the Government is providing financial lacking considerably, small-scale industrial units frequently become sick because of money not being available at appropriate time. To ensure this the entrepreneurs desire the Chamber to be consulted while preparing the district level credit plan.

(ii) Though the Reserve Bank had lowered the interest rate on loan, the same was not being implemented by the commercial banks. At the same time there was no uniformity in the interest rates of various banks. This requires to be rectified.

5. Telecommunications:

Knowing fully well that the industrial units depend on telecommunication facilities for growing as well as promoting and setting business to a great extent, the Chamber has been pressurising the authorities to improve upon the existing facilities and to provide additional facilities. Even though a time-bound programme was prepared to ensure this, it was not implemented.

The entrepreneurs complain that :

(i) Though with installation of electronic exchanges in some cities and STD facilities having been given to subscribers, the facility has not been of much help because of the exchanges having only a few lines. They want the exchanges to be expanded in line with the industrial development of the area.

(ii) Noting that even after payment of telephone bills as many as 500 telephones were disconnected in the area, the entrepreneurs want the Accounts Officer to visit on a fixed day every month each city to settle all accounts.

6. Transport :

In view of increased rail-road traffic as also necessity of air traffic facility following fast development of industries in Tarai and Bhabhar the Chamber desires:

(i) Provision of an air-strip at Kashipur, where there

is a large concentration of industries. Due to the close proximity of the Jim Corbett Wildlife Sanctuary, the strip will be a boon to tourists and thereby give a boost to tourist traffic leading to added economic advantage to the area.

(ii) Even though of late Rudrapur, Kashipur and Ramnagar, three main industrial centres of Tarai and Bhabhar, have been connected with broad gauge rail line, it is of little use to the industries, as the Railways do not provide them wagons on time. This situation needs an improvement in the wagon supply position.

(iii) Because of fast industrial development in the area there is heavy goods traffic on the roads leading to Moradabad from Kashipur, Rudarpur and Khatima, which leaves the roads in bad condition.The entrepreneurs want the roads to be maintained by hot-mix plant.

7. New Industrial Policy :

Consequent upon the New Industrial Policy launched by the Government the industries have been delicensed. This will make industries competitive. The entrepreneurs will automatically opt for areas where running of industries would be more profitable. This will harm the inaccessible and backward areas. Industries in Tarai and Bhabhar are likely to be affected also, which will undo what ever had been gained following the incentives and facilities provided by the Government for setting up industries in Tarai and Bhabhar.To obviate this possibility as also to maintain the tempo of industrial growth of the area the Chamber has suggested to the Uttar Pradesh Government that :

(i) Following the example of Himachal Pradesh, Sales Tax may not be imposed on new industries for 12 years.

(ii) Like Bundelkhand (in Uttar Pradesh) the industries be provided 50% rebate on electricity.

(ii) Half the expenditure be borne by the State Government on installation of generating sets.

(iv) On installation of unconventional and environment friendly power devices like wind-mills, 50% financial assistance be given.

(v) Fifty percent financial grant be sanctioned on installation of pollution control devices.

(vi) The Government of India be persuaded to accord five year tax holiday.

(vii) The State Government should provide 50% and 25% capital subsidy to electronic and other industries respectively.

(viii) Following the Himachal Pradesh pattern 2% State Capital Subsidy be provided on export.

(ix) Like Himachal Pradesh, North-Eastern States and Jammu and Kashmir, transport subsidy be raised to 90% from 75%.

(x) Continuous power supply be ensured.

(xi) Three percent interest rebate be provided by the financing agencies.

(xii) Banks be directed to make available Working Capital to entrepreneurs on time.

(xii) Interest rates of all banks should be the same.

(xiv) The industries be spared from the 'Inspector Raj'.

(xv) 'Single Window' be enforced for small scale indus trial units.

The members of Kumaon Garhwal Chambers of Commerce and Industry are of the view that for eco-friendly industrial development in Sub- Himalayan Tarai the following measures should be taken immediately:

(i) A separate Uttarakhand Industrial Policy should

be prepared which gives incentives like:

(a) Interest subsidy.

(b) Life long one percent Central Sales Tax to all old and new industries.

(c) Export incentive.

(d) State Capital Subsidy.

(e) Regular power supply at the lowest tariff rates.

(f) Extra incentives on Infrastructural Projects and Agro-based Industries.

(ii) Roads leading to industrial townships should be properly maintained.

(iii) Private investment in Hydro Electric Projects should be made and transmission as well as distribution of power should be privatised.

(iv) Allocation of sufficient funds be made for research and development in industrial plantations.

(v) Plantation activities should be encouraged in joint collaboration with the Forest Department and industrial units on a long lease.

The members of the Chamber also laid stress on the accountability of the Industries Department but were non-committal about their own accountability.

The picture of the industrial scene in Tarai and Bhabhar in fact is not as rosy as it appears to be. First of all after the deforestation of a large area of Tarai it had turned out to be a virtual granary of Uttar Pradesh. Staple food being the basic human necessity efforts to maintain it as such should have continued. Even if industries were desired to flourish along with agriculture, they should have been based on agricultural by-product only. This besides improving the finances of the inhabitants would also have provided ample employment opportunities. Additionally it would have turned the farm by-product, which otherwise goes waste and is also a health hazard,into useful products. Coming of all sorts of industries

It is also resulting in lessening in interest of the farmers in agriculture. Both factors are bound to affect adversely production of staple food-grain in the area, which will be a loss to the whole nation.

The setting up of a number of industries in the area has increased employment opportunities, but instead of satisfying the inhabitants, it has started to bring in disturbing social under-currents in the area. The locals feel that they are not only being denied the clout and influence in the area but are also being denied the new opportunities. This is for various factors. Almost all the industrial units being founded on the authority of the licenses issued by the State and Central Governments, the overwhelming majority of them are owned by outsiders. They are particularly peeved at this for the fact that even though many of them were aspirants for such licenses, for the reasons best known to the authorities, they were not favoured. These outsider entrepreneurs have brought their own men to man different levels of production processes. Even as labourers the locals are least favoured, because or their capability to counter the high-handedness of the employers. Thus the local people feel like having been cheated. A telling proof of this dissatisfaction is the defeat at the hustings of the politician who brought out this industrial development in the area.

Presence of outsiders in the area as also the swelling labour force consequent upon this development has heightened other social tensions also. There is an ever growing feeling of animosity against this new class which is bound to affect the social harmony. Already there is a feeling that in the garb of terrorism this element has been behind some of the anti-social activities. That incidence of thefts, assaults, plunders, molestations etc. are on the rise almost confirms this feeling.

Besides spoiling the social fabric industrial development is adversely affecting the physical environment of the area. Residents in the vicinity of the Century Paper Mill in the area complain of higher incidence of respiratory diseases, which indicates polluted air. Yet no one on the official side has cared to move against the factory. The Century Mill, Lalkuan owned by the Birlas has been in production since 1984. The mill located in close proximity to Lalkuan town and a few villages produces 165,000 quintals of writing and printing paper and 165,000 quintals rayon pulp per month. As per the factory management the mill is equipped with effluent treatment and air pollution prevention devices. Additionally the three chimneys of the mill are 40 m, 60 m and 65 m high to prevent diffusion of gases in the lower atmosphere.

The management maintains that the devices are operated regularly and it is only after proper treatment that the effluent is let out in a nullah which disgorges itself into the river Gola.

Not withstanding this claim of the factory the people complain that due to the mill there is water as well as air pollution. The pollution devices may have been installed by the mill, but they are not operated regularly, since the cost of running them is exorbitant. According to the residents of Lalkuan these devices are functional only when there is an inspection by the officials of the Pollution Control Board. Unfortunately, hitherto there have been no surprise checks or raids in the mill regarding the functioning of these pollution prevention devices by the concerned authority. Due to the air pollution the people in Lalkuan say that the birds have been found dead and that there is a marked depletion in their number owing to the foul air being emitted. They also say that the incidence of respiratory diseases among the nearby population is ever on the increase. A nauseating smell was felt by this writer also during his visit to the area especially when large clouds of smoke billowed from the main chimney.

The water pollution has taken toll of domestic animals and monkeys have died after drinking the nullah water. Irrigation channels have been taken out of this nullah, which also are the source of drinking water of the people. They complain that stomach diseases are on the rise in the area and many deaths have been caused only due to this factor. They also allege that the ground water has been contaminated due to the untreated effluent of the factory and the agricultural produce is declining.

There have been many agitations due to the water and noise pollution, which have been reported extensively in the local as well as the national press. Vijay Jaiswal a correspondent of the Hindi daily 'Amar Ujala' has put in a lone drawn fight against this pollution. In addition to the officials, the aggrieved people have met and reported to the Environment and Forest Minister, Government of India, Governor, Chief Minister and Chairman, U.P. Legislative Council in the past. The then U.P., Deputy Development Minister, Ram Sharan Verma aired his concern to the people of Lalkuan and strongly felt that due to the pollution being caused by the mill even the milk products in the nearby Milk Plant could be affected adversely.

It is intriguing that every time the pollution control devices have been inspected by the State Pollution Control Board experts, they have given a clean chit. Even though the air pollution control certificate given to the mill was cancelled earlier on 2.5.1989, till the time of the Assistant Engineer Environment Haldwani's inspection visits to the mill on 23.10.1989 and 4.11.1989, no remedial measures had been taken with the result that the mill is still causing pollution.

Surprisingly even after the denial of the certificate, the factory continued to function without undertaking any remedial measures. On the residents' complaints of ever increasing stomach and skin diseases in the area, the Medical and Health Department, Naini Tal got the water samples of ten hand pumps in the area tested by the U.P. State Health Institute, which found seven samples polluted. The Forest Department also got the factory effluent, which was supposed to have been treated, tested on 27.1.1992 by the Department of Environment, Pantnagar Agricultural University. They categorically stated that the effluent was injurious to animals, men as well as crops. The Forest Department threatened the mill with termination of its lease, but the owners have such a clout that the mill remained impervious to all these threats.

The aforesaid makes it abundantly clear that the local population is suffering due to the pollution from this mill. Even two State Agencies, viz. U.P. State Health Institute and the Pantnager University have clearly opined that water pollution is being caused by the mill. Curiously enough the State Pollution Control Board Engineers who are said to have inspected this mill several times have never confirmed the water pollution from the mill. It clearly indicates a connivance with the offender.

Apart from the Century Paper Mills, Lalkuan, the other industrial units which are responsible for causing pollution in Tarai and the adjoining areas are India Glycol Ltd, S.H. Sugar Mill, Straw Board Private Ltd, Belwal Spinning Mills, Banwari Paper Mill, Vishwakarma Paper Board, Jindal Udyog etc. Amongst the above mentioned units, Glycol India Ltd, is causing maximum pollution. It is disgorging its effluent in the Kosi river. This has affected the productivity of the adjoining area and its negative effects are also being felt on human and animal population in the Swar tahsil of the neighbouring Rampur district.

On the basis of a survey of Swar tahsil conducted with the help of Shanti Nabiyal, it was found that the agricultural yield of more than 100 villages in the region has been reduced and the water in the hand-pumps situated near the banks of the river Kosi has become contaminated. The villagers allege that several animals have died after consuming the polluted water of river Kosi.

On 12th and 13th February, 1993 a two day workshop was organized in Swar regarding the ecological hazards caused by pollutants. Thirty six volunteers form different villages, which had been affected by industrial pollution, attended the workshop and revealed the ill effects of pollution in the river Kosi. It has sparked a wave of anger amongst the residents of the area. On the water borne diseases caused by contaminated water, Dr. Sanjay Verma a leading physician of the area stated in the workshop that residents of several villages, whose source of drinking water is the Kosi river, are suffering from water borne diseases. He suggested that villagers should drink boiled water and add chlorine to it. The officers in charge of the veterinary hospital, Dr. Arun Kumar Agarwal, stated that animals were infected with worms and several other ailments. In the workshop it was suggested by him that to save cattle from waterborne diseases, vaccination of animals should be popularized and to treat calcium deficiency in cattle, they should be given lime water.

On 24th May 1993 it was reported that six animals had died in village Jaitpura of Murhapande Block in Rampur district after they had consumed the contaminated water of river Kosi. From time to time the villagers of Swar Tahsil have complained to the administration that their lives are threatened owing to the industrial waste being released in the river Kosi. They allege that the drinking water in the taps is often black in colour and sand as well as black particles can be seen suspended in it. As a result the villagers have been infected with stomach and skin diseases.

The villagers of Khampur village have submitted a memorandum to the Governor of Uttar Pradesh regarding their predicament caused by consumption of contaminated water of the river Kosi. Their grouse is that the contaminated water is posing health problems in their area and is responsible not only for stomach ailments, but other diseases like typhoid and cholera also. Further the polluted water has stifled the growth of grasses in their area, consequent upon which there is an acute paucity of fodder for the village cattle.

On visualizing their helpless situation and the nonchalant attitude of the Government regarding industrial pollution, the villagers of Swar tahsil decided to fight their own battle. Consequently the 'Kosi Pradushan Action Committee' was constituted which has evoked great response. The president of the committee Kausar Khan talks of ground realities and has summed up the objectives of the committee as:

1. To propagate consciousness amongst thepolitical leaders as well as the villagers regarding pollution problems of Kosi.
2. To organize such programmes through which the peo-

ple could be educated about the causes and effects of industrial pollution and find remedial measures.

3. To infuse a spirit of consciousness amongst the members of political, social and cultural organizations of the region and to create an atmosphere conducive to challenge the hazards of industrial pollution.

4. To inform all environmental organizations and environmentalists about the ecological problems caused by industrial pollution in the river Kosi and to muster their support as well as to seek their guidance.

5. To win the support of voluntary agencies,social organizations, non-governmental organizations and all interested organizations to make their cause a national issue.

The leaders of the committee strongly feel that through this approach they will be able to provide the movement a strong base and will succeed in making it a mass movement. Subsequently from within the movement and from the large spectrum of people associated with it they will be able to find a solution to their problem. They claim that this approach will also be helpful in advocating environmental consciousness and eco-friendly development.

The programme of the committee was launched on 1st April 1993 when its members organized a cycle rally and toured 150 villages in the area. They made a probe into the problems of the villagers and undertook a field study of the villages for ten days. Subsequently a report was prepared of the ecological problems caused by industrial pollution. According to the report the underground water on both banks of the river Kosi has been badly contaminated and a heavy loss has been incurred in the agricultural produce of the area. The pollution has also affected both human and animal population. In the report it has been suggested that the solid industrial waste accumulated on the banks of the river Kosi should be cleaned on a war footing and clean drinking water should be provided to the affected villages in the area.

The cycle rally culminated in the form of a general meeting on 10th of April 1993 and several villagers thronged the venue to extend their moral support. In the meeting it was decided that the energies of the people should be concentrated on a one point programme, to have a pollution free Kosi river and subsequently to sound the Ministry of Environment, Government of India of the actual situation in Swar Tahsil and of their one point programme. Concomitantly street meetings were held and a post card campaign was launched to inform the people outside the district of the sad plight of the villagers.

The Kosi Pradhushan Action Committee has evoked mass support from almost all political parties and a number of voluntary agencies, but it is intriguing that except for marathon meetings on the part of the Government regarding the problem, nothing fruitful has come out as yet and the pollution in Kosi river goes unabated. On the behest of the affected people, the District Magistrate of Naini Tal. Aradhana Johri organized a meeting of the officials and the people on 5th July, 1993, and instructed the State Pollution Control Board to check the level of pollution in the river Kosi. The State Pollution Control Board contends that the pollution in the river Kosi is within permissible limits, even though the affected people are suffering from water-borne diseases, the Government doctors admit that cattle population also is suffering, the wells on both sides of Kosi are polluted and the productivity of the land has been affected adversely. It shows that the Pollution Control Board has turned a blind eye to the miseries of the people and is inexplicably sympathetic to the industrialists.

Similar is the complaint of the Tanakpur residents against the stone crushers of the area, because of which the air is polluted to such an extent that they are suffering from various ailments. For the official apathy to move against the mills they have approached the judiciary, though so far unsuccessfully. If no heed is paid to these grievances and no remedial measures are taken it will make it abundantly clear that the declared environmental policies and programmes of the Government are mere rhetorics vis-a-vis the money power.

Of late the residents of village Faridpur in Moradabad district have taken up cudgels against industrial pollution caused by the Siddarth Paper Mill, Kashipur. They have been organized under the banner of 'Mazdoor Kalyankari Samiti,' a labour union. The villagers contend that the paper mill is releasing its untreated effluent in the river Daandi which has affected the productivity of the soil and is a health hazard to both human and animal population.

The labour union earlier approached the management committee to discuss the problems of pollution, but it was a futile exercise, because the management was impervious to the demands of the Mazdoor Samiti. As a sequel they decided to squat round the mill gate on 15th June 1994. According to the leaders of the labour union they had given information in this connection to both the civil administration as well as the management, though the mill officials claim ignorance of any such information.

In the morning at about 10 a.m. the union sent some villagers to erect a shamiana near the mill gate. It was however seized by the security guards and the villagers were forced to leave the place. After this incident the villagers with banners and loudspeakers proceeded on tractors and trollies to the mill. The security guards, according to the leaders were prepared to face the eventuality and they fired in the air. Subsequently three villagers, Sharafat, Mushtaq and Mubarak were pulled inside the gate and badly beaten up by the guards. The management on the other hand claims that these three in a fit of frenzy had jumped the gate and were actually hit by stones hurled by the villagers. They state that three of their officials Rajesh Bansal, Mahesh Patel and Ajay Singhal were also injured by the stones thrown by villagers. According to the local newspaper 'Amar Ujala' the police has refused that bullets were fired, but they have admitted that some villagers were beaten up by the security guards.

In the afternoon the injured villagers were arrested by the police owing to which there was lot of resentment against the police and to ventilate their ire the agitators raised slogans against the police for colluding with the mill management. Later they submitted a memorandum to the Sub-Divisional Magistrate, Kashipur regarding their plight and have demanded justice. The Sub-Divisional Magistrate has instituted an enquiry and instructed the police to look into the matter.

This is an other example of the local population having been subjected to the bane of pollution being caused by the mill. It is clear that they were suffering from the results of this pollution for long, which compelled them to take this course to ventilate their grievances. This leads one to conclude that the mill is either not having the pollution control devices (which is a very serious lapse), or is not putting them to use. Secondly, the State Pollution Control Board has failed to enforce the various provisions of the Environment Protection Act. Thirdly, the local administration failed to appreciate the grievances of the people and as such did no take preventive action.

These examples are sufficient to prove the general feeling that the industrial units in the area are causing water and air pollution. Though many of them might have installed pollution control devices, to avoid operational expenses, they are not put to use. In this the pollution rules enforcing and inspecting authorities appear to be hand in glove with the owners.

There is a feeling that this connivance has tacit political patronage also. If the owners, as cited above, were favoured unduly in sanctioning licenses, they can be favoured in this respect also. According to an official source this nexus between owners and politicians became evident in the case of verification of transport subsidy claims of various industrial units. As stated before 75% transport subsidy is admissible for transportation of raw material from rail head to factory site and carriage of the goods produced thereof from the factory to the rail head.

Previously octori paid at different points used to make possible for the industries department to check the authenticity of the claims. With the abolition of octroi in Uttar Pradesh the department was denied this check. The officials always had the feeling that the claims used to be inflated. To prevent this mal-practice they started checking on the veracity of the claims on the basis of sales tax and income tax paid by the factory owners. This not only made inflated claims difficult, but also brought out the mal-practices being resorted to by the factory owners in defrauding the state in the case of sales and income taxes. The authorities rather than objecting to this device of the industries department personnel should have appreciated this effort. Instead of commending its personnel, they were asked to desist from checking the sales tax and income tax accounts of the owners which clearly shows the politico-industrialist nexus.

Thus by the way of the transport subsidy the state exchequer continues to be cheated without any let and hinder. The number of beneficiary units which got transport subsidy are 180 and the amount paid in the year 1989-90 was Rs. 7,15,00,000. That 50% of the transport subsidy is claimed by the stone crushers is indicative of the loot of public money. It is notable that the area abounds in stones. As such there is no question of claim of transportation subsidy for carrying them as raw material.

Similar nexus became evident in the case of inspections of sick units by the local officials of the Industries Department. On inspection of 1,000 units, 200 of them were found to be sick. Of the 25 units in Bazpur Industrial Area all are sick. Out of 131 industrial units in Rudrapur Industrial Area, 54 are sick. Had the inspections been allowed to continue more glaring facts would have been revealed. It is curious that neither the inspections were allowed to be continued, nor were they allowed to be reported. Obviously the authorities did not want the facts to see the light of the day.

Just a sample of the fraud being played is the factory reported to have been operating on the outskirt of village Kundeshwari (Kashipur). It is owned by one big and influential political family of Uttar Pradesh plains. Though the factory building is still there, it has not been operational even for a single day. As such it is a factory only on paper designed to milch subsidies on various counts. Official sources also admit this trend when they themselves feel that nearly 50% units misappropriated the subsidies. In 1988 the Central Government allowed 25% investment subsidy to new industrial units in the area. The number of beneficiary units which got the Central Investment Subsidy is 551 and the amount released was Rs. 7,46,22,489. In the eventuality of the units closing before the expiry of five years, the subsidy was to be recovered . To avoid this penalty the pseudo-entrepreneurs used to approach courts, got stay and remain in litigation for years together. In the meantime five years passed and they automatically avoided the penalty.

With a view to provide incentive to new entrepreneurs the State Government has been sanctioning 25% Capital Subsidy to new units since 1.4.90. Additionally such units enjoy sales tax exemption for a period of initial seven years. Both facilities according to knowledgeable sources have been misused.

The extent to which these facilities were exploited rather improperly, the officials cite the example of a Photo Films concern, which was previously located at Gaziabad, U.P. The film was manufactured not in India, but in Japan. It was concerned only in cutting it to proper size, filling it in reels and selling it. The processes needed minimal effort and cost. While at Gaziabad it had enjoyed exemption in Sales Tax for five years. With the Government announcing special concession with a view to develop hilly, backward and zero industry areas, it just shifted to district Naini Tal, earned 25% capital subsidy as a new unit and further earned Sales Tax exemption for full seven years.

It is notable that except for the new premises the unit had only to shift its existing machinery from Gaziabad and earn 25% capital subsidy as if it had to make investment in new machinery and equipment. By the way of the development, its impact was nil as it did not involve manufacture of new material, nor did it help in development of any ancillary industry. As for providing employment to the people from the under-developed area, its impact again was negligible, as it was little labour incentive work. Whatever technicians it required, it brought with it from Gaziabad.

In a way it was just a front to reap ample concessions provided by the State. This is just an example. On investigation such examples may be many. Again such an investigation is not liked and therefore prevented also by the authorities that be. Thus there are many a units which instead of encouraging entrepreneurship in the area, give only fillip to the tendencies of deceit and fraudulent ways. That fails the very purpose of the intention of the State to bring up the under-developed areas in line with the other developed areas of the State.

Notwithstanding these drawbacks it is a fact that based on these incentives provided by the State, industrialization has made a head way in Tarai and Bhabhar. It has created a new awareness in the farmers, who have started industrial units to add to their income. Industrialization has provided an outlet for gainful utilization of otherwise useless agricultural by-product. It has also given them vocation for their spare time. To keep up the momentum as also to meet the demands of the Kumaon-Garhwal Chamber of Commerce and Industry, they should be provided raw material at the District Industries Centre, Haldwani or the nearest rail-head. At present they have to go as far a place as Gaziabad or Kanpur for the same. Additionally the State should provide marketing facility to the produce of their industries.

With a view to prevent any deterioration in environment only non-polluting and environment friendly industries should be encouraged in the area. Taking into account that deforestation on a gigantic scale was undertaken to settle the needy people there, which besides reducing the forest cover of the country, has also affected adversely the rain and weather cycle of the country, efforts have to be made to take corrective measures. With this end in view agro-forestry and forest-based industries should also be encouraged in the area.

In this connection a further point to be considered is the ever dwindling productivity of land in Tarai. In the early stages the land here was very fertile. This was due to the rich humus content of the soil, which was because of the land previously having being under thick forests since very long time. With intensive cropping along with heavy dressing of chemical fertilizers, the texture of the soil has been spoilt. This has resulted in lesser moisture retention capacity of the soil. Intensive cropping along with thus spoilt soil texture has adversely affected the soil moisture. Whereas previously there used to be little or none at all necessity of irrigation, now it has become a must.

With a view to undo the denudation of land caused due to promiscuous deforestation along with improving the soil texture, horticulture should be encouraged in Tarai and Bhabhar. Given the existing moisture and soil texture it should not be difficult to raise fruit tree plantations there This besides providing income to the farmers can produce material for running fruit preservation as well as other wood-based industries. As these industries would be in cottage, small and medium sectors, they are going to be labour incentive thereby providing employment to many. Such industries not being capital incentive, they will give fillip to local entrepreneurship, thus avoiding social tensions.

This type of approach will transform the economy of this area as besides supplementing their income from agriculture or horticulture, unemployment will no more be a problem. It will also be free from the existing social tensions. Additionally it will help in the betterment of the physical environment of the country. Thus Tarai and Bhabhar area of Kumaon region in Uttar Pradesh can be a torch-bearer of a new way of living.

8

Militancy in Tarai

Terrorism in its literal form is a relatively new phenomenon in India. However there is no commonly agreed definition of terrorism. It may vary and depend on the side of the ideological divide the problem is viewed from. The simplest definition is perhaps contained in the U.S. State Department's annual survey, 'Patterns of Global Terrorism, 1993', which states that, "Terrorism is premeditated, politically motivated violence perpetrated against non-combatant targets by sub national groups or clandestine state agents." It is a war of attrition fought by an invisible, but vocal army.

It may be difficult to define terrorism, but there is a broad agreement about its ingredients, which can be summed up as:

1. Terrorism involves a criminal act.
2. There may be killings random or selective.

3. The proximate target may be an individual, but the ultimate targets are the people. Terrorists kill one man to terrorise a thousand.
4. There is an element of surprise in terrorist actions.
5. Responsibility for violence is acknowledged to give publicity to the terrorist group and to create a public scare.
6. Terrorist actions are accompanied with demandsby way of redress or relief.
7. Terrorists thrive on outside support which may either be in terms of financial support or by harbouring and providing them sanctuaries.

The Sikh terrorism, though comparatively of a recent origin has acquired the dubious distinction of being the world's most lethal terrorist movement. In Punjab 247 people were killed in 1987 and the corresponding figure for killings in the first four months of 1988 plummeted to 777.

The Punjab militants when put under pressure in 1984 found a safe haven in U.P. Tarai, which has a sizeable Sikh population and concentrated their activities in the then Naini Tal district, where besides operating under forest cover, the hills were an added advantage. The Tarai belt in Naini Tal district is a large expanse of land adjoining the hills of Naini Tal, Garhwal and running along the border of Nepal. It has large farms, rivers, streams, forest and riverine areas, which offer ideal sanctuaries to terrorists and combating them here is a formidable task.

The main causes which have been responsible for disseminating militancy in Naini Tal Tarai according to the U.P. Police are:

1. The Tarai region in Naini Tal has a dense forest cover and is endowed with rivers, rivulets and nullahs which provide ideal hideouts to terrorists. Moreover, the rural areas are sparsely populated and the villages are

scattered owing to which it is easy for the terrorist to adopt surprise tactics, they strike and escape.

2. The proximity of Tarai with Punjab has also helped the militants in spreading their network. Most of the Sikh settlers here have relations in Punjab. These Sikh evacuees settled here after partition successfully reclaimed the Sub-Himalayan Tarai. In the beginning, when Tarai was being settled and rules were not strictly being abided by, some of the Sikh settlers encroached upon the territory of the tribals. It was with either force or cajolery. This encroachment was done at times with the connivance of the revenue officials. However, there is another aspect to it. In the initial stages when Tarai was being colonized, the officials did not check this tendency of land grabbing owing to the disdainful attitude of the Government in this context. Thus Sikh pockets have been established here and some of the Sikh settlers, who had sympathy with the militants, harboured them. The police allege that the sympathizers not only helped them financially, but also provided them food and places to hide.

3. When the militants in Punjab were put under pressure in 1984, they fled to U.P. Tarai. With the launching of 'Operation Rakshak' in Punjab in 1991, more militants took refuge here and since then there had been a rise in terrorist activities in Tarai.

4. During harvesting season March/October large combines come from Punjab to Tarai and the police suspects that some of these combines are used by militants to cross over to Tarai.

5. The rural areas in Tarai are sparsely populated owing to which the police stations are limited in number and are situated at a distance from each other. Thus the terrorist outfits got ample time and opportunity to promote their activities in this congenial environment.

6. The portion of Tarai bordering Nepal is a safe haven for the terrorists. Its length is about 795 km and except for the 200 km stretch in Pithoragarh district the rest is in the plains and easily accessible. Whenever pressure was mounted on the militants in Tarai, they crossed the border and escaped to Western Nepal.

7. The policy of the Panthic Committee has been to extend its activities outside Punjab, so that the attention of the Government is diverted and the overstretched police and paramilitary forces will have to operate in a larger area. As a sequel its would be easier for its protagonists to achieve the objective of Khalistan.

8. It seems that when the Bhartiya Janta Party was in power in U.P., special instruction were issued by the Pakistan Government to intensify terrorist activities here.

The militants have tried to propagate fanaticism by construing it as a social reform movement. To gain popularity they issued a code of conduct for the Sikhs and gave it wide publicity. The police officials allege that to intensify the publicity campaign, posters depicting the code of conduct were displayed outside Gurudwaras. It is also believed that the Code of Conduct issued by the militants was publicized during religious congregations. Some of the tenets of this code are:

1. It is essential for the Sikhs to become Armitdharis.
2. The Sikhs must abstain from having meat, liquor and other intoxicants.
3. Dowry is not to be given or accepted.
4. The marriage processions will not be attended by more than eleven persons.
5. The women should not wear any make up.
6. It is essential for Sikhs to sport turbans and to leave

their beard loose.

7. The Sikh girls as well as the ladies should cover their head with a 'dupatta' (unsewn cloth about two metres in length).
8. While attending school the boys should don white shirts, blacks trousers and a black turban. For girls it is essential to wear a black dupatta.
9. The priests must follow the teachings of Sikhism strictly.
10. The Sikhs should settle their disputes amongst themselves and avoid going to police stations or knock at the doors of the courts.

These spartan instructions were given to catch the imagination of common Sikhs and also to project a better image of the militants.

To understand militancy in Tarai, it is necessary to take into cognizance the July ordinance of 1959 aimed at evicting the Sikh settlers who had encroached upon forest and tribal land. In the ordinance the U.P. Government has labelled them as criminals. Even though land had been illegally occupied by other settlers also, only Sikhs were identified by the U.P. Government and blamed for this illegal occupation.

In the initial stages when Tarai was being settled, rules were not being strictly abided by. A sizeable number of settlers encroached upon the territory of the tribals. It was either through force or cajolery. According to the newspaper, 'Tribune', dated 5th October, 1981. "The Sikhs own most of the cultivated and culturable land in all the five tehsils of Tarai, most of it legally through duly registered deeds. But some of the land (about 80,000 acres, or 32,320 ha.) has been acquired by questionable means- for instance by persuading the Tharus and Buxas to sell, gift, mortgage or lease it through affidavits. In some cases the Sikhs entered into unlawful agreements with the tribals, stating that whatever the crop*, it would be shared on percentage basis. But the more belligerent amount the settlers from Punjab just roared in with their tractors on land which was not being cultivated". According to this article the Tarai tehsils had a total of 251 villages belonging to the Tharus and Buxas before the Sikhs moved in. In three decades after their arrival the latter literally grabbed 238 of these villages, leaving just 13 villages in the possession of the original owners. This statement however is an exaggerated version given by the U.P. Government.

The State Government asserts that the Sikhs settlers have browbeaten the tribals with a show of arms. According to the district administration the land occupied illegally by the new settlers is 1,70,000 ha. This data appears to be incorrect because there is a difference in the data provided by the U.P. Government and the district administration. This is probably owing to the fact that the revenue records have not been maintained appropriately by the concerned department in the wake of the drastic changes that have taken place owing the rapid development and the land ceiling laws. Any visitor to Khatima, Sitarganj, Bajpur and the interior villages cannot but notice the sharp contrast in the life style of the other settlers and the tribals. When the alienation of tribal land assumed serious proportions, the Social Welfare Directorate, Uttar Pradesh appointed a study team to probe into the living condition of the tribals. A detailed study report was prepared in 1978 which revealed that some 1300 settler families had grabbed land from the Tharu and Buxa tribals, who had owned it for a century or so.

Amir Hasan, the author of the book, 'The Buxas of Tarai', which was published in 1979 from B.R. Publishing Corporation,

---

** In this process known as share cropping the non-tribal took the land on 'theka' or contract for a specified period and gave a portion of the produce to the tribal. In practice when the lease period expired the lessees did not vacate the land. Subsequently the tribal had to run from pillar to post to get his land vacated, but did not succeed and was ultimately forced to give up the efforts.*

Delhi, has stated, "However, in the absence of any balanced, organized and planned programme for development of the tribals, their fortunes have been badly affected in course of the development process. Many outsiders, who were settled on vacant land and given funds and facilities to develop cultivation, did not confine themselves to the legitimate holdings. News spread that tribal and Government land could be encroached upon without fear of dispossession or penalty. The result: A large number of uninvited persons especially from Punjab and Haryana, namely relatives of earlier settlers swarmed into Tarai dispossessing the tribals from their ancestral land on a large scale, resulting in serious dislocation of tribal economy and disturbance of their social order". He further states that, "50% of the land-grabbers are Sikhs."

The administration those days being preoccupied with the development of Tarai just ignored the problem of land alienation. Moreover the tribals could not make their presence felt in the eyes of the administration and the police. The land-grabbers, the tribals claim behaved like an invading force. The tribals were taken by surprise and not being aware of the ways of their aggressive methods could not offer any resistance. Moreover being too feeble and peace loving they opted to retreat. In many cases the tribals admit that land was sold to the new settlers for a few bottles of liquor and they did not regret, because land was aplenty. In some cases they were made to put thumb impressions on papers when they were drunk.

The administration did not take any initiative in releasing the tribal land from illegal occupation. The officials advised them to approach the legal authorities and knock at the doors of the courts. Most of the tribals did not have the courage or money to file civil or criminal cases against the trespassers. In a few cases, where they mustered courage to go to the court of law, they did not succeed.

It is an established fact that tribal land has been occupied illegally by the new settlers. As already stated according to Amir Hsan, 50% of the land grabbers are Sikhs and the rest belong to other communities. During my survey I was also told by the tribals that not only people from Punjab, both Sikhs and Hindus, but residents of eastern U.P., released army personnel and people from other communities have also encroached upon their land. However the U.P. Government in an ordinance promulgated on 15th July, 1959 for ejectment from tribal land blamed only the Sikhs for illegal occupation and branded them as criminal tribes. They reacted sharply to the charges levelled against them and submitted a memorandum to the Prime minister on November 8th, 1959. Some portions of the memorandum are being cited below:

"On the 15th of July 1959 an ordinance has been promulgated by the U.P. Government to the effect that certain Punjabi communities may be evicted from their possession of lands in the districts of Shahjahanpur, Pilibhit, Naini Tal, Rampur and Bijnore, because they are dubbed as criminal tribes and are holding such land without title."

Tarai-Bhabhar is a long strip of land at the foot of the Himalayas running from Dehradun in the north-west to Assam in the north. Here we are concerned only with a narrow belt of the country immediately below the foot of the hills in Naini Tal, Pilibhit, Bijnore, Rampur and Shahjahanpur districts. It was a vast unproductive waste, overgrown with elephant grass and various kind of weeds, shrubs, reeds and trees. It was notorious for its most unhealthy malarial climate as also the number of tigers it harboured. Continuous heavy monsoons created ditches, ponds and swamps and these became the breeding grounds of mosquitoes causing malignant type of malaria. The condition here indeed has always been adverse to human habitation and agriculture. This area was then called the Andamans of U.P. Many times during the British regime, efforts were made to colonize it for agricultural purposes. All these efforts failed invariably. The scourge of malaria and vagaries of climate and soil could not be easily conquered and either the settlers had to perish in their attempts to reclaim land or they had to return to their homes ruined and broken hearted.

The scarcity of food caused by the Second World War compelled the Central and the Provincial Governments to speed up production of staple food-grains. Consequently the greatest and the biggest efforts were initiated in the Tarai region of Naini Tal district, Bijnore, Pilibhit and Rampur. In the beginning of 1947 the U.P. Government had requested the Punjab Government to send any number of peasants, landless cultivators and refugees who would like to settle in Tarai. Hence the sturdy and hard working cultivators of Punjab came forward, responded to this invitation and settled in Tarai and Bhabhar.

These cultivators were liberally allotted land by the Kham Superintendent incharge of Tarai and Bhabhar Government Estate, Haldwani in accordance with the provisions of the U.P. Tenancy Act 1939, vide G.B. Appendix No 2, Tarai and Bhabhar Kham Terms No.5687/IB-1212B/1947, dated 30.4.1948.

With the lapse of time there was a great rush for land and the lease was transferred from one cultivator to another. The Provincial Government issued instructions to the officer incharge of the Government Estate not to allot land to other than local residents. Thus the Punjabis started getting land from the allottees. Moreover most of the settlers having limited resources found themselves helpless after having sunk in this enterprise whatever they possessed and started looking for fresh capital and partners, so that allotted land started changing hands. The Kham Superintendent also allotted land in the forest areas, which were agricultural lands previously and if desired conferred hereditary 'rights.

In the year 1952-53 Mr. Bhawan Singh Bisht, the then Kham Superintendent, was transferred. He did not expect his transfer so soon and a large number of holdings occupied by such tenants remained unregulariged, on account of the above circumstances, the following categories of tenants emerged out:

1. Settlers who had joined hands with the original allottees and having invested their finances got their names registered in the revenue records. They have been in possession of the land for more than two years.
2. The allottees who didnot bring the land under cultivation strictly according to the terms and conditions to the allotment.
3. New cultivators who purchased land from the local Punjabi tenants and did not like to remain in the agricultural profession. This category is predominantly either agent proprietor or landless refugee tenants.
4. Those persons who reclaimed the fallow land without title and settled down on it and their names duly entered in the revenue records.
5. Such cultivators happened to be the accepted 'Assamis' (tenants) of the village Pradhan or headman.
6. Bonafide allotees who made extension in the land adjacent to their plots.
7. Cultivators who occupied the grants of land in the colonization area and were prepared to pay the outstanding Government dues.
8. Those cultivators who were settled in forest areas by the Kham Superintendent, but had no written record to support the allotment.

During the period of last five or six years more than five thousand notices of eviction were issued to the tenants by different courts of the districts under the U.P. Land Eviction Act 1953. Much time, money and energy was wasted and this created a sense of insecurity in the minds of a large section of tenants here. Food production was also adversely affected. The poor tenants who were hard hit by the Act 1953 resorted to a peaceful agitation and simultaneously made representations to the Revenue Minister who was prevailed upon to accept some of the categories of unauthorised occupants as tenants on payment of double rent, vide G.O. No. 580, dated

1.6.57.

Meanwhile a writ was filed in the Allahabad High Court against the Act. Thanks to the vigilance of the Allahabad High Court, the Act was declared ultra vires on 24.4.1959. This aggravated the situation still further and the State Government sharply reacted to it."

The priorities of the U.P. Government in the initial stages, when Tarai was being colonized, were to increase agricultural production and to solve the refugee problem. The Government invited people from Punjab for reclaiming Tarai. Those days when rules were not being strictly enforced, some of the settlers encroached upon tribal and Government land. There were people from different communities who were involved in this act of transgression, but the Sikhs alone were being blamed for this act. Moreover there is no denying the fact that it was owing to the Herculean efforts of the sturdy and hardworking Sikhs that Tarai was reclaimed. It is today one of the most prosperous agricultural belts in India the credit to a great extent goes to them.

The U.P. Government instead of appreciating their efforts labelled them as criminals.

The tenants who had been allotted land in Tarai before 1953 came under the purview of the U.P. Tenancy Act 1939 and had acquired hereditary rights over the land allotted to them. The Government had no legal ground to evict such tenants. It therefore explored new legal avenues of doing so and resorted to a special enactment to evict them. This brought forth the U.P. Land Eviction Act 1953. In continuation to this, the Government also issued a G.O.No. 408/IC-1422C/56, dated 7.4.1958 for intensifying further the eviction of these cultivators who were declared as unauthorized occupants under the aforesaid Act of 1953.

This G.O. implied, "The eviction cases should be disposed off with top speed and at least 36000 acres (1454.4 ha.) of land or near about should be resumed every year. The Government considers that there should be two whole time officers of the rank of Tahsildars exclusively for this work, but pending the consideration of this proposal the Board may impress upon the Deputy Commissioner concerned to ask the existing officers to carry out their duties in connection with eviction cases as expeditiously as possible."

It was perhaps on account of this deliberately inconsistent policy of the U.P. Government about eviction that the Planning Commission commented, "In some States, large scale ejectment of tenants and voluntary surrenders which are open to doubt as bonafide transactions have taken place."(Second Five Year Plan, 1956).

The U.P. Government did not succeed in its design owing to the writ filed in the Allahabad High Court subsequent to which the Act was declared ultra vires on 29.4.1959. The Government reacted sharply and in a haste managed to promulgate the U.P. Land Eviction and Recovery of Damages Ordinance 1959, which has a pronounced bias against the Sikh settlers. To add insult to injury, the eminent politician, Dr. Sampurnanand, the then Chief Minister, U.P., called the Sikhs as infiltrators. In a letter written to Sardar Hukum Singh, Deputy Speaker, Lok Sabha, New Delhi from Lucknow, dated 29.8.1959 he has stated, "They (Punjabis) infiltrated into the State uninvited and in many cases had absolutely no right to the land which they are occupying". The statement of Dr. Sampurnanand was contradicted by a member of the Legislative Council, U.P., Banwari Lal of the Praja Socialist Party. He stated in the Council, "The Government itself had invited these settlers to occupy the land and develop it when Pandit Govind Ballabh Pant was the Chief Minister here. It is strange that the Government is now going back on its promise to them". (U.P. Council Proceedings, 14th August, 1959).

A conference of the Sikhs under the auspices of the U.P. Sikhs Pratinidhi Board was held on 1st April 1960 at Rudrapur to protest against the action of the Government. The conference was presided over by Master Tara Singh, the then President of Shiromani Akali Dal and Shiromani Gurudwara Prabandhak Committee. In his presidential address he condemned the action of the Government and called upon the Sikhs to unite in the hour of distress. He stated, " We are today meeting under a dark shadow and the uppermost feeling that we all are carrying within our breasts concerns the plight of our brethren—— Through this cruel move, the Government of this State has not only thrown all considerations of human values to the winds, they have shocked conscientious citizens of the country by their narrow parochial spirit. Their brutal action in this matter has been so utterly disdainful of the basic fundamentals of the Indian constitution and the underlying spirit of national unity, that it deserves condemnation from all right thinking people.

"On the one hand, those at the helm of affairs swear by the high idealism of a casteless and classless society and stand for an indivisible India; on the other, as manifested through their actions they are clearly guided by a provincial and clannish narrow outlook."

"Visualize the picture of these vast tracts of land some years back before the sturdy Sikh farmers came forward to reclaim it. It was a vast jungle, unproductive, inaccessible, overgrown with weeds, shrubs, reeds and trees. The heavy monsoon added to the miseries of the new settlers as this area has been a perpetual home of malignant malaria as well as other deadly diseases and frequented by lions and tigers. The Sikhs settlers withstood all these natural calamities and hardships and turned this rugged tract into an area of smiling gardens with their own sweat and blood. And now, when their labour has begun to bear fruit, a thankless Government is asking them to quit."

"And adding insult to injury, this sturdy stock of Sikhs who reclaimed the land have been categorized as 'criminal tribes of erstwhile Punjab'. Is it not a heinous crime against all sense of democratic traditions to draw out such distinctions and to discriminate one citizen from another. —— Therefore, such a discriminatory treatment meted out to the Sikh settlers in Tarai, borne out of Hindu imperialism of Uttar Pradesh Governmental high-ups will only weaken our national solidarity."

"The Khalsa took its birth to defend the weak and the oppressed and we are not going to stand any such repression based on such communal or provincial considerations, resulting in the ruin of our brethren in any part of India."

Various efforts to check land alienation have failed because of politics and other factors. In June 1981 an ordinance was promulgated again which aimed at the eviction of unauthorized occupants of land belonging to the tribals and this brought the Sikh settlers and others in direct confrontation with the U.P. Government. The ordinance promulgated ostensibly in pursuance of the Prime Minister's resolve to undo the injustice done to the scheduled tribes and scheduled castes, generated social tensions. There were apprehensions that attempts to dispossess the settlers of the land, the ownership of which vests with the tribals according to revenue records, may lead to clashes.

The June 3rd ordinance is in fact an amendment in the land law rule. It bans the sale of tribal land and empowers district officials to prosecute illegal occupants of tribal land. As the objects and reasons explain, the bill seeks to remedy the disturbed social equilibrium in the Tarai region. The ordinance gave wide ranging powers to the district authorities to evict those who had grabbed the land of the tribals. Reoccupation of the land was made a cognisable and non-bailable offence. It was further made punishable with imprisonment for a term which could extend to three years and also with fine which could extend to Rs. 3000.

The settlers from Punjab as well as from other States, panicked. The ordinance forced them to set up the Krishak Sangh as a spokesman of the Sikhs and others. But while the Revenue Department recognized the Rana Parishad of the Tharu tribals, it did not grant recognition to the Krishak Sangh as a spokesman of the new settlers. The refusal to grant recognition to the Sangh was obviously a clear move to prevent Sikhs from joining hands with other communities and seeking political patronage.

In a way the move paid off and no party actively associated itself with the Tarai Krishak Sangh. The Sikhs owed allegiance to the Akali Dal (Longowal) the settlers from Bengal looked upto the C.P.M., while those from Bihar and Eastern U.P. had the support of the C.P.I.

Taking advantage of the situation, the authorities evicted early in August 29, families in five villages. Land measuring about 24.5 ha. was resorted to 40 tribal families. The villages involved were Kushalpur, Khukrela, Gurkhura,Chanmola and Govindpur.

But the eviction was a sham operation. In the evicted areas the Tahsildar turned up with the tribals together with some policemen and told the illegal occupants to vacate the land. Subsequently a tribal meekly came forward and gave his thumb impression on certain documents. It was then announced that the land had been legally transferred to the tribal and after the announcement the officials left. As soon as party moved out the tribals were forced to leave the land either through force or cajolery.

Discreet enquiries made in the Revenue Department revealed that the State Government itself had not covered a major flaw in the ordinance which made the eviction eventually a farce. The ordinance is silent on what has to be done to the dwelling units of non-tribal dwellers on land belonging to the tribals in case of eviction. The tribals in the situation would find themselves in possession of their land with families of big farmers right in their middle with their farm houses. Moreover the district authorities suffered from a handicap. No proper force had been made available to them to carry out the eviction operations.

The Ministry of Agriculture it seems had forewarned the State Government of the eventuality, but the Government did not take cognisance of it. Moreover the experts in the Ministry of Agriculture also felt that transferring of land to the tribals those days would lead to wild growth in Tarai again because firstly the Tharus and Buxas according to them have no love for the land and secondly they are averse to modern methods of agriculture. However this is not true, they do lack enterprise but if given the opportunity and proper incentive they can work hard.

Both the tribals and the Sikhs are outsiders. The former fled from Rajashthan as per their tradition, a long time ago to escape the Mughals, while the latter came to this malarial infested jungle area at the invitation of the then Chief Minister of U.P. Responding to the call, farmers from Punjab, Bengal, Bihar and other parts of the country came virtually running. The biggest group came form Punjab since partition had deprived many Punjabis of their fertile lands in West Punjab-their principal means of livelihood. These sturdy farmers had still plenty of will to work with their hands rather than languish as beggars in refugee camps. The then ruling Congress(I) was apparently not united on the issue. Even while the then Revenue Minister of U.P., Baijanath Kureel reiterated the Government's resolve to restore land to the tribals, Ranjit Singh Sethi, a Sikh minister of State, who was later dropped from the ministry, openly announced at a meeting in Khatima, "Mrs. Gandhi has stayed the operation of the ordinance". Inquiries at the District Magistrate's office and the Kumaon Commissionery show that there was no such directive from Delhi.

The Sikhs on the other hand are in a defiant mood. They claim that the revenue records are defective and as such cannot form the basis for dispossessing them. Some settlers also state that several tribals had of their own volition sold land to them. How could the Government thus invalidate such transactions ? The Sikh leaders who have been living in Tarai for the past four decades, contend that the Government should regularize the occupation of the settlers. They argue that the Sikh settlers had reclaimed the inhospitable land after undergoing considerable risks. The Government should thus reward them for their labour.

There seems to be an element of truth in their claim. Govind Ballabh Pant, a shrewd politician, knew that none else than the farmers from Punjab could clear the region of wild growth and forest and make it cultivable - a stupendous task which the tribals had not been able to accomplish. His assessment was correct, about a decade later in 1957, Bajpur,Sitarganj, Gadarpur, Khitima and Kichha tehsils stood in the forefront in agricultural output.

By and large the Sikh settlers are in no mood to surrender the land. This is evident from the fact that whenever an eviction has been carried out, the Sikhs who claim to be the rightful owners, have re-occupied the land as soon as the police and officers were withdrawn. Moreover some of the Sikhs are armed to the teeth. They have weapons of almost every type which are enough to scare the tribals.

In spite of the diverse groups of people settled in the Tarai region, there is no doubt about the dominance of the Punjabis, especially the Sikhs. They are rich and their affluence has incurred the jealousy of other communities. However the fact remains that some Sikh and other settlers have illegally occupied tribal land, but the results of the Government's reprisal were foiled mostly by the Sikhs. They have developed a good network of road transportation, small industries and servicing industries. As a result of all these developments, the Tarai and Bhabhar region is humming with activity. The mosquitoes, wild animals and bandits of yester years have disappeared and there are thousands of hectares of lush green land, growing paddy wheat and high yielding variety surgarcane of excellent quality.

In the wake of these developments the tribals have become a victim of the land greed of the new settlers. Moreover, almost total exclusion of the tribals from the fruits of Tarai development has meant the loss of the most important economic outlet for the common people within the region. This has heightened their sense of helplessness. The Buxas and Tharus have no leaders or organization which can fight for their rights or look after their welfare. No doubt the Buxas have formed a Buxa Parishad, but it is absolutely inactive and inert. The Tharus on the other hand, have formed the Rana Parishad. In private conversation, several Tharus are extremely critical of the Rana Parishad. Their contention is that an individual family has formed this Parishad and it does not care for the general welfare of the Tharus.

Even as the controversy rages, curiously no political party has taken any initiative to sort out the problem. This is because almost all political parties and their popular leaders today get strong ballot and financial support as well as muscle power from the new settlers to help their cause of election, while these tribal communities have none to offer or no capacity to negotiate their offer of ballots. The leaders have failed to organize the tribals under a commonly acceptable popular leadership of their own community. The failure may be explained not only by the limited character of their organizations, but also by the weak financial base. Politicians have rightly assessed the divisions within tribal groups and obviously they favour the land grabbers which have both force and guile to support the politicians.

The ruling B.S.P. and S.P. combine in U.P. which was supposed to champion the cause of the downtrodden no interest in the tribals of Tarai. The Congress (I) is silent on the issue, though its tilt is towards the new settlers. The Bhartiya Janta Party and the Janta Dal are scrupulously avoiding taking sides. The Communists find themselves in a curious situation. An eminent Marxist leader, who is a big farmer himself, openly champions the cause of the new settlers. The Marxist leader contends that the ordinance is undemocratic. The so called kulaks in the Tarai region have their biggest champion in this Marxist leader. The C.P.I. has its own problems. Revenue records show that two prominent members of the district C.P.I. own over 80 ha. of land. An important C.P.I. leader here allegedly had some 63 ha. of farmland registered in the name of his pet dog.

But today the problem of infringement by settlers on tribal land and forest land, according to Government records has taken a complex form. Be that as it is the essentially agrarian problem has acquired political overtones with the circulation of the Khalisatan map, drawn by the Canadian Sikhs showing the Tarai region as a part of Khalistan. " We will give up our life, not our land". This forceful statement of Sikh farmers sums up their defiant mood. Given the rigid stance of the tribals and the Sikh settlers, the State Government has a tough problem on its hands and it remains to be seen what transpires.

In the initial stages some Sikhs in Tarai were swayed by the terrorist ideology especially those Sikhs who had been issued eviction orders for occupying tribal land illegally and some who had marginal holdings. After Operation Blue Star in 1984 as mentioned earlier, several terrorists fled Punjab and took refuge in U.P. Tarai. The same year it was reported that a training camp for terrorists had been started by the former head constable of Punjab Police, Sewa Singh in the forests of Hatiya Sot in Pauri Garhwal. Subsequently in 1984 six incidents of terrorism were reported in Tarai. In 1985 the number plummeted down to six again. Concomitantly with the rise of militancy in Punjab, its repercussions were felt in U.P. Tarai also. The frequency of incidents increased here also, details of which are cited below:

Year	Incidents reported
1987	10
1988	22
1989	29
1990	40
1991	182
1992	294

Source : U.P. Police.

The steep rise in the number of incidents during the years 1991 and 1992 was a result of the pressure the Punjab militants were put to with the deployment of army there. Subsequent to which several terrorists from Punjab took refuge in different states. The nature of criminal activities of the terrorists as reported by U.P. Police during these years is given below:

S.No.	Name of crime	Year 1991	Year 1992
1.	Murder	66	55
2.	Bank dacoity	4	3
3.	Arms dacoity	17	8
4.	Capturing of vehicles	12	12
5.	Looting of petrol pumps1	-	
6.	Kidnappings	18	27
7.	Bomb explosions	7	9
8.	Extortion	2	-
9.	Encounters	47	85
10.	Miscellaneous	8	95
	Total	182	294

Between 1984 and 1992, 583 people were killed by terrorists in the State. Amongst the killed 65 were policemen, 82 terrorists, 99 Sikhs and 337 non-Sikhs. However the gory killings witnessed in Rudrapur then in Naini Tal Tarai have been the worst hitherto. The militants exploded a bomb during the Dusshera festival when maximum people had assembled to witness the Ramleela celebration on the evening of 6th October 1991. In this blast 44 people were killed and 159 sustained serious injuries. Subsequently there were bomb blasts in Haldwani and Kashipur.

The comparative data of terrorist activities between 1984 and 1992 as furnished by the U.P. Police has been detailed below:

Nature of crime	1984	1985	1996	1987	1988	1989	1990	1991	1992	Total
Murder	-	-	1	4	4	3	19	66	55	552
Bank dacoity	3	1	-	-	1	1	-	3	3	12
Attempts to	-	-	1	-	1	1	2	1	-	6

loot banks										
Looting of arms	-	1	-	1	1	8	-	17	8	36
Capturing of Vehicles	-	-	1	-	1	5	1	12	12	32
Looting of petrol Pumps	-	-	-	1	3	2	-	1	-	7
Other lootings	-	1	-	-	3	1	-	-	4	9
Kidnappings	-	-	-	-	1	1	18	26	46	
Explosions	-	-	9	-	1	1	3	7	8	29
Extortions	-	-	-	-	-	1	-	2	-2	3
Encounters with attempts to kill	-	1	-	2	2	2	10	47	84	148
Miscellaneous	3	2	3	2	5	4	3	8	95	125
Total	6	15	6	10	22	29	40	182	295	605

The terrorist activists in the last few years clearly indicate that the militants have been able to organize themselves in U.P. Tarai and are being trained and guided by terrorist outfits in Punjab. These extremists are also laundering arms and ammunitions to them. In the terrorist prone areas they are trying to cajole and allure the people to their ideology. Together with this to win the support of the local population they are creating a psychological fear through terrorism and the Police Department feels that they have succeeded in their objective.

From the information gathered by the Police Department it appears that the militants are armed with latest weapons like mortars, rocket launchers, automatic weapons and the lurking fear is that they have entered into a conspiracy for liquidating important people, policemen as well as mass killings. It is therefore felt that a vigil should be maintained throughout the year for averting such mishappenings and the police force should be increased. To support their view point the Police Department has furnished the following details of different districts in U.P. which were affected by terrorism and have been declared as sensitive areas:

Name of the district	Area in square km	Population	Sikh Population	Police force	Number of Gurudwaras	Number of Sikhs with licensed weapons.
Naini Tal	6794	1,200.000	125,000	2153	148	1247
Pilibhit	3499	1,100,000	100,000	1302	110	1500
Shahjahanpur	4575	1,700,000	30,000	1809	110	30
Bareilly	4120	2,400,000	30,000	2721	14	250
Moradabad	5967	3,500,000	12,000	3270	25	90
Rampur	2367	1,300,000	45,000	1423	100	15
Bijnor	4849	2,100,000	30,000	2034	73	300
Dehradun	3088	900,000	0,000	1641	47	79
Pauri Garhwal	5440	700,000	1,200	-	8	70
Lakhimpur Kheri	7650	2,100,000	38,000	1681	103	977
Haridwar	2460	1,100,000	6390	1119	31	183
Muzaffarnagar	4176	2,800,000	1,735	1618	61	122
Sharanpur	3200	2,300,000	15,277	1913	49	58

The major militant outfits which are active in the Tarai region of Naini Tal are:

S.No.	Name of Outfit	Ring leader	Area of operation in Tarai (Police Stations)
1.	Bhindranwale Tiger Force of Khalistan (Chhanda)	Satnam Singh Chinna.	Sitarganj, Kashipur, Khatima, Nanakmatta.
2.	Bhindranwale Tiger Force of Khalistan.	Sukhdeo Singh Chinna	Khatima, Sitarganj, Nanakmatta.
3.	Khalistan Commando Force (Panjwar group)	Balvinder Singh Kali.	Kashipur, Jaspur, Ramnagar.
4.	Khalistan Commando Force (Zafarwal group)	Kulwant Singh, alias Kanta.	
5.	Bhindranwale Saffron Tiger Force of Khalistan.	Swaran Singh Jaiwanda	Rudrapur, Sitarganj Kichha.
6.	Khalistan Liberation Force.	Surjeet Singh alias Gurumeet.	Jaspur, Ramnagar, Kashipur, Bajpur,
7.	Khalistan Liberation Army.	Dilip Singh alias Dipa	Jaspur, Ramnagar, Bajpur, Kashipur.

Besides Naini Tal Tarai, the operational area of the above mentioned militant groups extends to other districts of U.P.

like Pilibhit, Shahjahanpur, Bareilly, Lakhimpur Kheri, Bijnor, Haridwar, Rampur and Dehradun.

The U.P. Police claims that apart from the above mentioned terrorist outfits there are some other groups as well. They do not stay permanently in Tarai. After indulging in one or two activities, they either escape to Punjab or become inactive for a certain period.

The activities of the militant outfit, Khalistan Commando Force, Zaffarwal group have been reduced in Naini Tal Tarai after the elimination of Randhir Singh, alias Bijli alias Chhotu.Similarly the group Babbar Khalsa International has been flushed out from Tarai after the killing of its leader Jaswinder Singh, alias Sher Singh Ghora and the hard core militant, Sukhwinder Singh, alias Pola.

The following table gives details of the arms confiscated from militants in different districts of U.P. between 1984-1992:

District	AK 47	AK 56	Rifles 315 bore	SLR	303	Guns DBBL bore	SBBL	Pistols Factory	Local made	Revolvers made
Bijnor	3	3	3	1	4	3	4	2	1	4
Naini Tal	7	4	2	1	3	4	1	-	3	3
Bareilly	-	-		-	1	-	4	1	-	1
Shahjahanpur	2	3	-	1	1	-	-	-	296	2
Pilibhit	1	6	2	1	-	3	2	-	-	3
Moradabad	-	-	-	1	-	-	-	-	-	2
Rampur	1	3	-	3	1	3	2	-	2	5
Dehradun	1	1	-	-	-	1	2	4	-	2
Lakhimpur Kheri	1	-	4	3	-	2	1	1	1	4
Total	**16**	**20**	**12**	**12**	**10**	**16**	**16**	**10**	**306**	**23**

Militant tactics :

The following terror tactics were adopted by the militants in Tarai :

1. Murders.
2. Economic crimes
3. Perpetrating fanaticism in the name of reformation to win the confidence of people.
4. Demoralizing the police force and to render the administration ineffective.

The different forms of killings as adopted by militants to achieve their objectives are:

1. Killings with an objective.
2. Random killings.
3. Mass killings.
4. Liquidation of important people.

In the initial stage the militants resorted to economic crimes like looting of banks, kidnappings and extortion. The bank dacoities were committed mostly in banks situated in rural areas, but a substantial amount could not be procured from these banks. Subsequently they concentrated more on kidnappings for ransom and extortion. Incidents of extorting money from the Sikh farmers as well as businessmen have come to light according to the Police Department. It is also being alleged by the police officials that the Sikh farmers were made to part with one tenth of their agricultural produce to the militants.

To demoralize the police force and to make them ineffective they were ambushed and killed. In 1991 the extremists organized 23 raids on the police force and killed 30 police officials. In 1992 as many as 18 police men were killed. Apart from the attacks on the police, the movements of the police officials were monitored and mines were laid on their routes. They also attempted to create an environment of fear by sending anonymous letters to officials. In consonance with their terrorist tactics the militants kidnapped a Sub Divisional Magistrate and a Lekhpal (revenue official) from Rampur district on 26th December 1990, though later they were released.

The militants wanted to create communal disharmony between the Hindus and the Sikhs in Tarai. They advocated and tried to instil a feeling amongst the Sikhs that they were different from the Hindus. To win over the Sikhs they warned the administration that if their brethren had to face any repression in Tarai, the consequences would be serious. However, when they resorted to indiscriminate killings of innocent people they did not distinguish between the Hindus and Sikhs.

In the beginning the police was caught unawares and the militants had a definite upper edge. Moreover the police, which is essentially equipped to handle law and order situation not terrorism, could not contain militancy in Tarai. Some other factors also contributed in fomenting militancy in the region. The police in the initial phase of terrorism had neither cared to instil a sense of security in the masses nor tried to secure their cooperation. On the contrary their handling alienated the Sikh masses. They were victims of police high handedness. Most of them having been in the area for over four decades, had little to do with the terrorists, yet they were also subjected to humiliation. The militants resorted to indiscriminate killings, looting and, at a later stage kidnappings for ransom and extortion. Soon the people realized that the terrorists in Tarai were not fighting for Khalistan. Their demand for a separate identity was only a cover for extortion, abduction and loot and their avarice had been whetted by the economic prosperity of the region. Moreover operating under forest cover with the vast expanse of land in Tarai and hills of the region was an added advantage.

The so called militancy in Tarai gave the small time criminals an opportunity to become heroes by projecting themselves as militants. It also helped people to settle their personal scores. A glaring example of personal vendetta which was being misconstrued as a case of militancy is that of Gurbachan Lal Sharma* and Sardar Cheema. Pandit Gurbachan Lal, alias Pandit a big farmer from Bajpur, who wielded both financial and political clout, was made a Special Police Officer (SPO) by the local police in 1992, though it is alleged he had a criminal record and the Police Department was privy to it. Sharma exploited his new status by combining it with the anti-terrorist rhetoric to settle old scores with some of the Sikh farmers.

He revelled in the fact that he had killed Shamsher Singh, a younger brother of the highly decorated Major General Shubeg Singh, hero of the Bangladesh War of 1971 and subsequently a very close associate of Bhindranwale. Shubeg Singh was also killed in the Operation Blue Star. Shamsher Singh had been murdered by Pandit's musclemen several years ago, long before Shubeg Singh had turned towards Bhindranwale.

Pandit like the terrorists was also generating a feeling of animosity between the Hindus and the Sikhs and some fanatic Hindus did rally round him. For some time he was projected as a hero by the fanatics and it is alleged that funds were collected and given to him for buying arms and ammunition. While Pandit was basking in this new found glory he received an extortion demand of Rs. 500,000 from the terrorists in the beginning of 1992. Sharma refused to yield to the terrorist demand.

They retaliated by ambushing a car coming from Sharma's house in which two persons were killed.

The situation however took a volatile turn on the morning of April 27th when the terrorists kidnapped seven persons in Garappu, a village in Tarai, ostensibly for a ransom. Amongst the kidnapped were Pandit's son and nephew together with five industrialists from the area. The terrorists on discovering

---

* *And the nemesis is the murder of Pandit- allegedly by the Cheema group on 7th February 1995 at 9.30 am.*

the identity of Pandit's relations killed them and released the rest on payment of a heavy ransom on May 2nd.

Pandit though unaware that his son and nephew had been killed retailated by attacking the paper mill of his neighbour and arch political rival Sardar Cheema the same evening. It is alleged that Cheema had links with the militants and had tipped them about the anti-terrorist stand of Pandit. It is also rumoured that he used to extend pecuniary assistance to the militants and to settle old scores with his rival got his son and nephew murdered.

Pandit picked up Cheema's younger son Gurdayal Singh from the paper mill in the presence of several people with the intention of using him as a bargaining chip with the terrorists. Some Sikhs protested by lodging a FIR against Pandit. It is believed that in the meantime Pandit came to know about his relations' deaths and to avenge their murder killed Cheema's son. Some believe that he died during torture and his body was found the next morning in a field.

Ten days later at the bhog ceremony of Gurdayal Singh, several prominent Sikh leaders openly criticized the police inaction and condemned the partisan attitude of the Deputy Inspector General of Police. The police responded by implicating Cheema in terrorist reprisals and registered a case of TADA against him.

On September 23rd, a Maruti gypsy was blown up in Bajpur in which six policemen were killed. Concomitantly the police arrested six prominent Sikh citizens under TADA and accused them of master minding the operation. Prominent among them was Sardar Harcharan Singh Brar, aged 75 who had been operated upon for by-pass surgery six months back.

In this case the police initially said that these arrests were made at Deen Dayal Bhullar's farm on 24th September, where they were allegedly celebrating the blast with the dreaded terrorist Jaivanda. On second thought after realizing that Bhullar had been provided police security, the police amended its statement to shift the site of the celebration to Sardar Mohan Singh's farm.

Again according to the police these six were accompanied by six terrorists in the festivities. The terrorist made good their escape in the ensuing firing that followed after the police swoop. It is intriguing that no one was injured in the firing and that there were no traces of the salvos on the boundary wall. It is notable that Sardar Mohan Singh's farm is having a 2.2. m security wall in which the escape route is only the solitary gate. With the load of arms and ammunition the terrorist are reported to carry, it would not have been easy for any of them to escape uninjured by scaling this high wall in the face of police bullets.

The police on the other hand alleges that they cannot be blamed totally for their highhandedness. In the beginning they claim that some Sikhs in Tarai had sympathy with the terrorists. They considered them as their Saviours and were swayed by the Khalistan movement. Some of them even harbourd terrorists and used them to settle their personal scores and long standing disputes. Many a times the militants took refuge in forest houses (Jhalas) which were owned by some Rai Sikhs and have all modern amenities. The militants relaxed here during the inactive period and whenever the police approached these jhalas, they were forewarned by the Rai Sikhs from a distance.

The following month, on October 20th, five persons were killed near Belwal Spinning Mills in Naini Tal district, near the Jim Corbett National Park. The next day Pandit and his sons stormed a courtroom and went on a shooting spree in which four people lost their lives. A leading social worker of the area, Gurunarain Singh Bhatti sustained serious injuries. Pandit was finally arrested, but only after the Punjab Chief Minister, Beant Singh called up his counterpart those days, Kalayan Singh.

Rivalry among the numerous mafia gangs operating in the Tarai region in Uttar Pradesh added a new dimension to terrorism in the area. Feuds were settled in the only way known to the mafiosi ruthlessly. Retribution was frequently resorted to. The groups had rather well defined areas of operation-land grabbing, hooch, forest produce, and so on. But when their paths crossed, as they inevitably did, the balance of terror where once maneaters prowled, only the law of the jungle- the survival of the fittest prevailed.

The situation however has changed today. Militancy has been brought under control, though it lingers in the minds of the local people.

That the police have got an upper hand in Tarai since 1994 is evident from the fact that 12 policemen were killed in 1992, this number came down to two in 1993 and in 1994 no such incident occurred. Similarly the number of civilians killed in militant violence also came down form 68 in 1991 to 47 in 1992 and five in 1993. In 1994 no such incident was reported. The list of the dreaded militants who were killed by the U.P. Police in The Sub-Himalayan Tarai is detailed below:

S.No.	Name & Address of the militant	Year	Police station where killed
1.	Sarvjeet Singh, S/o Shri Iqbal Singh, Lalangalean, Batala, Punjab.	1989	Kichha
2.	Dharam Singh, alias, Dharam, S/o Shri Pyara Singh, Police Station, Kastival, Batala, Gurudaspur, Punjab.	1989	Kichha
3.	Unknown militant	1990	Bajpur

4.	Lakhwinder Singh Cheema	1991	Haldwani
5.	Balwinder Singh, alias Binda, Police Station, Marori Bilsanchha, Pilibhit, U.P.	1991	Jaspur
6.	Bassan Singh, alias Zafarwal.	1992	Jaspur
7.	Unknown militant	1992	Ramnagar
8.	Balkar Singh, Police, Station Ajitpur, Kashipur.	1992	Kashipur
9.	Joginder Singh, S/o Shri Kundan Singh, Police Station, Mitawala.	1992	Jaspur
10.	Yadvendra Singh, alias Yadu.	1992	Khatima
11.	Paramjeet Singh, alias Pamma.	1992	Khatima
12.	Amarjeet Singh, alias Amba, Police Station Betkheri, Bajpur	1992	Consumed cyanide capscule at Hapur in U.P. while being chased by the Naini Tal police.
13.	Gurbachan Singh, alias Gora, S/o Shri Trilok	1992	Haldwani

	Singh, Police Station, Hayatnagar, Khajuria, District, Rampur, U.P.		
14	Two unknown militants killed in a bomb blast during police chase.	1992	
15.	Asar Singh, S/o Shri Trilok Singh, Police Station, Betkheri, Bajpur.	1992	Bajpur
16.	An unknown militant	1992	Haldwani
17.	Onkar Singh, S/o Shri Balbir Singh, Police Station, Sidhara, Bilaspur, Rampur, U.P.	1994	Bajpur
18.	Heera Singh, alias Sahab Singh, Patrampur, Jaspur.	1994	Bilaspur, (Rampur)
19.	Nirmaljeet Singh, alias Nimma.	1994	Bilaspur

Source : Naini Tal Police

During the period 1984 to 1994, 20 militants were killed by the U.P. Police in Naini Tal Tarai in 62 encounters while 20 policemen died in action. The police also rounded up 140 suspects either for terrorist activities or for having links with the militants. The catchet of arms and ammunition confiscated by U.P. Police in Naini Tal Tarai during the years, 1992-93 was one of the factors responsible for containing terrorism:

S.No.	Name of the weapon	1992	1993
1.	AK 47 rifle	1	1
2.	AK 56 rifle	3	-
3.	Assault rifle	4	-
4.	Carbine	1	1
5.	Rifle 315	2	4
6.	Rifle 303 bore	3	4
7.	Rifle 300 bore	1	-
8.	Revolver	5	2
9.	SBBL gun	1	9
10.	DDBL gun	4	1
11.	Rocket launcher	1	-
12.	Bombs	6	1
13.	RDX	-	20 kg
14.	Thirty spring rifle-	1	

Source : Naini Tal Police

In 1994 two AK 56 rifles, one 303 bore rifle, one bomb and one S.J.R. was seized.

The police also tried to win the confidence of the local populace, especially the Sikhs. The strategy paid dividends and militancy has been checked to a great extent. The police has been able to flush out almost all the major outfits active in the Tarai region. Though a few might still have escaped the police dragnet, so far they are inoperative. However notwithstanding these achievements of the local police, a very senior police officials feels that constant vigil has yet to be maintained to prevent future regrouping of the militants in the region.

Based on extensive field study of the area this writer feels that in the past when the area was free from terrorism some of the police officials minted money from some Sikhs and small time criminals by threatening them with arrest under

TADA. The blackmailing attitude of these police officials and nonchalance of political parties have fomented religious schism, which in future is likely to pose a greater threat than terrorism. Tarai was known for its religious harmony, but in the recent past both Hindu and Sikh diehards have started fanning communal feelings. Some bloody incidents in the past clearly indicate the new type of polarization, ramifications of which have not been clearly understood. Together with this the combination of crime has had the effect of reducing this once peaceful territory with a cosmopolitan character to a communal tinder-box. Some of the police and paramilitary forces frequently working at cross purposes used the National Security Act and the Terrorist and Disruptive Activities Prevention Act rather indiscriminately. Small wonder that when militancy was at its peak, some Sikhs had begun moving out of the region. It is intriguing that no political or social leader condemned terrorism in Tarai. Had the social and political leaders come out to stem this trend, it could have been halted much before.

Apart from the U.P. Police, the Special Task Force, B.S.F., C.R.P.F., Naga Police and the U.P. Armed Constabulary was deployed in the area to combat terrorism. However, there was no coordination between these forces. Their energies were being frittered away for the lack of such coordination. Also there was no common policy to achieve the objective. Moreover ego clashes among the officers of these forces were so pronounced that they had started percolating down to the rank and file level.

Ideally there should have been an IG Operations, staying with the forces in the terrorist infested area itself. No doubt the I.G. of PAC posted at Moradabad, in addition to his regular duties had been given this charge. But his regular duties kept him as busy that he had little time to look into this aspect.

The U.P. Police as before is ill-armed as compared to the militants and its counterpart in Punjab. This had an adverse effect on the psyche of the local population. The police stations are ill-equipped. Even the jeeps are not in good working condition. Moreover the promotion avenues are few. A number of appointments at the middle level have been guided by politics. The police officials often complain that they become a target of criticism when they falter, but when they achieve something for the society, their efforts go unnoticed. Even when they die in action their sacrifice goes unobserved, unheard of and unsung.

Militancy cannot be contained by force only. It requires mustering the good will of the locals. Of late the U.P. Police has made commendable efforts in this direction. However the local youth should also be taken into confidence, since the militants have a potential to win over the local unemployed youth and lead them astray. Already there have been reports of their having engaged Buxas, a primitive tribe and local youths for their errands. Such youths instead of being allowed to be a tool in the hands of the militants, can be drafted for the Special Task Force specially raised for this purpose and to maintain a vigil against the revival of militancy in Tarai. Being thoroughly acquainted with the people as also the topography of the place they can be of immense help. Instead the Force is primarily comprised of personnel seconded by the U.P. Police or PAC and as such are susceptible to the weaknesses of the system.

Beside the police and para-military forces, other departments also have to play a vital role in the crusade to eradicate terrorism. In Tarai at present all criminal activity revolves around illicit timber trade and encroachment upon Government land. Most of the encroachment is either on forest land or on river beds. The people involved in illegal timber trade or encroachment on Government land have at times harboured the militants. Thus the departments like Revenue, Forest, Irrigation etc. should also help the police in curbing such activities.

9
An Overview

As the end of the Second World War was in sight the question of the demobilized military personnel began to loom large. At the instance of the Government a detailed topographical contoured survey of Tarai and Bhabhar areas of Uttar Pradesh was undertaken and a scheme prepared for the colonization of ex-servicemen there, following which released military personnel were allotted land in the villages around Bajpur, Kashipur, Haldwani and Kaladhungi etc.

Additionally with the end of the Second World War, the scarcity of food compelled the Central and State Governments in India to take up urgent measures to increase production of staple food grains. Consequently herculean efforts were initiated in the Tarai and Bhabhar region, and land, hitherto under forests, was allotted to different communities for agriculture.

The Government was trying to cope with this situation that India achieved Independence and with it came the partition. Thus in and after 1947, a wave of refugees from West Punjab (now in Pakistan) and East Pakistan (now Bangladesh) came to settle down in the Sub-Himalayan region of Tarai and Bhabhar. With these new settlers a new era of permanent settlement dawned in Tarai and Bhabhar. This besides resulting into shrinkage of forests also meant its denudation.

To give a fillip to agricultural production, dams and barrages were constructed in this region which led to further destruction of forests. The area of sal forests felled for the construction of these reservoirs was 20696.46 ha.

Further a large area was deforested in Sub-Himalayan Tarai for Shardasagar and Lohia Power House. Large areas of the project sites are still under illegal encroachment and serving as the nuclei of destruction of adjoining forest areas and harbouring of criminals.

Today the whole region is one of the most prosperous agricultural belts in India, but it is at the cost of depletion of thousands of hectares of dense forest. The negative effects of deforestation in the sub-montane forests of Tarai and Bhabhar are being felt in the montane and sub-tropical forests of Himalaya region also, because most of the supply of timber and fuel for the population in the foothills is being provided from the rapidly diminishing forests of the Lesser Himalayan region. Hitherto on the basis of the data available, it can be concluded that a vast area of forest has been cleared owing to the extension of land under agriculture. The agricultural table given below of the 10 blocks of Tarai and Bhabhar, wherein agriculture accounted for negligible area prior to its colonization vividly indicates the present day dilemma of agricultural land nibbling at the forest:

Block	Total area in ha.	Area under cultivation in ha.	Forests in ha.	Waste land in ha.
Kotabagh	13347	5883	126	3581
Haldwani	152558	12099	208	2121
Ramnagar	14430	11567	267	1417
Kashipur	18517	16383	222	8
Jaspur	23229	17742	571	1654
Bajpur	28646	23405	547	1548
Gadarpur	23326	19160	474	2189
Rudrapur	31153	25597	134	1104
Khatima	35157	26429	1885	3159
Sitarganj	33244	24609	3404	2423
Total	236307	182874	8838	20241

With cultivation surrounding the forests everywhere, the Forest Department claims, it is difficult to control illicit fellings in the remaining forests, owing to the deep rooted traditional beliefs of the villagers that the forests are primarily intended for fulfilling their requirements. Moreover, illegal timber trade has become a lucrative and regular business. The data available of illicit felling it given in the next page.

Year	Illicit felling number of trees	Fine realized in rupees	Value in rupees of seized timber
1985-86	1,600,000	540,000	1,114.600
1986-87	1,500,000	500,000	1,077,000
1987-88	2,600,000	500,000	1,300,000
1988-89	5,750,000	400.000	2,000,000
1989-90	6,676,711	1,066,753	2,000,000

Source : Forest Department, Western Circle, Naini Tal

The data of illicit timber seized in the financial year from April 1993 to March 1994 is detailed below:

Month	Value in rupees of of seized timber	Month	Value in rupees of seized timber
April	2,339,868	October	271,671
May	4,965,816	November	536,730
June	2,335,076	December	659,816
July	2,718,290	January	457,669
August	1,811,175	February	993,364
September	336,529	March	800,536
Total		**18,226,540**	

This is however just a tip of the iceberg. Curiously enough the forest and the police departments, which have been able to apprehend a few of the culprits, are unable to check the thefts, moreover the fires in the timber godowns during the last decade have raised doubts and controversies regarding the cause of these fires.

In private conversation during the field survey I was told that atleast 35 to 40 truck-loads of illicitly felled timber passes illegally through the main check post in Tarai and Bhabhar everyday and each truck contains atleast 80 to 120 quintals of timber. The timber which is pilfered is mostly khair (Acacia catechu). In Tarai and Bhabhar at the moment there is a nexus between the politician, police and timber mafia and all criminal activity revolves around illegal timber trade. Politicians are chary of getting on the wrong side of the timber mafia, which has proved to be extremely generous to them during election time. Only last year 40 trucks loaded with khair were retrieved by some honest police officials in Lalkuan, but political clout and slackness of rules prevented stern action against the culprits. In the recent past, most of the cases of illegal timber trade, which were referred by the Forest Department to the court, the criminals were either released scot free or a minimum penalty was imposed on them. This attitude has encouraged the criminals and within five years in the Western Circle alone, 14 forest officials have been murdered and 36 fatally wounded in their bid to prevent illicit timber trade. Even dropouts from schools and colleges and some villagers are involved in the illegal timber trade, because they have realized that it is very lucrative to fell a green tree and sell it to middlemen of timber merchants from Delhi and other far flung places. It is said that the police mostly helps the timber mafia and is alleged that for postings in Haldwani and Lalkuan, which are regarded as plum postings for inspectors, since illegal timber trade is rampant there, the police is willing to cough up substantial amounts, Rs. 300,000 for Haldwani and Rs. 150,000 for Lalkuan, as they are confident that they will soon recover more than their initial investment.

A few of the more enterprising farmers have started forest based industries like plywood, card-board and craft paper without taking into account the regeneration capacity of the forests. This has further added to deforestation in this area. At present there are six large and medium sector units operating in the Tarai region. Apart from these, there are at present 183 registered forest based small sector units functioning in the Tarai and Bhabhar region as well as 125 saw mills. Recently the Century Paper Mills has been commissioned in Lalkuan and the Forest Department is supplying 145,000 cubic metres of eucalyptus annually to the paper mill. This will not only add to the already fast depleting forests, but will also encourage in the neighbouring areas the planting of eucalyptus trees which are known for creating a dry micro-environment. Since Sub-Himalayan Tarai has been declared as industrially backward area, owing to the subsidy and other fringe benefits, more industries are going to come up in the near future causing more devastation to forests.

Encroachment on forest land by organized groups of unsocial elements, as mentioned earlier, has not only caused ecological degradation, but is also threatening the very existence of these forests. The most unfortunate part is that, the encroachment is being done in an organized manner and the Forest Department has become a helpless spectator to it. No Government or politician with a desire to continue in power is going to oust the encroachers and the forest officials dare not enter the region for fear of their lives.

Terrorism also has led to deforestation. The forest officials were scared to enter the thick forests unarmed and thus the timber mafia, allegedly patronized by the militants, dealt freely in illegal timber trade. This is not always true. In 1992 an honest forest officer was killed in the area. Actually he was killed by those involved in illegal timber trade, but militants were blamed for the murder. Yet this is a fact that owing to the fear of the militants the forest officials avoided entering the forests. The timber mafia is taking advantage of all such situations and dealing in illegal timber trade with impunity.

Impact of deforestation on the Marginalized population :

The residents of the Khattas and the Gujjars are forest dwellers, for them forests are their livelihood, their very existence. They are in love with forests, but their love is beset with many problems especially after deforestation in Tarai and Bhabhar.

As mentioned earlier the Khatta dwellers and the Gujjars graze their cattle in Tarai and Bhabhar. Since the British days the Forest. Department had followed a system of levying grazing fee in order to regulate the number of cattle. In 1822, the grazing tax in Tarai and Bhabhar was 19 paise per buffaloe, 13 paise per cow and 6 paise per ox. In 1921, the following rates were fixed per annum:

Buffaloes	-	Rs. 2 per animal
Cows	-	Rs. 1 per animal
Oxen	-	Rs. 1 per animal.

These rates were doubled in 1981. The latest rates are as follows:

Number of animals	Grazing fee per animal (Rupees)	Lopping fee per buffaloe per season (Rupees)
Upto 10	8	20
11-20	10	25
21-30	12	30
Above 30	16	40

The following are the rules for lopping of branches.

1. Only ordinary sickle (hansia) can be used for lopping.
2. No lopping of trees of less than 30 cm girth is permitted.
3. No branch cutting from the upper half of the umbrella of the trees is permitted.
4. Branches exceeding 7.5 cm in girth cannot be cut and no leading branch can be chopped off.
5. Lopping of lone trees on slopes is banned.
6. Cutting of branches of trees within 30 metres on either side of the roads and in the vicinity of buildings is prohibited.
7. Lopping is not allowed in areas brought under plantation.
8. Lopping of trees on the periphery of grass blanks is prohibited.
9. Lopping of sal (Shorea robusta), semal (Bombax ceiba), haldu (Adina cordifolia), khair (Acacia catechu) shisham (Dalbergia sisoo), tun (Cedrella toona) tendu (Diospyros tomentosa), jamun (Syzygium cumini), bamboo and allenthus is not permitted.
10. No lopping of trees, falling within the permitted cat-

egory is allowed in the vicinity of the forest inspection houses.

Deforestation has affected the vocation of both the Khatta dwellers and the Gujjars. They have been reduced to a state of abject poverty. The area under reserved forests has shrunk in Tarai and Bhabhar consequent on the coming up of Pant Nagar Agricultural University and large farms, especially in southern Tarai. This has restricted considerably the areas available for cattle grazing. Additionally in these areas lopping is not being permitted; moreover large tracts in Tarai and Bhabhar have come under eucalyptus, teak, shisham and khair plantations, species which are commercially useful. For such plantations clear felling becomes necessary and moreover grazing in plantations is prohibited.

The Khattas :

Consequent upon the rise in the price of land in Tarai and Bhabhar as also the improved facilities for the sale of milk and its products, human and animal, both populations have risen in these Khattas. This has resulted in clash of interests of the residents in these areas. vis-a-vis forest conservation. There have been several representations to the Government from these areas for the for removal of their grievances. The Government has been sympathetic to them, but hitherto no steps have been taken to improve their condition.

The herdsmen of the Khattas took up the membership of the Milk Society of Lalkuan and thereby tried to organize the trade of milk. Simultaneously the Milk Federation has also put demands for the improvement in their economic status. The following are the problems and demands of the Khattas put forth from time to time before the Government :

1. As grass does not grow under eucalyptus, their plantations have caused difficulty in grazing.
2. Plantations may not be raised around Khattas and the areas where plantation have not been raised, they may be excluded from plantations.

3. With the coming up of new plantations, many families residing in them had to be settled elsewhere which has subjected them to considerable difficulty. Considering that on the one hand the Government is settling the landless and others in Tarai, on the other old inhabitants are being displaced which is not rational. The problem of displacement affects even the general population and causes them unprecedented hardships. But in the case of the Khatta dwellers the hardship is even more severe and has special ramifications. The displacement brings them under acute socio-cultural strain. Further, a low level of literacy and their traditional life-style of isolation get in the way of their speedy and genuine resettlement and make it difficult for them to earn their livelihood.
4. If the grazing lands of the Khattas have to be restricted, the inmates will have to be settled elsewhere and new pasture lands to be identified for them, which is not feasible and extremely difficult.
5. As the milk producers do not own any land, they can neither produce food for themselves nor raise for their animals. Every herdsman should therefore be allotted 0.202 ha. of land for each cattle to enable them to raise better fodder for them. This land has to be given on long lease.
6. Every family be allotted on permanent basis about 73.03 ha. of land for agricultural purposes.
7. Land be allotted on permanent basis for human and animal residence. As the herdsmen are not allowed to raise permanent structures, they as also their cattle reside in highly unhygienic conditions. Frequently they become victims of forest fires, which almost ruins them and owing to which they are reduced to perpetual poverty. Considering this the Forest Department should allow construction of permanent structures for them as also their cattle.

8. Roads leading to Khattas are in a bad shape, which puts the residents to considerable trouble and it is also difficult for the milk vans to ply on them. The Forest Department should construct the main as well as approach roads.
9. Drinking water poses a great problem to the inmates and their cattle, particularly because the Forest Department does not permit them to sink tubewells in the forest. Every Khatta should be provided with a tubewell.
10. The Forest Department auctions the milk 'bhattis' annually which stifles the progress of milk cooperatives in the Khattas and encourages middlemen. The Forest Department should not auction the 'bhattis' and cream separators in the Khattas as some of them are already members of the Milk Producers Cooperative or propose to be one.
11. Every Khatta should be allotted common land for community purposes like cowshed, herdsmens' residence, milk room, school hospital, play field etc.
12. The Forest Department realizes road tax from the Milk Federation vehicles on their visits to the Khattas for collection of milk, which is ultimately passed on to the poor milk producers as they are members of the cooperative organization. Cooperative institutions should be exempted from this tax.
13. These Khattas have no postal, medical, rationing and educational facilities.
14. The residents of the Khattas should be given forest produce like timber and grass for construction of thatched huts.

The cheap grazing facility as desired by the forest dwellers is not feasible and will result in further deterioration of forest cover. It will mean an uncontrollable rise in the number of cattle which will lead to reduced grazing facility, a decline in the quality of cattle and rearing of more cattle to counter the decreasing milk yield. The belief that the wealth of a farmer is measured by the cattle owned by him, is at the root of the unhappy condition of our cattle. This has to be countered if improvement in this direction is desired. It is also necessary to save our forests which is in the interest of the locals as also the whole nation. The proximity of a village to forest areas should not allow its inhabitants to play with the interests of the whole nation, nor should they be benefited at the cost of national interests.

The percentage of uneconomical cattle in the Khattas is also quite high about 55 per cent, which are a big drain on the ever dwindling fodder resources. It is imperative that the number of uneconomical cattle should be drastically reduced and a programme for introduction of improved varieties of buffaloes and upgradation through artificial insemination or cross-breeding should be worked out. Stall feeding should also be popularized and shortage of fodder to an extent can be met by having only pedigree cattle.

The demand of the Khatta dwellers of allotting 0.202 ha. of land for each animal is not possible. According to the 1973 data the number of animals in the Khattas is 106,920. This means the total land allotted to the Khatta dwellers for their cattle to enable them to raise better fodder for them would be approximately 213,840 ha. which is not possible. This demand is according to the number of cattle in 1973, in 1994 their numerical strength has increased though the correct data is not available. However, atleast one ha. of land should be allotted to every family for growing fodder, residential purposes and to construct sheds for their cattle. Once land is allotted for growing fodder then strict restrictions should be imposed upon grazing of cattle in the forests. At the same time new settlers should be strictly prohibited.

The Khatta dwellers should be provided with education, health, veterinary, postal and rationing facilities. Together with this they should be connected by proper roads and their demands of not auctioning milk 'bhattis' annually should be met with. Potable water should also be supplied to them.

There can be another alternative. Many urban localities have sprung up within or in close proximity to the Tarai forests. They are equipped with all the amenities of modern life. If these Khattas are shifted on the periphery of these towns, their demands of these facilities would be met without any extra expenditure. To meet their requirements for water either separate tubwells can be sunk or they can be provided water from the existing supply. To meet their requirement of fodder they can either be allowed to raise green fodder crops in the near eucalyptus plantations or procure from the villages and farms in the vicinity. From these localities they will have market for their milk and milk produce with the aid of the cooperative societies. Such an arrangement besides meeting all the requirements of the Khatta dwellers will also save forest. The project similar to this being undertaken in the Rajaji National Park will be of considerable interest.

However, the Khattas opting for the new settlements should be shifted to these centres where the cooperative societies will cater to their needs. But the Khattas dwellers satisfied with their present conditions can continue to stay at their existing sites and to enjoy the present facilities as well as the new ones.

In the meantime with a view to curtail illicit extraction of wood from reserve forests, fellings in them should gradually be banned completely. Madhav Gadgil, the famous environmentalist writing in the 'History of Forestry in India' - a book edited by this writer- opines, "For as long as fellings continue in these forests, it would be very difficult to control illicit felling and destruction. A total ban would be far easier to implement, especially if we involve local people on a wide scale in its execution."

A ban on such fellings in the reserve forests and association of the locals in their functioning will also check many mal-practices. With openness, loosening the hold of corrupt politicians and bureaucrats and more checks and balances from those employed on the scheme and voluntary agencies working with them, the EGS (Employment Guarantee Scheme) could also serve as an important course around which the powerless could become organized and acquire some clout. Such openness will thus undo the politician - bureaucrat - illicit timber trade mafia, responsible for destruction of our forest wealth as also deaths of many foresters.

As given above Tarai forests were clear felled to provide gainful employment to the demobilized military personnel, evacuees from Pakistan, freedom fighters, landless laboures etc. In this process immense harm has already been done, which should be stopped forthwith. With a view to generate more avenues of employment the forests should be allowed to grow naturally. Such vibrant forests beside being reservoirs of genetic diversity will also be a tremendous source of usufructs, which can be a useful source of gainful employment to many more persons. It is in this connection that Madhav Gadgil has recommended launching of Employment Guarantee Scheme based on such material forests. On the employment generation capacity of usufructs as against the forest based industries, he writes, "The paper mills may have created fewer jobs than they destroyed with declination of bamboo for thousands of artisans dependent on it. The plywood mills may have generated less employment than was lost through the liquidation of mango and many other minor forest producing trees."

Plantations are being raised and fellings are resorted to with a view to meet the requirement of forest- based industries as also to cater to the small timber requirements of the locals. Quick growing plants should be raised on village common land to meet the fuel, fodder and small timber requirements of the locals. To supply raw material to the forest-based industries farmers should be encouraged to grow trees on their degraded or marginal farm-land. Supporting this suggestion with data Madhav Gadgil says, "The biomass needs of this population (villages), plus the biomass needs of the industry should be met from tree production on privately owned and cultivated land ... The total biomass demand of such land may be called upon to fill annually could be 80 million tonnes for fuel and 20 million tonnes for industrial requirement. This 100 millions tonnes could very reasonably be produced on 10 million ha. out of 150 million ha. of land under cultivation in this country; a very reasonable level of demand."

The Gujjars :

When the Gujjars came to Tarai and Bhabhar, there were abundant forests, whereas the number of their buffaloes was small. In 1921-22, e.g., the number of buffaloes of the Gujjars was 150 which increased to 628 in 1926-27. In 1936, the number of buffaloes belonging to the Gujjars increased from 1000 to 2000. This was found to be excessive and in 1946 the number was subsequently reduced to 800, vide Commissioner Kumaon's Order No. 2942/mi-78, dated July 10, 1946.

Previously there was little biotic pressure on the forest resources. According to the Forest Department, about 20 years back, there were about 150 Gujjar families in Tarai and Bhabhar with cattle numbering 2500. But today there are more than 400 families living in Tarai and Bhabhar and the number of their cattle has soared upto 16,000. The Gujjar families are scattered over the forests and every family claims grazing monopoly in forests around their dwellings, which has further added to the biotic pressure on the forests. Considering that a large number of Gujjar settlers live in forests and subsist on milk trade only, the situation has become extremely difficult for them to eke out a living. Initially when milk was in abundance, the Gujjars used to sell milk products like butter and ghee, but with the reduction in yield, they sell only milk today. Most of the Gujjars are steeped in indebtedness of businessmen to whom they sell their milk cheap. This reduction in their pecuniary status has come within the last two decades owing to the rapid shrinkage of forests and their inability to switch over to other professions. Lack of education has also prevented them from adapting themselves to the changing environment. There are no educational institutions in close proximity to the Gujjar dwellings. Only in exceptional cases a few Gujjar families have sent their children to school. However, no Gujjar has passed high school and there are only seven children who have studied upto class five.

During my survey I observed that some Gujjars have started cultivating small patches of forest land, but being extremely honest, a simple warning from the forest officials is enough to prevent them from encroaching upon or cultivating forest land unlike many other communities in Tarai and Bhabhar. However a few of the Gujjars are financially well off and have purchased land in Chorgalia.

In the past the Gujjars used to move to the hills during summers, thus giving rest to the forests in Tarai and Bhabhar for about six months. But since 1962, the Gujjars in Tarai have stopped migrating to the hills with the result that saplings do not get the time to grow and owing to the dependence of Gujjars on these forests for such a long period, they have been damaged considerably. Previously when fodder was in abundance, the Gujjars used to comply with the regulations of lopping; but in recent years, on account of the increase in the number of cattle and the decline in the grazing areas, the Gujjars have resorted to excessive lopping, branch cutting and even cutting of young shoots of trees. They are heavily penalized by some of the forest officials for their negligence and at times they have to bribe them with milk and chicken, which in Gujjar parlance is known as 'Haq Pani'.

It is true that the practices adopted by the Gujjars are damaging the forests which have to be protected in the larger interest of the country. But we should also accept the fact that the Gujjars are a tribe and that they have practised nomadism for a long period and their main occupation is buffaloe breeding. Thus dairy farming must form the focal point of any economic development project for the Gujjars. The following recommendations can be made on the basis of field survey:

1. The Forest Department should either undertake a scheme for fodder development in the vicinity of

Gujjar settlements or land should be allotted to the Gujjars both for agricultural purposes and fodder. Most of the Gujjars in Tarai and Bhabhar, unlike their brethren in other parts of India are interested in agriculture. So a scheme should be prepared for their permanent settlement in Tarai and Bhabhar. It is suggested that those Gujjars, who are desirous of getting land for fodder raising, may be allotted land in plantations free of cost for first five years and those opting for agriculture should be allotted land on half rates. It is hoped that given such incentives, the Gujjars will raise enough fodder for their buffaloes and gradually start stall feeding them.

The idea of a complete ban on grazing inside the forests is not a viable proposition until the Gujjars are given permanent settlements. In the meantime fodder areas can be developed for their animals by the Forest Department. In the past in Tarai and Bhabhar there used to be 'Chaurs' or grass blanks in the forests where animals used to graze without damaging the forests. Owing to deforestation and increase in biotic pressure these Chaurs have vanished. However like these glades, fodder areas could be developed inside the forests or on the fringe areas and this fodder development should become an integral part of the Gujjar developmental schemes.

2. A programme for introduction of improved varieties of buffaloes and up gradation through artificial insemination or cross breeding should be worked out. Together with this the number of animals should be restricted. It is beneficial for the Gujjars to have only good milch buffaloes, but they are not going to go by this advice immediately, as the numerical strength of cattle is regarded as a status symbol among them, especially for marital alliances. Stall feeding should also be popularized and shortage of fodder can be met to an extent by:

(a) Having only pedigree cattle.

(b) Limiting the uneconomical cattle.

(C) Feeding the cattle on green fodder and other nutritive feeds.

Castration of local degraded he-buffaloes should be resorted to limit the number of uneconomical cattle. Such cattle should be segregated from others and gradually disposed off. Purchase of these buffaloes should also be stopped.

3. It is noticed that pedigree cattle brought from outside start losing their milch capability and are susceptible to local diseases like river flu, foot and mouth, render pest, mistitis and haemorrhagic septicemea. To counter this problem it is advisable that besides purchase of better breed cattle, efforts to upgrade the local breed should also be made. For this purpose cross breeding should be undertaken. This can be achieved by using better breed male buffaloes for breeding the local buffaloes. In the initial stages preferably good cross-breed male buffaloes should be used and switching on to pure bred animals can be done in the later stages. Thus at minimal cost a large number of buffaloes can be upgraded resulting in good milk yield. This experiment has already been successful at Vikas Nagar in Dehradun district, Ranikhet and Almora. The cross-breeding in Tarai can deliver the desired result only when matched with simultaneous animal nutritional programme, so that the required balance of feed and fodder is made available to the cross bred animal from the very beginning. By raising the standard of feeding, the production, of indigenous animals can be increased to a large extent and thereby also preventing deterioration in their good qualities.

Establishment of a separate organization for development of pasture and grassland is needed, so that systematic improvement of pasture and grass can be undertaken with latest techniques available in the country and abroad. This will not only benefit the forest dwellers, but will also maintain the ecological balance in the region. In the beginning some areas, where plenty of fodder is available during rainy season, may be selected and fenced for fodder growing. This fodder may be collected before flowering season and bailed in the form of hay and stored in the neighbouring settlements. The Gujjars living in close proximity may be supplied this fodder on subsidized rate on the condition that they will not graze their animals in the forests and will participate voluntarily in the programme. The Gujjar women in particular should be motivated to participate in this programme to make it a success.

Regulation of grazing is also to be introduced in the region. It is already being practised very successfully in several high altitude communities, such as those in Sikkim and Kameng, the Bhotias of Uttar Pradesh and the highland communities of Himachal Pradesh. Rotational grazing will have to be worked out by the Gujjars in consultation with departmental experts of the Forest and Animal Husbandry Department, keeping in view the carrying capacity of the tract taken for experimenting. Subsidies for this purpose may be considered and a five year rotation should be adopted to allow for regeneration of grass.

Regulation of grazing should be combined with regeneration or replantation of degraded forests. The replanting programme should concentrate on fodder trees or on quick growing fuel species. Fodder forests produce a considerable higher sustainable yield per hectare of fodder than the grassland, and it also produces green fodder at seasons when there is no grass available. Varieties of fodder trees will have to be identified, nurseries for multiplication established in each eco-development unit and a massive programme for plantation launched. The Gujjars should be taken into confidence and be made responsible for planting and maintenance, but technical guidance would have to be provided and the saplings distributed free for an initial period of five years, so as to complete the first rotation cycle. Besides this, community rights should be maintained in those Gujjar settlements which are in close proximity under the above mentioned measures of development.

4. A cooperative scheme should be preferred and executed for:
   (a) Animal feed
   (b) Purchase of milk cattle
   (c) Processing of milk
   (d) Marketing of milk and milk products
   (e) Credit needs
   (f) Consumer needs

5. Animal Husbandry and Cooperative Departments should prepare schemes for improvement of animal breed and raising fodder crops. They should also provide technical advice, including the latest dairy technology, financial assistance and better breed of animals for Gujjars.

6. The Gujjars, who have established a permanent settlement on their own in the forests, their habitats should be connected by roads by the Forest Department. This will help development of dairying on cooperative basis amongst them, as vehicles of the Cooperative Federation will be able to collect milk from them during all seasons. At present they are being subjected to exploitation by the middlemen, because of lack of transporting facilities.

7. The Gujjar women constitute an important segment of the population and work more than their male counterparts. But they are extremely backward, hence

vocational-cum-literacy classes should be started for young girls and women. They have also to know a lot about personal hygiene and here the village level workers can play an important role by working with them and educating them.

8. Schools and Primary Health Centres should be opened in close proximity of Gujjar habitats.

9. The main problem is to wean away the Gujjars from nomadism, which is detrimental to the regeneration of forests. They should be grouped together in milk cooperatives and settlements congenial to their particular social and cultural needs. Together with providing them means of livelihood their cultural heritage should also be preserved.

10. The Gujjars are suffering in their capacity of milk production owing to the inadequacy of water supply for drinking and washing etc. In all the Gujjar settlements which I surveyed there was only one source of water, a hand pump. No settlement had more than one hand pump. In the past the Gujjars were migratory, but now in the Sub-Himalayan Tarai they are more or less sedentary. Therefore it is essential that adequate water should be provided to them or they should be permitted to sink more hand-pumps in their area.

11. No utilization of faecal material of the livestock population of the Gujjars is being done hitherto. This cattle dung can be used for compost or for bio-gas or even for burning as fuel in the nearby villages. The Gujjars can make some extra-earning by selling the compost as manure and dry cowdung as fuel in the nearby villages.

12. Introduction of cottage industries based on forest usufruct among them will also add considerably to their earning. Additionally it will make them interested in the vibrant and thriving forests. This will help in limiting the destruction of forest to a great extent.

13. Latest fuel efficient and smokeless 'Chulahas' should be popularized among them by free or subsidized distribution of such ovens to the Gujjars. This will minimize the necessity of cutting trees for fuel wood.Further they should get fuelwood free of cost, which can be in the form of fallen and dried wood.

14. The Gujjars should be taken into confidence and actively involved in preparing a comprehensive programme for their development.

15. Finally the Gujjars of Sub Himalayan Tarai should be enlisted as Scheduled Tribes so that steeped in poverty and ignorance, they can reap the benefits of the provisions under the tribal development. Unlike their brethren in other states, they have not been included hitherto as Scheduled Tribes in Uttar Pradesh though they are in the process of being considered as backward.

Article 342 of the Constitution provides that the President may with respect to any State Union Territory specify the tribes or tribal communities which shall be deemed to be Scheduled Tribes in relation to that State or Union Territory. Interestingly but sadly the anthropologists, sociologists, social workers, administrators and others who have been involved with the tribes and their problems either on theoretical plane or on practical grounds are still not on the same wave length regarding the concept and definition of tribes. From 1917 to the 1931 census, for instance the nomenclature referring to tribes underwent successive modifications such as aborginals or depressed classes. After Independence they were standardized as 'Adivasis' and Scheduled Tribes, but this standardization did not remove all ambiguity.The Gujjars of Uttar Pradesh are a victim of this ambiguity though the concept and definition of tribe have certainly narrowed down to an appreciable extent now. It is imperative that the Gujjars of Tarai should be redeemed from the shackles of definitions and ambiguity and should be enlisted as a Scheduled Tribe keeping in view their forest dwellings, their geographical isolation, economic backwardness, common culture, common ancestry and their least desire to change.

Deforestation and tribes :

Destruction of forests has dwindled the forest base and concomitant loss of natural resources, thus adversely affecting tribal economy. Further with the increase in agricultural land in Tarai, the tribals, Tharus and Buxas, could not compete with the new settlers. In the initial stages when Tarai and Bhabhar areas were being colonized and rules were not being strictly enforced, a sizeable number of new settlers encroached upon the territory of the tribals. According to the district administration of Naini Tal in 1951 the Tharu and Buxa tribals owned about 250,000 ha. of land, today only about 30,000 ha. is in their possession. In most of the cases land grabbing was done through force or cajolery. The tribals were forced to gift, mortgage or lease land through affidavits. They were also subjected to harassment, so that ultimately they were forced to leave their village or make a compromise with their tormentors by agreeing to be cheap landless labourers to grow food crops in the land previously owned by them. It is a pity that even though in the revenue records they continue to be owners of the land, but so many years having passed in the meantime they cannot claim it.

The following methods were used by the new settlers to terrorise them:

(a) Cattle of tribesmen were lifted at night or even during day time.

(b) Their animals were not allowed to graze on traditional forest land.

(c) Their fields were encroached upon and false cases were registered against them.

(d) However the more belligerent amongst the new settlers just roared in with their tractors on fallow land to occupy it.

When the land alienation of tribals assumed serious proportions, the Social Welfare Department of the State Government appointed a study team to probe into the living conditions of the tribals. A detailed study report was prepared by it in 1978 which revealed that some 1300 settlers' families had grabbed land from the tribals, who had owned it for a century or so. The complicity of the concerned authorities at this game of grabbing the tribal land became evident when inspite of this report no action was taken against the land grabbers.

The land grabbing was done more often than not with the connivance of the revenue and police officials. Moreover the land revenued authorities have not been able to keep pace with the rapid development of agriculture in Tarai and Bhabhar in maintaining the records. They are in an absolute mess and it has been observed that in several cases the recorded tenant is not the actual occupant of the land. The worst affected by this motivated inefficiency of the revenue authorities are the tribals. The inefficiency is at the root of most of the difficulties of the tribals. Innocent as they are, they do not know the wily ways of the unscrupulous officials.

The tribals claim that when they heard of the partition in 1947 and the sufferings of the refugees, they received them with open arms when they were rehabilitated here and gave them food to eat. Together with this they welcomed other settlers like the Jats, the freedom fighters, agricultural graduates, released military personnel and others also, little realizing that some of the new settlers would forcibly occupy their land. Thus they became victim of their own generosity.

Land grabbing was also done through unscrupulous money lending by 'banias' (local traders), 'banjaras' (roving traders, who trade mostly in cereals) and some of the new settlers, who could not use muscle power. They snared the tribals into usury and took possession of their land and crop through deceit.

The process of money lending has reduced the tribals to a hapless condition and the incidence of indebtedness has assumed serious dimensions. While in the old days the money lenders were content with the high rate of interest or payment in kind, the present day money lenders have an eye on their land. Before 1950, when the money lender caused harassment to the tribals, the Kham Superintendent use to intervene and exempted the tribals from either payment of interest or fixed easy installments of repayment.

Every thing however has changed with the influx of outsiders. The money lenders from cities in and outside Tarai discovered the tribal area of Tarai as a paradise for usury during the first three decades of post-Independence period. They were extremely unscrupulous and the rate of interest charged by them was exorbitant They were not merely interested in charging excessive interest on loans advanced by them, as had been the practice earlier, but had a much more dangerous intention of grabbing tribal land by tempting them to obtain easy money from them on loan. It is disturbing to find that more than half of the tribals were not able to repay the loan and had to borrow again to make the repayment.

There were two ways for obtaining loans for repayment. In the first mode the tribals took loan from one money lender to repay another. In the second mode the same money lender changed the pronote. In these transfers all sorts of malpractices were indulged in with the result that the borrower could hardly pay the interest. There was always a divergence between the loans actually taken and loans shown on papers. The tribals who then had land aplenty with no idea of its value, did no realize the repercussions of parting off with a portion of the land to the land grabbers. In the beginning it is said that there were instances of tribals bartering away their land for even a bottle of liquor.

Contact with the new settlers, which was sudden and all embracing, has caused great socio-economic tension creating a dislocation in their cultural matrix. The inroads of money economy have perpetuated the assertion of individual authority, consequent upon which joint family is giving way to nuclear families. A sizeable number of people now prefer to cultivate their own land independently, spend their income on their own family and live as separate units. The fragmentation of land holdings has taken place and the number of landless labourers is increasing.

A vital problem which the tribals are now facing is the disintegration of their culture. The rich tradition of folk music and dance, which manifests the aesthetic value of the tribals, is waning. Their growing contact with the new settlers and coming within the reach of the electronic media has played havoc with their cultural, social and ethical values. It is having a wrong impact on their personal as well as social life. Crime, which was unknown previously, has seeped in and cases of theft and murder have been reported. Even then the tribals have still preserved their old virtues of honesty, simplicity and hospitality. With the growth of new consciousness the younger generation has developed a sense of apathy towards their oral traditions, with the result that tribal songs and dances are being replaced by film music and dances.

Imposition of ideas by Indian 'Sadhus' (mendicants), christian missionaries, reformers, do-gooders, social workers and even Government officials are having a negative effect on their basic cultural values, which makes them feel small and perplexed regarding their indigenous culture. The insistence upon abandonment of old customs and rites under the pressure of Hindu contact has brought the custom of dietary restrictions and taboos. Further the pride in claiming a higher social status, wearing of the sacred thread and conforming to the tenets of Hinduism in some form or the other are all indicative of a change that is coming over the tribals. By inviting the Brahmins in various ceremonies like birth, marriage and death etc. under the influence of Hindus, the tribes have to incur unnecessary expenditure.

Deforestation has also affected the status of tribal women who enjoy a higher status in the society than their male counterpart. Amongst the Tharus and Buxas there is a belief that their women are of royal descent and they came to Tarai in the medieval period with their retinue of servants to escape the onslaught of Mughal brutality. With the passage of time they married their servants, but even after marriage they retained their superiority. With the vicissitudes of time there is an unmistakable evidence of men folk trying to dominate the women on the pretext of safeguarding their honour from aggressive settlers. The younger generation is active in trying to curb their freedom by imposing a ban on their going to weekly markets and fairs. In this it has been considerably influenced by the social set up of the neighbouring communities, where women have a subordinate role. They are also egged on by the non-tribals who ridicule them by stating that they are dominated by their women. The women-folk however have reacted to this infringement upon their rights and have openly defied the ban imposed on them. As men do not have much control over their women owing to their inferior status, the situation has fomented trouble in the tribal community which has resulted in family bickerings and has marred the marital happiness.

Deforestation has depleted those shrubs and trees which bear edible fruit. Some of these were used as medicines by the tribals in the past. A few among such plants are guler (Legerstroomic indica), phalsa (Grewia sapida), bel (Aegle marmelos), jamun (Syzegium cumini), bahera (Terminalia belerica) etc. It has also reduced the number of livestock. Tree leaves which were used as fodder, were wantonly destroyed creating problems for forage.

It can be concluded that the biggest problem which the tribals are facing with the rapid development of agriculture and destruction of forests is land alienation. In view of the fact that the tribal indebtedness is closely linked with land, it would be necessary to enact a law to meet the needs of land-owning indebted tribal families. As a matter of fact in sensitive tribal areas private money lending should be banned. The Government has already taken steps to prevent transfer of land from tribals to non-tribals and to regulate money lending, but this has to be backed by a strong executive action. For the moment however, their debt upto a particular date can be waived off and for this a proper debt redemption programme can be launched.

The tribals who still have good sized land holdings, should be encouraged to take agriculture on scientific lines. They should be familiarised with a package of improved agricultural practices, including irrigation, training in crop management, animal husbandry, good seeds, fertilizers, implements, insecticides and pesticides. They should also be encouraged to take up social forestry. Families which have small or marginal holdings as well as landless labourers should be given assistance and trained in animal husbandry, poultry farming and cottage industries.

Further small multipurpose cooperative societies with exclusive tribal membership should be organized, so that they are managed by the tribals themselves. These societies should meet the credit, agricultural inputs, essential commodities and marketing needs of the tribals.

To remove economic imbalance in Tarai, the development of tribals at a rapid pace is the need of the hour. A special cell should be created which would constitute of Government officials, social workers and experts who have worked on different aspects of tribal life. It is essential that preferably the people and organizations which are interested in tribal welfare programmes should be involved.

Today illiteracy is the main bane of the tribals. The rate of drop-outs at each stage from class one onwards is very high. To eradicate illiteracy, schools specifically for the tribals should be opened. The Servants of India Society is doing laudable work in dissemination of education amongst the tribals, but at the Government level the implementation of schemes is very tardy. Timely distribution of scholarships, money,books and notebooks is lacking. The solution to a great extent lies in the rapid educational progress of the tribals.

Protection, regeneration and collection of minor forest produce should be optimized. The tribals should be helped to process them, so as to earn higher income from sale. For this institutional arrangements be made for its marketing. Together with this the formation of forest villages at par with revenue villages be taken up. It will help the tribals to process usufruct produce. The tribal economy be considered within the parameters of the forest policies of the State and Central Governments. To make this beneficial to the tribals as well as the State, they should be encouraged to play the role of guardians of the forests. This can be achieved by making them aware of the sustainable and vibrant forests being in their own interest. Such an enlightened approach pre-supposes two conditions. Firstly, the foresters should be sympathetic to the tribal aspirations and should be capable of counselling them properly. Secondly, through education and proper extension methods the tribals should be encouraged to look to the forests as their source of sustenance and hence their self-interest in the protection of the forests.

Taungya problem :

Another burning problem is of the landless agriculturists of taungya villages.Taungya cultivation or agro-forestry derives its name form the Burmese word 'taungya' or hired cultivator system. This was used by the Forest Department to raise food crops in plantation areas, till the time that the trees were four to five years old. For this purpose landless labourer families were employed in forests as taungyas. Taungya cultivation was started in the Sub-Himalayan Tarai in 1932 in the sal (Shorea robusta) forests which were considered to be fit for taungya.

Taungya cultivation was discontinued in the Sub-Himalayan Tarai in 1955 and since then the problem of settlement of these cultivators has posed a serious problem.

Kota Range in Ramnagar Forest Division has three villages of Taungya cultivators viz Rampur, Leti and Chopra which were established in 1932. These villages were settled primarily to facilitate taungya cultivation. There were 130 families in the villages and the inmates worked as casual forest labourers also. They had been allotted 0.22 ha. to 1.32 ha. of land per family for their personal use. In the initial stages they rendered satisfactory service, but after 1947 they started demanding allotment of land. According to the Forest Department, from 1947 to 1955 these cultivators worked perfunctorily in the plantations, but after 1955 they totally stopped working and renewed their demand of allotment of land. Taking into consideration their demand, the Forest Department referred the matter to the State Government with a rider that if their demand is met with, it would set up a wrong precedence. Subsequently the State Government ordered the eviction of taungya cultivators from the villages on forest land. The Forest Department initiated steps to vacate the land in the light of the orders of the State Government, but the move was strongly resisted by the taungya cultivators. As a sequel the department deferred the action temporarily.

To this day the situation is nowhere near a solution. A solution has been only a topic of correspondence between the Forest Department and the Uttar Pradesh Government. Even after nearly a decade of deliberations, nothing has come out of it. While the Forest Department on its part is not ready to cede the forest land for agriculture, the Government also does not want to set up a precedence and thus open Pandora's box. In this connection a moot point worth consideration is that the taungya cultivators made their appearance in the Tarai forests not on their own, but only on the behest of the Forest Department. They have been there for the last six decades and therefore it will be unjust to ask them to leave the forest and fend for themselves.

The Forest Department and the U.P. Government are morally bound to resettle them. The more the delay in settling the problem, the more complex it becomes. With the reputation gained by India of having resettled a vast number of refugees from the West and then East Pakistan in the aftermath of Independence, given a will it should not be difficult to provide them a basis for their livelihood.

The main grouse of the taungya cultivators is that the land which they have been cultivating for several years has not been transferred in their name hitherto. Their contention is that the Forest Department is prepared to lease them land since 1973, whereas taungya cultivation had started in Tarai from 1932 onwards and they have been in the villages ever since then. Further, land revenue is to be charged at the present market rate which the poor cultivators cannot afford to pay. Moreover land lease is not transferable and after the father's demise it cannot be transferred in the name of the direct descendant.

Their other demands are medical and veterinary facilities, opening of an Intermediate College in their area, construction of roads and drinking water as well as irrigation facilities.As deforestation has a direct effect on the women folk and their health, the cultivators strongly feel that they should be given old age and widow's pension as admissible to other citizens.

Industrial Development :

The new settlers, a lot of whom came from erstwhile West Pakistan, very soon made a big success of their acquisition with the result that the area in a few years turned out to be the food granary of the whole country. This made the farmers to diversify their food produce and in addition to the cereal crops they went in for cash crops like sugarcane. The change in the pattern of agriculture heralded in the coming up of agriculture based industries in the area. Already some rice and flour mills were functioning in the area, though only on cottage and small scale basis. Abundance in food production as also new found affluence of the new settlers resulted in establishment of other industrial units. Cooperative movement and the incentives provided by the Government to the entrepreneurs gave further boost to the industries based on agricultural produce.

Of late there has been a diversification in the industries in Tarai. This has been made possible for two factors. Firstly, the neo-rich, who had been looking for more lucrative avenues to make money, have started non-agro based industries. This besides their comparative affluence was made possible for expanded training facilities as also concessions provided by the Government for setting up industries in the hills and industrially backward districts of the country. Secondly, setting up of a few industrial estates by the State Government, wherein a host of facilities are provided to entrepreneurs, has given further boost to industries in the area.

However the picture of the industrial scene in Tarai in fact is not as rosy as it appears to be. First of all after deforestation of a large area of Tarai it has turned out to be a virtual granary of the country. Cereal crops providing the basic human necessity, efforts to maintain it as such should have continued. Even if industries were desired to flourish along with agriculture, they should have been based on agricultural by-product only. Coming up of all sorts of industries in Tarai is resulting in the shrinkage of area under agriculture. It is also resulting in lessening the interest of big farmers in agriculture. Both factors are bound to affect adversely production of staple food grain in the area, which will be a loss to the whole nation.

The setting up of a number of industries in the area has no doubt increased employment opportunities, but instead of satisfying the inhabitants, it has started to bring in disturbing social undercurrents in the area. The locals feel that they are not only being denied the clout and influence in the area, but are also being denied the new opportunities. This is for various factors. Almost all the big industrial units being founded on the authority of the licences issued by the State and Central Governments, the overwhelming majority of them are owned by outsiders. The locals are particularly peeved at this for the fact that even though many of them were aspirants for such licences, for the reasons best known to the authorities, they were not favoured. These outside entrepreneurs have brought their own men to man different levels of production processes. Even as labourers, the locals are least favoured, because of their capability to counter the high-handedness of the employers. Thus the local people feel cheated. A telling proof of this dissatisfaction is the defeat at the hustings of the politician who brought out this industrial development in the area.

Besides disturbing the social fabric, industrial development is adversely affecting the physical environment of the area. This has been caused due to the industrial units either not at all being fitted with the pollution control devices or not operating them. It results in air and water pollution causing considerable worry to the local population. A glaring example is provided by the Century Paper Mill, Lalkuan. The residents in the vicinity of the mill complain of high incidence of respiratory diseases, which indicates polluted air. Yet no one on the official side has cared to move against the factory.

The management maintains that the devices are operated regularly and it is only after proper treatment that the effluent is let out in a nullah which disgorges itself in the river Gola. Not withstanding this claim of the factory, the people complain that due to the mill there is water as well as air pollution. The anti-pollution devices have been installed by the mill, but they are not operated regularly, since the cost of running them is exorbitant. According to the residents of Lalkuan, these devices are functional only when there is an inspection by the officials of the Pollution Control Board.

There have been many an agitations due to the water and noise pollution, which have been reported extensively in the local as well as the national press. Vijay Jaiswal, a correspondent of the Hindi daily, 'Amar Ujala' and the residents of Bindu Khatta have put in a long drawn fight against this pollution. They complain that stomach diseases are on the rise in the area and many deaths have been caused only due to this factor.They also allege that ground water has been contaminated due to the untreated effluent of the factory and the agricultural produce is declining. Recently on 17th June 1994 on the recommendations of the enquiry committee headed by the Sub Divisional Magistrate, Haldwani, different samples of drinking water from Ghornala in Bindu Khatta were tested by the Lucknow branch of the State Heath Institute. In its report the institute has mentioned that the water in some of the hand pumps is contaminated and not fit for drinking.

Apart from the Century Paper Mill, the other industrial units which are responsible for causing pollution in Tarai and the adjoining areas are India Glycol, S.H. Sugar Mill, Straw Board Private Ltd., Belwal Spinning Mills, Banwari Paper Mill, Vishwakarma Paper Board, Jindal Udyog, Siddharth Paper Mill etc. Amongst the above mentioned units, India Glycol is causing maximum pollution. It is disgorging its effluent in the Kosi river. This has affected the productivity of the adjoining area and its negative effects are also being felt on human and animal population in the Swar tahsil of the neighbouring Rampur district.

From time to time the villagers of Swar tahsil have complained to the administration that their lives are threatened owing to the industrial waste being released in the river Kosi. They allege that the drinking water in the taps is often black in colour and sand as well as black particles can be seen suspended in it. As a result the villagers have been infected with stomach and skin diseases. But the administration beyond mouthing platitudes has taken no action against the industrial unit.

On visualizing their helpless situation and the nonchalant attitude of the Government regarding industrial pollution, the villagers of Swar tahsil decided to fight their own battle. Consequently the 'Kosi Pradushan Action Committee' was constituted which has evoked great response and has generated mass support from all political parties and a number of voluntary agencies. But it is intriguing that except for marathon meetings on the part of the Government regarding the problem nothing fruitful has come out as yet and the pollution in Kosi river goes unabated.

Similar is the complaint of the residents of Tanakpur against the stone crushers of the area, because of which the air is polluted to such an extent that a large number of people are suffering from various respiratory diseases. For the official apathy to move against the owners they have approached the judiciary, though so far unsuccessfully. If no heed is paid to these grievances and no remedial measures are taken it will make it abundantly clear that the declared environmental policies and programmes of the Government are mere rhetorics vis-a-vis the money power.

Of late the residents of village Faridpur in Moradabad district have taken up cudgels against the pollution caused by the Siddarth Paper Mill, Kashipur. They have been organized under the banner of 'Mazdoor Kalyankari Samiti', a labour union. The villagers contend that the paper mill is releasing its untreated effluent in the river Daandi which has affected the productivity of the soil and is a health hazard to both human and animal population.

The pollution rule enforcing and inspecting authorities appear to be hand in glove with the industrialists. There is also a feeling that this connivance has tacit political patronage. If the owners were favoured unduly in sanctioning licences, they can be favoured in this respect also. According to an official source this nexus between owners and politicians became evident in the case of verification of transport subsidy claims of various industrial units. A transport subsidy of 75% is admissible for transportation of raw material from rail head to factory site and carting of goods produced thereof from the factory to the rail head.

Previously octroi tax paid at different points used to make possible for the Industries Department to check the authenticity of the claims. With the abolition of the octroi tax in Uttar Pradesh the department was denied this check. The officials always had the feeling that the claim used to be inflated. To prevent this malpractice they started checking on the veracity of the claim on the basis of sales tax and income tax paid by the factory owners. This not only made inflated claims difficult, but also brought out the mal-practices being resorted to by the factory owners in defrauding the state in the case of sales and income taxes. The authorities rather than objecting to this ingenuity of the Industries Department personnel should have appreciated this effort. Instead of commending its personnel, they were asked to desist from checking the sales tax and income tax accounts of the owners which clearly shows the politico-industrialist nexus.

Thus in the way of transport subsidy the state exchequer continues to be cheated without any let and hinder. The number of beneficiary units which got transport subsidy are 180 and the amount paid to them in the year 1989-90 was Rs. 71,500,000. That 50% of the transport subsidy is claimed by the stone crushers is indicative of the loot of public money. It is notable that the area abounds in stones and as such there is no question of claim of transportation subsidy for carrying them as raw material.

Similarly nexus became evident in the case of inspections of sick units by the local officials of the Industries Department. On inspection of 1000 units, 200 of them were found to be sick. Out of 131 industrial units in Rudrapur Industrial Area, 54 are sick. Had the inspections been allowed to continue more glaring facts would have been revealed. It is curious that neither the inspections were allowed to continue, nor were they allowed to be reported. Obviously the authorities did not want the facts to see the light of the day.

Not withstanding these drawbacks it is a fact that based on these incentives provided by the State, industrialization has made a headway in Tarai and Bhabhar. It has created a new awareness in the farmers,who have started industrial units to add to their income. Industrialization has provided an outlet for gainful utilization of otherwise useless agricultural by-product. It has also given them a vocation for their spare time. To keep up the momentum as also to meet the demand of the Kumaon-Garhwal Chamber of Commerce and Industry, they should be provided raw material at the District Industries Centre, Haldwani or the nearest rail head. Additionally the state should provide marketing facility to the produce of their industries.

With a view to prevent further deterioration in environment only non-polluting and environment friendly industries should be encouraged in the area. In this connection a further point to be considered is the ever dwindling productivity of the land. With intensive cropping along with heavy dressing of chemical fertilizers the texture of the soil has been spoilt. This has resulted in lesser moisture retention capacity of the soil. Thus to undo the denudation of land caused due to promiscuous deforestation and improving the soil texture, horticulture should be encouraged in Tarai and Bhabhar. Together the with this agro-forestry and forest-based industries should also be promoted in the area.

Militancy :

The militants when put under pressure in Punjab in 1984 found a safe haven in U.P. Tarai. In the beginning the police was caught unawares and the militants had a definite upper edge. Moreover the police, which is essentially equipped to handle law and order situation, and not terrorism, could not contain militancy in Tarai. The police in the initial phase of terrorism had neither cared to instil a sense of security in the masses nor tried to secure their cooperation. To the contrary their handling alienated the Sikh masses. They were victims of police high handedness. Most of them having been in the area for nearly four decades, had little to do with the militants, yet they were also subjected to humiliation. The militants resorted to indiscriminate killings, looting and at a later stage kidnappings for ransom and extortion.

Rivalry among the numerous mafia gangs operating in the Tarai region added a new dimension to terrorism. Feuds were settled ruthlessly. Retribution was frequently resorted to. The groups had rather well defined area of operation, but when their paths crossed, as they inevitably did, the balance of terror was upset with disastrous consequences. The timber mafia reaped the maximum advantage of the situation. As the forest officials were too scared to enter the forest unarmed, the timber mafia had a field day in pilfering timber and at times under the garb of militancy.

The situation however has changed today. Militancy has been brought under control, though it still lingers in the minds of the local people. The police has been able to flush out all the major outfits active in Tarai. Even though a few might still have escaped the police dragnet, so far they are inoperative. However notwithstanding these achievements of the local police, a very senior police official feels that constant vigil has yet to be maintained to prevent future regrouping of the militants in the region.

Militancy cannot be contained by force only. It requires mustering the good will of the locals. Of late the U.P. Police has made commendable efforts in this direction. However the local youth should also be taken into confidence, since the militants have a potential to win over the local unemployed youth and lead them astray. Such youth instead of being allowed to be a tool in the hands of the militants, can be drafted for the Special Task Force specially raised for the purpose and to maintain a vigil against the revival of militancy in Tarai. Being thoroughly acquainted with the people as also the topography of the place they can be of immense help.

Deforestation brings in meteorological hazards :

The Central Himalaya with its foothill, the Tarai and Bhabhar has been the nature's own unique factory which has been nourishing the agriculture of the Indo-Gangetic plain. The natural ecosystem of these hills and foothills had been formed through millions of years of continuing natural processes, which formed the top soil, vital for sustaining the life line along the plains. During the monsoon, rain water and glacial water carried this top soil down the mountain slopes. The comparatively unproductive rocks, sand and debris were deposited in the Bhabhar and Tarai belt at the foothills and allowed most of the fine silt,rich in the top soil to flow down which would rejuvenate the natural fertility or productivity of the agricultural land down stream in the plains. Thus the periodic floods had become a welcome feature during the past, which had sustained the great Gangetic civilization during the past thousands of years.

But gradually Man started interfering with this long standing natural process of the life line. Increasing demand for renewable natural resources, both for sustaining an increasing human population and for supporting their gradually changing life style denuded the vital ecosystems in these critically important hill slopes. One after another, hitherto inaccessible areas were made accessible and forests were wantonly destroyed.

To add to this due to demographic reasons most of the Tarai belt was gradually brought under the plough to increase agricultural production. This myopic decision ushered in an era of unprecedented floods in the plains. The loss of natural forest cover on the hills has already been instrumental to increased frequency of floods. And now the reclamation of the Tarai and Bhabhar let loose a torrent of flash floods, which carried incalculable quantity of unproductive stones, sand and other debris, which caused lowering of natural agricultural productivity in the plains. With heavy monsoon rains in the upper catchment area water rushes down the hill slopes and then through the Tarai belt without any obstacle and causes havoc not only locally, but all along the agricultural plains. The damage caused by floods in the three districts of Kumaon region in 1993 is being detailed below:

S.N.	Name of District	No. of Tehsils affected	No. of villages affected	No. of families deaths	Total No. of human	No. of animals
1.	Naini Tal	13	997	20101	21	343
2.	Almora	4	1276	17360	23	199
3.	Pithora-	6	500	3740	19	89
Total		**23**	**2773**	**41201**	**63**	**631**

S.N.	District Pucca	Houses damaged fully Kachha	Pucc	Houses partially damaged damaged Kachha		No. of schools
1.	Naini Tal	370	1638	7252	11279	120
2.	Almora	561	-	2376	-	376
3.	Pithor-agarh	235	-	552	-	110
	Total	**1166**	**1638**	**10180**	**11279**	**606**

S.N.	District	No. of Government roads damaged	Roads damaged of local bodies
1.	Naini Tal	30	205
2.	Almora	44	-
3.	Pithoragarh 30	-	
Total		**104**	**205**

Source : Office of the Commissioner, Kuamon Division, Naini Tal.

In the name of increased forestry production for the people and to sustain various industries, the basic principle of Forest Management on sustained yield basis was pushed aside through political and bureaucratic patronage and the natural crown density got severely depleted. The forester's view point was never granted due weightage and in fact most foresters as S. Deb Roy, Retired Additional I.G., Government of India puts it, had to join the band wagon, under systematic pressure generated by utter short sighted policy for immediate gains. Total land use planning, which should ideally have been the matter of top most priority in overall planning, got one of the least priority.

The present situation probably calls for central planning for restriction of resource utilization as per stark reality on the ground. It is true that the forester anywhere in the country has been totally alienated from the rural users. Because of his 'policing' role common man looks upon him as one who invariably stands between him and his natural resources, vitally required for his subsistence. For the villager the forester can provide him nothing except threats of prosecution under various laws.

The foresters hitherto have not taken the people into confidence, owing to which forestry even today is not a peoples' movement. Vibrant forests ensure a conducive environment and to revive them the planners and policy makers will have to reach the people. For the success of forestry programmes it seems that the attitude of the foresters, the villagers, politician, policy maker and all those involved with creation, maintenance and utilization of the natural resources must change and they should make forestry a programme, literally for the people, by the people and of the people.

The depletion and degradation of natural forest cover in this crucial area of Tarai is already proving disastrous. Dense forest covered Tarai meant perennial and constant flow in our river systems. Tampering with it is inviting catastrophe. It must be realized that this apparently wild looking area had been designed by nature to ensure real sustainable productivity and to reclaim it for boosting agricultural production was a short sighted and suicidal attitude. This area with its natural ecosystems is precious beyond any description to humanity and should be saved from further deterioration.

The forest areas in Tarai have almost all through been looked upon as a source of unending utilizable resource. Even most working plans of the Forest Department have sought to prove their worth and efficiency by prescribing greater yields, which has resulted into destruction of ecosystems. Now we are left with no choice, but to protect the area from further destruction by developing unconventional energy sources and propagating them. Meanwhile during the transition period some tough measures seem to be inevitable to protect such areas from deforestation and illegal timber trade.

The watershed management schemes must also be viewed with extreme seriousness and taken up in the area. Together with this social forestry should be granted very high priority, as the successful plantations raised by social forestry, though may not replace the ecosystems, will provide much sought after alternate resources and help the traditional forests gain some respite from further deterioration.

In a bid to repair the damage done, the Forest Department has introduced programmes of social forestry in Tarai and is doing commendable work. But instead of indigenous species, fast growing species like eucalyptus are being propagated. Moreover no steps are being taken to prevent illicit felling as well as illegal timber trade.

The Forest Corporation at present is only propagating mechanized plantation and agro-forestry. The other two components of social forestry, viz rural and urban forestry have been overlooked absolutely. To meet the fuel, fodder and shelter needs of the rural people, plantation of trees on community lands, degraded forest, roads and railway sides, canal banks and other vacant lands should be taken up. Programmes for the creation of tree reserves in the towns of Tarai and Bhabhar should also be taken up. Municipal laws for new constructions should also provide for compulsory tree plantation. Just as there are rules governing the built in area and the vacant area in a housing plot, there should be a provision for tree plantation also. Cutting down of such trees should be punishable with discontinuation of electric and water supply.

Hitherto, no effort has been made by the Forest Department for extension activities in Tarai and Bhabhar to catch peoples' attention and to enthuse them to take up social forestry on a large scale. One of the immediate needs in social forestry programmes is to build up a good extension work. It should aim at convincing the people of the importance of forests to them and their duty to protect, conserve and develop it. The people have to be made aware of the fuel saving devices like fuel-efficient stoves. Additionally they have to be helped to take up cottage industries based on forest usufructs. This will make them aware of their own interests in the protection of forests and will also save agriculture nibbling of forest land. The idea of limited family also should be brought home to them. This besides ensuring their own welfare will also prevent deforestation.

Tarai, prior to denudation of its rich forest cover inspite of its being smaller in size, has been a giant in as much as that it has been the basis of the fertility of the Gangetic plain as also it has ensured the perenniality of its rivers. It can even now turn out to be as such, provided of course that its human as well as natural resources are utilized appropriately. Given a sympathetic and humane treatment its forest dwellers - the Gujjars and the Gothias have the capacity to bring in a white revolution, besides working as the protectors of its forest wealth. The tribals, Tharus and Buxas, can also serve as custodians of our forests. With social and agro-forestry along with the farmers taking to horticulture in a big way the vanishing green cover of Tarai can be retrieved and replenished considerably. This can give a fillip to the forest and horticulture based industries in the area, which will be satisfying also to the burgeoning entrepreneurship among its settlers. Such industries being lesser capital incentive and more labour absorbing will ensure wide dissemination of ownership, thus preventing the present day animosities in the society.

Select Bibliography

1. Home Department, Public, September 16, 1802, File No. 8, National Archives, New Delhi.
2. Home Department, Public, September, 16, 1802, File No. 9, National Archives, New Delhi.
3. File No. 3 Volume 125, Letter dated October 3, 1834, State Archives, Lucknow.
4. File No. 11, Volume 115, Letter dated September 11, 1834, State Archives, Lucknow.
5. Batten, J.H.- A Few Notes on the Subject of the Kumaon and Rohilkhand Turaee, Journal of Asiatic Society of Bengal XIII, Pt 2, 1844.
6. Report on the Administration of N.W. Provinces, 1868-69 and 1873-74, Board of Revenue, Allahabad.
7. Beckett, J.O.B.-Report on the Settlement of Kumaon district, Allahabad, 1874, State Archives, Lucknow.
8. Ramsay, Henry - Report on Beckett's Kumaon Settlement, Allahabad 1878, State Archives, Lucknow.
9. Pauw, E.K. - Report on the Tenth Settlement of Garhwal District, Allahabad 1896, National Archives, New Delhi.
10. Hutton, C.H. - Report on the Tarai Canals, Government Estates, December 18, 1897, Kumaon Commissionery, Naini Tal.
11. Box No. 78, File No. 15, Department No. IV, Report of Tarai District, Regional Archives Naini Tal.
12. Letter of C.H. Hutton, Executive Engineer, Tarai and Bhabhar Canals, dated December 18, 1897, Kumaon Commissionery, Naini Tal.
13. Department XI, Government Properties, letter dated August 26, 1904, State Archives, Lucknow.

14 Letter dated April 24, 1906, from M. Mumtaz Ali Khan, Officiating Superintendent, Tarai and Bhabhar to Dep-

uty Commissioner, Naini Tal, Kumaon Commissionery, Naini Tal.

15. Department X, File No. 10, Serial No. 2, 1906-1907, Regional Archives, Naini Tal.

16. Letter of J.W. Hoss to Chief Secretary, S.P.O., Donnell, United Provinces, dated March 10, 1909, Kumaon Commissionery, Naini Tal.

17. Letter from J.C. Robertson, Special Malaria Officer, Bareilly to J.W. Holmes, Chief Secretary, United Provinces, dated June 7, 1909 Regional Archives, Naini Tal.

18. Box No. 87 File No. 39 Regional Archives, Naini Tal.

19. Letter of J.W. Hoss to Chief Secretary, S.P.O. Donnell, dated October 27, 1911; Regional Archives, Naini Tal.

20. Department XI, File No. 29, Box No. 103, Regional Archives, Naini Tal.

21. Revenue Department, Serial No. 2, File No. 762/1910, State Archives, Lucknow.

22. Department No. 1, File No. 4, Letter No. 2971, dated May 15, 1912, Regional Archives, Naini Tal.

23. Revenue Department, Serial No. 1, File No. 369/1913, Regional Archives, Naini Tal.

24. Revenue Department, File No. 2 Volume 125, Regional Archives, Naini Tal.

25. Report on the Tarai and Bhabhar Development Committee, March 1947, Naini Tal , Kumaon Commissionery, Naini Tal.

26. Uttar Pradesh Ke Arthik Sambhagaun Ke Janpadvar Aakre, Uttar Pradesh, Lucknow 1992.

27. Agriculture Statistics at a Glance, Ministry of Agriculture, Government of India , New Delhi 1993.

Books

1. Allami, Abul Fazl, - The Ain-i-Akbari volume II, Translated by Jarrett, (Reprint) Calcutta, 1978.

2. Atkinson, E.T. - Kumaon Hills (Reprint) Cosmo Publications New Delhi, 1974.

3. Basham, A.L. - The Wonder that was India, New York, 1953.

4. Bhanu, Dharam - History and Administration of the N.W.P. Agra and Oudh. Agra, 1957.

5. Bingley, A.G. - History, Castes and Culture of Jats and Gujjars, 1899.

6. Buckland, C.E. - Dictionary of Indian Biography, Bloomburg 1906.

7. Boase, Frederick - Modern English Biography, London, 1965.

8. Clay, J.M. - Naini Tal, Allahabad, 1928.

9. Chaturvedi, M.D. - Working Plan for the Tarai and Bhabhar Estates, United Province 1934-35 to 1948-49, Volume I, Naini Tal, 1936.

10. Chattopadhya, Kamla Devi - Tribalism in India, New Delhi, 1978.

11. Crooke, N. - The Tribes and Castes of North Western India, Vol. II (Reprint), Cosmo Publications, New Delhi.

12. Hasan, Amir - A Tribe in Turmoil, New Delhi, 1986.

13. Ibbetson, Denzil - Castes, Races and Tribes of the People of Punjab (Reprint) Cosmo Publications, New Delhi 1981.

14. Kayastha, Devi Das - A Short Memoir of General Sir Henry Ramsay, Almora, 1897.

15. Majumdar, D.N. - Races and Cultures of India, Bombay 1961.

16. Munshi, K.M. - The Glory that was Gujar Desh, Part I, Bombay 1955.
17. Nevill, H.R. - Naini Tal : A Gazetteer, Lucknow, 1922
18. Pande, Badri Dutt - Kumaon Ka Itihas, Almora, 1937.
19. Pande, G.C. - Role of Kumaon University in Animating a Socio-economic change in the Himalayan Society, Uttarakhand Bharti, Naini Tal, 1976.
20. Pande, G.C. - Travails of Tribal Change and Related Administrative Change, Seminar Papers, "Tribals in Kumaon", Naini Tal, 1980
21. Pande, G.C. - Economic Development of U.P. , Uttrakhand Bharti, Naini Tal, 1983.
22. Powell, Henry Baden - The Indian Village Community (Reprint) Cosmo Publications, New Delhi, 1972.
23. Raturi, H.K. -Garhwal Ka Itihas, Dehradun, 1928.
24. Rawat, A.S. - Man and Forests, New Delhi, 1993.
25. Sherring, M.A. - Hindu Tribes and Castes Vol. II (Reprint) Cosmo Publications, New Delhi, 1977.
26. Woodyatt, Nigel G. - Regimental History of the 3rd Gurkha Rifles, London, 1929.